Pickles and Preserves

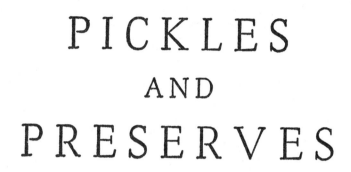

PICKLES
AND
PRESERVES

BY MARION BROWN

AVENEL BOOKS • NEW YORK

CONTENTS

THE SWEET AND THE SOUR   1

GENERAL INSTRUCTIONS   5

SPICES, HERBS, SEEDS, AND OTHER
    SEASONINGS   10

1. Pickles   15

2. Fruit Pickles   53

3. Pickles and Preserves from Frozen Foods   65

4. Miscellaneous Pickles   70

5. Relishes   89

6. Bottled Foods   114

7. Brandied Fruits and Syrups   138

8. Preserves   150

9. Conserves   175

10. Jams   182

11. Marmalades   194

12. Crystallized and Glacéed Fruits; Preserved
    Flowers   206

13. Jelly   219

14. Fruit Butter   241

15. Meats and Sea Food   245

vi   CONTENTS

WEIGHTS AND MEASURES—APPROXIMATE
    EQUIVALENTS   272

DENSITY OF SUGAR SYRUP   275

YIELD OF FRESH AND DRIED FRUITS BY
    MEASURE   276

INDEX   277

The Sweet and the Sour

THE CONSERVATION OF FOOD BY PICKLING AND PRESERVING IS AN old and honorable art that grew out of man's need to conserve in times of plenty for times of want. Pickles and preserves may be made for pleasure as well as for profit. They add zest and variety to meals as they please both the eye and the palate. Only the person who has looked upon her own shelves of sparkling glasses of jelly, deep rich preserves surrounded by amber and ruby sirup, colorful jars of pickles and relishes "put up," perhaps a few at a time with love and care, will know the satisfaction derived from this art.

It is to the early Colonists that we owe our inherent taste for "the sweet and the sour" as well as the basis for many good and practical recipes for conserving the bountiful produce of the United States. Helen Bullock, in *The Williamsburg Art of Cookery*, says of preserving and pickling: "Pickles, preserves, jellies, sweetmeats, conserves and relishes were such staple table delicacies in

1

Colonial Virginia that one can rarely examine the inventory of any person's estate without finding preserving-kettles, stone and earthen jars, jelly glasses, pickle dishes, corner dishes, and an abundance of utensils for making and serving them."

The purpose of this book is to bring together a collection of recipes—both old and new, and for large and small quantities— that may be used by the homemaker, the chef, or the commercial packer.

The recipes have come to me from all parts of the country and some from other countries. With few exceptions, the fruits and vegetables are grown throughout the United States. From Eliza B. K. Dooley's *Puerto Rican Cook Book* several recipes dealing with tropical fruits that are grown both in Puerto Rico and the United States have been selected. There are a few recipes calling for Mexican ingredients—also available in this country. Some early English recipes that are interesting and practical have been included. Recipes from my *The Southern Cook Book*, copyright, 1951, by the University of North Carolina Press, Chapel Hill, N.C., have been so identified.

While each recipe furnishes concise instructions, general instructions are given for each major section of this book. The general instructions should be carefully read.

Before the discovery of good grain vinegar and refinement of sugar, vegetables and meats were pickled in a form of brine or fermented fruit juices. Preserves were made with honey or sweet reed sirup (cane, bamboo, etc.). However, until the invention of hermetically sealed containers, much food was wasted by spoilage. The making of pickles and preserves was arduous and hazardous.

Today any homemaker can make pickles and preserves with comparative ease and assurance that the finished product will be safe from spoilage.

Those who have space for a garden and a few fruit trees have the advantage of conserving the surplus yield perhaps more economically than those who must buy produce from retail markets. Those who raise poultry and stock may process meats by pickling, salting and smoke curing. Delicious and unusual by-products can be made from the less popular cuts and parts of fowls and animals

—souse meat, scrapple, hogshead cheese, goose cracklings, are but a few.

The American markets have extended their vast services so that now there are fresh vegetables, fruits, meats, and seafood available to anyone who wishes to conserve food. The city cliff-dweller may make pickles and preserves for family consumption as simply and almost as economically as his rural neighbor. In most sections of this country during certain seasons there is a surplus of fresh produce, meat, and seafood. The wise conserver will look for locally grown produce as it matures, and preserve by one method or another in times of plenty.

There are frozen fruits and vegetables that may be bought in large and small quantities that can be quickly made into pickles and preserves. Canned fruit, vegetables, and juices may often be substituted for fresh or frozen produce. Many markets offer stock brined cucumbers that can be turned into pickle, thus saving the pickle-maker from the long and tedious process of brining.

Herbs, spices, and other seasonings, so necessary in the making of pickles and relishes, are now standard stock in almost all good food stores. (See pages 10–13: Spices, Herbs, Seeds, and Other Seasonings.) Many herbs can be grown in the home garden or even in an apartment window flower box or in flower pots.

The manufacturers of hermetically-sealed containers now design jars, glasses, and bottles in large and small sizes to safeguard and enhance home-made products. When selecting containers it is well to remember that the graceful and eye-appealing jelly glasses, jars, and bottles will be welcome on the table as well as for gifts, and are as easy to come by as the ordinary. Small earthenware crocks filled with fruit butter, jam or liver paste; sparkling glasses of jelly, preserve, jam, conserve, marmalade, or *mélange*; decorated wooden boxes of candied fruit peel or fruit paste; wicker-encased wine bottles topped off with a cap made of heavy aluminum foil filled with home-made catchup (or catsup or ketchup, as you will), sauce, or fruit syrup—these are a few of the many ways in which home products may be gift-dressed.

Many of these containers may be salvaged after they have

served other purposes. To cap bottles with foil, take a circular piece of foil and center it over the cork, pressing down all around—it folds like an umbrella. Now, take an oblong piece of foil, wrap it around the neck of the bottle, and secure it with Scotch tape to conceal the folds of the first piece. Similar foil topping may be put on jelly glasses; then dress the glasses with individual decorative labels.

Elaborate kitchen equipment is not necessary in the making of pickles and preserves. It is important to include in the standard equipment an enamel cooking vessel or regulation preserving kettles for vegetables and fruits that are acid-producing. Wooden spoons should be used for stirring. While it is not always necessary to use kitchen scales, they are essential when dealing with recipes that call for weighing.

Manufacturers of preserving and pickling equipment and of containers usually furnish complete instructions for the proper use of their products. It is always advisable to read these instructions and to follow them.

Perhaps in no other form of cookery is there more freedom for the play of the imagination than in pickling and preserving. In this book there are many basic recipes with sugggestions for variations. Thus, the imaginative cook may try her hand at discovering an entirely new "dish" from another's recipe. As Brillat-Savarin wrote more than a century ago, "The discovery of a new dish does more for the happiness of mankind than the discovery of a new star."

MARION BROWN

Brownlea
Burlington, North Carolina

General Instructions

FOR PICKLING AND PRESERVING

BEFORE PROCEEDING WITH ANY OF THE RECIPES PRESENTED IN OUR book, it is a good idea to read these general instructions. Here you will find important and useful information that can save time and prevent waste and that will prove continuously helpful.

As you will see, these instructions and cautions apply variously to the pickling and preserving of vegetables and fruits and to the preserving of meat, to the equipment needed for these processes, and to the packaging and storing.

1. Each fruit or vegetable should be in perfect condition. Examine each piece for dark or bruised spots. Remove all such spots and test, by smell and taste, any doubtful piece. Give tomatoes extra attention, for they often appear to be in good condition when they are not. If in doubt, discard the piece. One bit of soured produce can spoil the lot.

2. The produce should be washed or cleaned just as for cooking. Fruits with high acid content, such as pears, apples, and so on, should be dropped into cold water as they are peeled.

3. Do not pick fruits or vegetables right after a rain, for they will be water-logged and inferior. If possible, wait at least 12 hours after a heavy rain. Then use the produce the same day or refrigerate it.

4. It is best to work with small quantities when making jelly and preserves.

5. Use enamel, porcelain, agateware, wooden, or special metal preserving vessels for pickling and preserving. Use wooden spoons or forks for stirring.

6. An old wives' warning is "Never put your hand in a pickle brine, for if you do, the entire lot will spoil." Use a long-handled

fork or spoon. Grease in pickle brine will cause the pickle to spoil. If scum forms on the brine in the crock of preserved food, skim at once.

7. For best results in making jelly, heat the sugar before it is added to the fruit juice. Put the sugar in a bowl and heat in 300° F. oven until warm all the way through.

8. Use an open kettle for the final cooking of pickle, jelly, and preserves unless specific instructions direct otherwise. Fruits to be cooked for juice extraction are almost always cooked in a covered vessel and cooked slowly.

Liquids will evaporate faster in a wide-mouthed kettle than in a deep narrow one. Within a specific cooking time, therefore, the contents of a wide-mouthed kettle will be reduced more than the contents of a deep kettle. Some kettles will cook preserves down to a thicker consistency than others. A relish or chutney containing items indicated by the number rather than by pound can vary by as much as a quart or two. The same is true of cucumber pickle.

If syrup must be cooked to a full rolling boil, use a vessel that has a volume at least three times the volume of the combined ingredients to be boiled. Unless otherwise stated, use a wide-mouthed open vessel for cooking.

9. All jars, tops, and other canning equipment should be sterilized before the food is packed and sealed. A good home-made sterilizer is a large kettle. Place all equipment in water to cover, bring to a boil, and boil for at least *fifteen minutes*. Let stand in hot water to cover until needed. Invert jars and drain. To keep the jars hot after they are drained, stand them upright in hot water, put the tops on lightly, and keep them covered until time to fill.

10. Be sure there are no nicks or broken places in jars or tops.

11. To seal jars means to make them airtight. This is done by the use of screw-top jars with rubber rings or automatic-sealing tops, paraffin, bottle caps, corks, or other means. Preserves and pickles are usually packed in screw-top jars. Jelly, jam, conserve, and other thick mixtures are usually packed in jelly glasses and sealed with paraffin, but they may be sealed in screw-top jars. Fruit butters are sealed in screw-top jars. Juices, sauces, and syrups

are either bottled or packed in screw-top jars. Brandied fruits are packed in screw-top jars or in crocks, according to the recipe. Pickles may be stored for limited periods in crocks. The final, and best, way to pack all conserved fruits and vegetables is in airtight containers.

12. To seal a screw-top jar, turn the top down on the rubber ring until it can be turned no farther; then have it tested by someone with a firm grip to see that it can no longer be turned. If any air bubbles appear, the top is not airtight.

13. Boil rubber rings and automatic-sealing tops according to manufacturer's directions. *New* rubber rings or automatic-sealing tops *should be used* each year.

14. *To pack hot*: Drain the hot jars quickly on clean, soft, thick cloth or several thicknesses of absorbent paper. When ready to pack, invert jars and if not hot enough, stand them upright in a shallow pan of hot water. Fill one jar at a time and seal according to individual recipe instructions. Set the jars to cool on a thick cloth or slab of wood. Never set them on cold metal; they may explode or crack.

Some commercial packers recommend that preserves be given an additional hot-water bath after sealing. Unless a recipe calls for this extra processing, do not process in a hot-water bath. As a rule, preserves are ready for use when they have finished the open-kettle cooking and need no further processing.

15. *To pack cold*: Allow preserves to cool in the kettle in which they were cooked or pour them into shallow pans for fast cooling. Drain sterilized jars on clean, heavy, soft cloth or several thicknesses of absorbent paper until cool. When ready to fill, turn the jars upright. Fill immediately and seal immediately.

16. To seal with paraffin, the contents of the jar should be cool. Melt paraffin and keep it hot in a small container with a lip, such as a metal pitcher or individual frying pan. As each jar is to be sealed, run a silver knife blade down around the rim of the preserves to a depth of ¼ inch. Remove the blade and quickly pour on a thin coating of paraffin. Allow the paraffin to set for several seconds. Add a second coat, and repeat until a coating about ⅓ inch deep completely covers the surface of the contents. When the

paraffin is thoroughly set and cool, the container may be further sealed with extra closures, such as caps or tops, or it may be covered with heavy wax paper or aluminum foil and tied securely with twine.

17. Sealed preserves should be stored in a dark, dry place. As an alternative, wrap each jar in heavy brown paper. If preserves are exposed to light, they will lose their natural color.

18. In many recipes in this book the contributor will suggest the use of "good" vinegar. Only good vinegar should ever be used to make pickle, for inferior or weak vinegar will cause spoilage.

A "good" vinegar is of 40 to 60 grain strength with a 4 to 6 percent acetic acid. Many manufacturers prefer a distilled vinegar. If fruit vinegar is used, it should first be filtered through standard filtering paper or through double thickness of flannel cloth. Unless you can determine the grain strength, *do not use home-made cider vinegar.*

As a rule the volume of vinegar, plus the sugar and spices, should be one third the volume of the ingredients to be pickled; that is, 1 gallon of vinegar syrup will pickle approximately 3 gallons of whole vegetables, such as cucumbers.

19. If vegetables are properly brined, there will be no need to add hardening or coloring agents, since the vegetables will be firm and crisp and take on a deeper green color. This is especially true of cucumbers.

Some feel the necessity of adding alum or lime when making pickle of fermented produce. This is not considered good practice by experienced picklemakers.

The practice of "greening" cucumbers by heating them in a copper kettle is denounced by such an authority as Dr. Edwin LeFevre. He says: "Experiments have shown that in this treatment copper acetate is formed, and that the pickles take up very appreciable quantities of it. *Copper acetate is poisonous.* By a ruling of the Secretary of Agriculture, made July 12, 1912, foods greened with copper salts, all of which are poisonous, will be regarded as adulterated."

20. The yield, or quantity, of packed pickles and preserves is difficult to determine. Many things must be considered: the con-

dition of the vegetables and fruits; the water content; the size of the product; and the rate of cooking. The type of cooking vessel also plays an important role. In many instances in this book, the "yield" is omitted because of the undetermined size of vegetables or fruits to be used. (See table of yields, page 276.) In other instances, the basic quantity to be prepared is optional. It is better, when making pickles and preserves, to think of the yield in approximate terms.

21. In making pickles and preserves, a pair of kitchen scales and an adequate set of measuring implements and vessels are essential.

22. *To bring to a slow boil*: To put on cold and bring to a gradual boil.

To bring to a rolling boil: To cook rapidly until the whole mass boils up in the kettle.

23. *To stand overnight*: To stand at least twelve hours.

Spices, Herbs, Seeds, and Other Seasonings

SPICES, HERBS, SEEDS, AND OTHER FRESH AND DEHYDRATED SEASONINGS are assets to many foods. The descriptions given here apply mainly to their function in the making of pickles and preserves and in other foods described in this book. Unless identified here with some other part of the world, these herbs and seasonings can be grown anywhere in the United States.

allspice: so called because the flavor resembles a blend of cinnamon, nutmeg, and cloves; used in pickles, relishes, mincemeat, catchups, chili sauces, spiced fruits, fruit butters, preserves, etc.

anise seed: ground seed which adds flavor to seafood pickle.

basil: an herb, especially tasty in any tomato catchup or sauce.

bay leaves: used whole or crushed in vegetable pickles, sauces, and some relishes; bitter if cooked too long; should be used sparingly.

canell: early spelling of cinnamon.

caraway seed: often used in cabbage pickle and to season sauerkraut.

cayenne: grown mainly in Africa; very hot; gives warmth and color to sauces, pickles, relishes, etc.

celery salt: used in vegetable pickles, relishes and sauces.

celery seed: excellent for vegetable pickles, relishes, and catchups.

chervil: grand tomato seasoner.

chili powder: used in Mexican sauces, many tomato sauces, etc.

cinnamon: inner bark of the cinnamon tree; ground or in stick form; used in fruit and vegetable pickles, preserves, fruit butters, chili sauces, tomato catchups, spiced fruits, jellies.

cloves: whole or ground, used in pickles, preserves, fruit butters, brandy fruits, chili sauces, catchups, etc.

10

coriander seed: an aromatic herb; good for any pickle containing cabbage.

crab boil: a mixture of hot spices used principally for sea food or other hot pickles; contains red pepper pods, whole cloves, allspice, ginger root, basil, sage. It is packaged and can be bought in any good market dealing in spices.

creole pepper: Louisiana pepper, similar to Cayenne; very hot and used in all hot Creole sauces; good in catchups.

curry powder: well-known East India condiment; a mixture of many herbs and spices; used in pickles, relishes, chutneys, etc.

dill, fresh: sprays are used to flavor dill pickle or any brine for dill pickle; can be used dried.

dill seed: used in dill pickle, dill brine, and the like.

fennel seed: a plant of the parsley family, tasting a little like anise; very good in Italian sauces or any tomato sauce.

garlic: pungent seasoning for various types of pickle.

garlic salt: good in garlic pickles.

ginger: from Jamaica, British West Indies, other tropical lands; whole or ground, crystallized or dried in roots; used in pickles, preserves, jellies, chutneys, jams, conserves, fruit butters, etc.

hickory smoke salt: gives hickory flavor in curing meat.

horseradish: powdered dry root or fresh grated root; very hot.

hot salt: highly seasoned salt for any tomato sauce.

lemon verbena: good for flavoring jellies; use fresh leaves.

liquid spices: especially good for fruit pickle, since they do not turn the fruit dark; can be purchased at drugstores and markets; fine for peach, apricot, and melon pickles, fruit butters.

mace: highly aromatic East India spice made from the covering of nutmeg seeds; ground or whole; used for pickles, preserves, sauces, etc.

mint: essence and fresh leaves used to flavor jelly and other fruit preserves calling for mint flavoring.

mustard, dry: ground yellow mustard seeds; used in mustard pickle, sauces, mixed vegetable pickles, salad dressings, tomato sauces, etc.

mustard seed: white, yellow, and black seeds; used in vegetable pickles, relishes, etc.

nutmeg: aromatic seed covered by mace, from the Molucca Islands; grated or ground, used in preserves, conserves, pickles, sauces.

oregano: native to Italy, Spain, and Mexico; often called "wild marjoram"; good in Mexican sauces; is in all chili powder.

paprika: a mild seasoning, used for mild flavor and color in pickles, relishes, and so on; the Hungarian variety is considered superior.

parsley: used fresh or dried, for seasoning tomato sauces, etc.

pepper, green bell: has sweet fine flavor; used in relishes, chutneys, pickles, sauces; a mixture of red and green peppers gives color to mixed pickles and relishes.

pepper, ground red: little hotter than Cayenne, but used in same manner.

pepper, red bell: same as green bell peppers.

pepper, white ground: has a spice flavor and is fine for mild vegetable pickles and sauces.

pepper pods, red hot: long, thin type of pepper having very hot flavor; can be used fresh or dried, whole or crushed, in hot pickles, relishes, etc. The green pod is the same, but not quite so hot.

peppercorns, black: pepper berries from the Far East; they are sun-cured and have fresh hot flavor; use whole or ground in vegetable pickles.

pickling spices: mixture of whole spices, containing all the required flavors; used in making pickle. It is often compounded of seventeen or more spices and is usually purchased already mixed in various combinations.

poivre aromatique: French blend of spices; especially good in catchups and chili sauces, tomato juice, etc.

rose geranium: same as lemon verbena.

rose petals, rose calyx: good for jellies, preserves, honeys, wines, etc.

rosemary: once known as "Mary"; used in mixed spices for pickles and sauces; fine in sausage and other ground meats; mild and aromatic like thyme and marjoram.

saffron: from Mediterranean regions; has a yellow color and subtle flavor; used in mustard pickle, curry sauces, and the like; has been scarce for years; should be used sparingly.

sage: highly aromatic herb used to season sausage and other pre-served meats, tomato sauces, and so on; should be used sparingly unless a strong flavor is desired; Dalmatian sage is considered the finest.

savory: Spanish herb of the mint family; used in same way as rosemary.

sesame seed: an Oriental seed; good in vegetable pickles.

sweet marjoram: a perennial herb of the mint family; often used in catchups, chili sauces, soup mixtures, etc.

turmeric: ground spice of yellow color; used in many pickles, such as mustard or "yellow" vegetable pickle; a good substitute for saffron.

Preserved Fruits

. . . Take of Barberries as many as you will, boil them in spring water till they are tender, then having pulped them through a sieve, that they are free from stones, boil it again in an earthen vessel over a gentle fire, often stirring them for fear of burning, till the watery humour be consumed, then mix ten pounds of sugar with six pounds of this pulp, boil it to its due thickness. . . .

Conserves and Sugars

. . . the flowers of Water Lilies, red Poppies, Peony, Peach, Primroses, Roses, . . . Violets, with all these are conserves made with their treble proportion of white sugar: yet note, that all of them must not be mixed alike, some of them must be cut, beaten, and gently boiled, some neither cut, beaten nor boiled, and some admit but one of them, which every artist in his trade may find out by this premonition and avoid error.

The Complete Herbal and
English Physician Enlarged
by Nicholas Culpepper, London, 1653

1. Pickles

*Cucumber Pickles, Mixed Cucumber-Vegetable Pickles,
Other Cucumber Combinations*

ALMOST ANY VEGETABLE OR FRUIT CAN BE PICKLED IN SOME FORM
or other. Some, however, take to pickling better than others. The
most common fruits for pickles are peaches, pears, apricots, melon
rind, cherries, and similar meaty fruits. Cucumbers rank high as a
vegetable pickle; others are onions, carrots, cauliflower, peppers,
beets, artichokes, cabbage, broccoli stalks, string beans, corn, and
so on.

Vegetables and fruits are pickled whole or cut, as desired.
Chopped or ground combinations are known as relish. Under
the heading of relishes are chutney, chowder, hash, chow-chow,
salad, soy, mélange, and so on. Pickles and relishes add zest and
flavor to any meal and are considered an important low-calorie
food. Many pickles and relishes are basically the same; they differ

15

only in the combinations of fruits and vegetables, the spicing, and the manner of preparing.

Vegetable pickles may be stored for limited periods in crocks. For indefinite storing they should be packed in sterile jars and sealed as are any canned vegetable or fruit (see Preserves for canning and sterilizing).

There are two general ways to make pickle: the short brining process and the long fermentation process. All vegetables should be placed in brine and processed before being made into pickle. Fruits may be conserved in brine, but they need no brining process before being made into pickle.[1]

A certain amount of fermentable sugar is present in all vegetables and fruits—especially in cucumbers and cabbage (see Sauerkraut). When vegetables are put into brine, the salt draws out the fermentable sugar by the process of *osmosis*. As a result an acid brine is formed that acts upon the vegetable tissues, producing a hardening and firming effect and a "cured" taste. The acid brine checks the action of organisms that would otherwise cause the vegetables to spoil. Produce that is properly brined will keep indefinitely.

As a rule relish mixtures, which contain an assortment of whole or chopped vegetables, are processed by the short method, and some pickle made of cucumbers may be quickly processed. Most authorities and experienced picklemakers, however, are convinced that cucumber pickle should be fermented by the long process before being made into the finished product. (See brine solutions below.)

Vegetables may be brined in small or large quantities. The most convenient and satisfactory container for making small quantities in the home is a stone jar, for stone absorbs objectionable odors and flavors. Small kegs or large glass jars may be used. The most popular size is a 4-gallon stone crock, which holds about ¼ bushel of produce.

Watertight kegs or barrels are best for making large quantities

---

[1] Dr. Edwin LeFevre, of the Bureau of Chemistry, U.S. Department of Agriculture, has written an excellent bulletin, *Farmers' Bulletin* 1438, on fermented pickle. The bulletin is recommended to picklemakers, especially to those who make pickle in large quantity.

of brined pickle or sauerkraut. When they are used, they must first be thoroughly washed or charred to remove any foreign odor or flavor. Potash or soda lye solutions, made according to directions given by the manufacturer, simplify the cleansing task. Pour the solution into the container and let it stand for 2 days. Then drain out solution and wash thoroughly.

All brining containers must be covered while the produce is being processed. Boards, about 1 inch thick, of any wood except yellow or pitch pine make the best covers. The boards should be cut round and should have a diameter about 1 to 2 inches less than that of the container, so that they may be removed easily and the salt added without disturbing the contents of the container. Dip the boards in melted paraffin; then hold them over a flame so that the paraffin will fill the pores of the wood. This process makes it easy to wash the boards. Heavy earthenware platters may be used as a substitute for board covers.

The covers should be further protected by a heavy, clean white cloth to keep out dust and insects. Grape or cabbage leaves spread directly over the vegetables or over the cover give added protection and flavor to pickle. This is especially true of dill pickles.

If vegetables are treated by the long fermentation process in a weak brine and are to be kept for any length of time in the same container, it must be sealed. The best and cheapest way is to pour a coating of melted paraffin, at least a half inch thick, over the surface of the vegetables. Cover the paraffin with a lid, weight down, and store the container in a cool, dry place.

If paraffin is applied before active fermentation stops, gas bubbles will form and break through the paraffin. In this case, remove the paraffin, reheat, strain, and pour again on pickle.

The safest way to preserve produce brined in a weak solution is to transfer it to sterilized Mason jars, pour over fresh brine to cover, and seal as for any canned produce.

Brined Cucumbers—Small Quantity

Since cucumbers are more frequently brined by the long fermentation process, they are used as an example for explaining the process.

> 4-gallon stone jar, crock, or other suggested container with cover
> ¼ bushel fresh cucumbers of uniform size
> 6 quarts 10 percent brine (22½ ounces of dairy or dry flake salt to 6 quarts water, 40 degrees reading on salinometer scale)
> Extra salt

Wash the container thoroughly with hot soapy water, rinse and dry. Wash the cucumbers and dry them thoroughly. Pack them in a container. Cover with cold brine. (*Never use hot brine for processing cucumbers or any produce*, since hot brine will retard or stop formation of the acid necessary to ferment the pickle.) Let stand covered overnight. On the next day add 1 pound of salt to each 10 pounds of cucumbers (1 pound 3 ounces salt for ¼ bushel cucumbers), in order to maintain the strength of the brine.

At the end of 1 week, and of each succeeding week for 5 weeks, add ¼ pound of salt. Add the salt by pouring it on the lid of the container. By so doing the salt will gradually sift into the solution and not sink to the bottom of the container.

As the pickles ferment, a scum will form on the surface of the brine. This scum is injurious to the acidity of the brine and should be skimmed off as it forms.

While fermentation is taking place, gas bubbles will form, and the brine will be in motion. When fermentation stops, the brine will be still and the cucumbers ready for further use. This takes from one to three weeks. Cucumbers may then be cured in the same brine and container, or they may be removed and combined with vinegar, spices, and sugar and made into many varieties of pickle.

If cured in the same brine, the finished product is known as "salt" or "salt stock." If made in small quantity (the same amount as given for brining—¼ bushel), add salt as indicated for brining. Keep the cucumbers thoroughly submerged in the brine, and keep them covered. They should be cured in about 6 to 8 weeks, according to the quantity and condition of cucumbers being processed.

Brined Cucumbers—Large Quantity

1 large keg or barrel with cover (40 to 45 gallons)
Cucumbers
40-degree brine (22½ ounces salt to every 6 quarts water, 40 degrees on salinometer scale)
1 quart vinegar
Extra salt

Prepare barrel and cover as for long fermentation. Wash the cucumbers and dry thoroughly. Mix the solution of brine in a large container, and pour about 6 inches of brine into barrel. Add vinegar. As cucumbers are gathered from the garden (or purchased), put them into the brine. Adjust the lid and weight it down. Let stand overnight. Next day add salt at the rate of 1 pound of salt for every 10 pounds of cucumbers.

If cucumbers are added slowly to the barrel, no extra solution of brine need be made and added, for the brine will draw out enough juice from the cucumbers. If they are added rapidly, make additional 40-degree brine to keep the cucumbers covered.

When the barrel is full, add 3 pounds of salt each week for 5 weeks. Add salt by pouring on lid as for small quantity.

Do not stir the brine while the pickles are processing, for this action may cause air bubbles. In adding pickle to the barrel it is best to use a clean white cloth or piece of clean white paper to handle the cucumbers. Drop them in gently.

Skim the surface as scum forms.

If cucumbers are to be cured in same brine and container, process as for small quantity.

Brined cucumbers or the salt-stock pickle may be made for home consumption or may be sold to commercial picklemakers or retail food merchants. There is a great demand for this product, and it is an economical and easy way for the cucumber grower to make extra money on the crop.

Maximum acidity of brine is reached at, or soon after, the close of the active fermentation stage. After this the strength of the acidity decreases gradually. The stage of active fermentation continues from 1 to 3 weeks, depending upon the temperature, the sugar content of the produce, the strength of the brine, and other factors. While fermentation is taking place, gas is formed and a froth appears on the surface. When fermentation stops, the brine becomes still.

To determine whether the brine is acid, dip a piece of litmus paper, obtained from any drugstore, into brine. If the paper turns pink or red, the brine is acid. It is impossible, however, to determine the degree of acidity by this method. Those who do not have the equipment and instructions with which to make chemical tests on brine should follow the instructions on maintaining brines given under Brined Cucumbers in Small Quantity and Brined Cucumbers in Large Quantity in preceding pages.

The volume of brine necessary to cover vegetables should be about one half the volume of the vegetables. Thus, it will take about 2½ gallons of brine to process a 5-gallon jar of vegetables.

While vegetables are in fermentation, it is important to store one container in a place where the temperature will remain at about 86 degrees Fahrenheit. This is especially important when fermenting sauerkraut or any vegetable processed in the late fall or in winter. A low temperature will retard and sometimes completely stop fermentation, and the produce in the brine will spoil.

Many of the recipes in this book give specific proportions for the brine. But the following directions will be helpful in other recipes. In all brines, dry flaky salt, called *dairy salt*, should be used, although table salt may be used if it is more convenient. Dairy salt may be purchased at any farm-supply store.

One of the most frequently used brines is a 10 percent brine. This is familiarly known as brine "strong enough to float an egg." Such brine is strong enough to allow slow fermentation of vegetables. Produce kept in a 10 percent brine will not spoil. To make: dissolve 1 pound of salt in 9 pints of water.

To make a 5 percent solution, dissolve ½ pound of salt in 9 pints of water. Vegetables in a 5 percent brine will ferment rapidly, but will spoil within a few weeks if not sealed.

Spiced Vinegar Scale

To 1 gallon of vinegar add:
> ½ ounce each allspice and cloves
> 1 stick cinnamon
> 1 piece mace
> 1 pound sugar for sour pickle
> or
> 2 pounds sugar for less acid pickle
> or
> 4 to 6 pounds sugar for sweet pickle (granulated sugar is always best)

Tie spices in muslin bag, drop into vinegar, add sugar, and boil for 15 minutes. Pour spiced vinegar in a large glass jar, cover, and store for 3 weeks before removing spice bag. One gallon of vinegar will pickle ¾ peck of cucumbers.

From: Pickling, *by Rose Ellwood Bryan, Extension Circular 362, N.C. Agricultural Extension Service, N.C. State College of Agriculture and Engineering of the University of North Carolina, and the U.S. Department of Agriculture, cooperating.*

Cooking Brined Cucumbers

To make pickles of brined cucumbers, combine vinegar, spices, and sugar in a cooking kettle. Bring to a full rolling boil. Drop in a few cucumbers at a time. Bring back to a full rolling boil. Skim out cucumbers and pack them tightly in large stone crocks or glass jars, leaving room at the top for at least ½ inch of vinegar to cover the cucumbers. Pour the hot vinegar syrup over them. Let stand overnight; if more syrup is needed to cover cucumbers, make an additional amount. Keep the pickles in large jars until they will absorb no more of the vinegar syrup. Pack in smaller commercial jars, completely cover with syrup, and seal. See individual recipes for variations of this recipe.

Celery Vinegar

Celery vinegar is excellent for pickling vegetables, seafood, and combinations of both. It is a tasty salad-dressing base and is often used in the same way as catchup.

> 1 quart fresh celery, finely chopped, or
>   ¼ pound celery seed
> 1 quart cider vinegar
> 1 tablespoon salt
> 1 tablespoon sugar

Place the chopped celery or celery seed in a sterilized jar. Heat the remaining ingredients and pour boiling hot over the celery. Let cool, seal, and set aside for 2 weeks; strain if fresh celery has been used. Pour the liquid into a bottle, cork, and seal.
From Mrs. Norman Riddle, Burlington, N.C.: An old family cook book.

Mustard Vinegar for Pickle

Mustard vinegar is good for any sweet mustard pickle and is especially good for mixed cucumber and onion pickle.

> ¾ pound salt
> ¼ pound dry mustard
> 2 tablespoons each of celery seed, white mustard seed, ground cloves, cinnamon, allspice, black pepper, and ginger
> 4 pounds sugar
> 1 gallon vinegar

Mix the dry ingredients and make into a paste with a little cold vinegar. Mix the paste into the remaining vinegar and bring slowly to a boil, stirring constantly. When the mixture thickens, remove it from the heat and put it in a stone crock. Toss in pickles, or use according to individual recipes. Makes about 3 gallons of pickle.

Grape-Leaf Pickle Brine

Grape or cherry leaves add a delicate tang to any cucumber pickle if they are packed with the cucumbers in the brine. Pickles made by this method may be used direct from the brine or may be reprocessed into vinegar pickles.

In a stone jar or crock place a layer of grape leaves and a layer of freshly washed cucumbers. Alternate layers until the container is filled. Add a few grapes if desired. Fill with a brine made by adding ½ cup of salt to 1 gallon of water. It should not be too salty. Weight down the cucumbers with a stone on top of an inverted saucer or platter, and cover the jar with a clean cloth. Let stand for about 4 days. The pickles should be used at once or further processed in vinegar.

An old Dutch recipe.

Dill Pickle

Dill pickle may be made in much shorter time than the regular long-fermented pickle, since the addition of dill and spice makes it unnecessary to ferment the cucumbers until a "cured" taste has been reached. However, inasmuch as they may be cured in a weak brine to hasten the process, the pickle must be sealed to prevent spoilage.

> 4-gallon stone crock or jar with cover (as for Brined Cucumbers)
> Dill
> Spices
> Grape leaves
> Cucumbers to fill jar to within 3 inches from top
> 1 pound salt
> 1 pint vinegar
> 2 gallons water

Wash crock thoroughly, rinse, and dry. In the bottom of the crock spread a layer of grape leaves, a layer of fresh dill sprigs, and a thin layer of mixed pickling spices. Wash and dry the cucumbers and pack in the crock. Cover with a brine made by dissolving the salt into the combined vinegar and water. *Do not heat the brine.* Cover the crock with a lid and store it in a place with a temperature of about 86° F. The pickles should be ready for use in 10 days to 2 weeks.

Remove the pickles from the crock and pack in glass jars. Pour brine into an enamel or porcelain vessel and bring to a boil. Remove it from the heat and cool it to about 160° F. Pour it over the cucumbers to fill the jars. Add a sprig of dill and additional spices if desired as the jars are packed. Seal the jars airtight.

Lazy Dills

This is a cold-pack sweet dill that is amazingly easy to make.

> 6 large commercial dill pickles, thinly sliced crosswise
> 3 cups sugar
> 4 cloves garlic
> 1 teaspoon whole allspice
> 4 bay leaves

Combine the ingredients in a stone crock, cover, and let stand at room temperature for 24 hours to dissolve the sugar. No vinegar is needed, since the pickles have already been in brine. Chill thoroughly before serving.

VARIATION

> Dill pickles, already processed
> 1½ cups vinegar
> 1 teaspoon salt
> 2 teaspoons white mustard seed
> 1½ cups brown sugar

Cut the dills into pieces and pack in sterilized jars. Combine vinegar, salt, spices, and sugar and bring to boil. Pour hot over pickles. Seal and let stand for 2 weeks before using.

Kentucky Dill Pickles

This method may be used to dill cucumbers, okra, or green tomatoes.

> Cucumbers (or fresh okra or green tomatoes)
> Finely cut dill
> Hot pepper pods (red or green)
> Garlic cloves
> 1 gallon vinegar
> ½ gallon water
> 2 cups salt, *noniodized*

Scrub the cucumbers well with a brush and drain. Pack in quart jars. To each jar add finely cut dill to taste, 1 pod of hot pepper, and 1 clove of garlic. Blend the vinegar, water, and salt in a kettle and bring to a boil. Insert a silver knife blade in jar of cucumbers, then pour in hot brine to fill the jar. Withdraw the knife blade and seal the jar. This amount of brine will pickle about 3 gallons of cucumbers.

VARIATIONS

Tiny okra fresh from the garden dilled this way is wonderful. Cherry stone green tomatoes may also be dilled. They look exactly like olives—but taste better.
From Mrs. Harris W. Rankin, Paducah, Ky.

Kosher Dill Cucumbers or Tomatoes

> 10 pounds small whole cucumbers or small round green tomatoes
> Cloves of garlic
> Hot red pepper pods
> Peppercorns
> Fresh dill
> 3 quarts water
> 1 cup salt
> 4 cups vinegar

Wash and dry vegetables and pack in sterilized quart jars. For each jar add 1 peeled clove garlic, 1 hot red pepper pod, 4 to 6 peppercorns, and 1 generous sprig of fresh dill. Combine water, salt, and vinegar in saucepan, bring to a boil, and pour at once over pickle. Seal jars. If there is not enough vinegar brine, make more. The number of jars obtained depends on the size of the cucumbers or tomatoes.

Dill Gherkins

Tiny fresh gherkins (immature cucumbers)
Fresh dill
Mustard seed
Bay leaves
Alum

Scrub the cucumbers, rinse, and dry. Pack them in jars, alternating cucumbers and fresh dill sprigs, and put 1 teaspoon of mustard seed on each layer of cucumbers. On top of the pickle in each jar, place 1 bay leaf and 1 piece of alum the size of a garden pea.
Combine in a saucepan:

1 cup vinegar
2 cups water
1 tablespoon salt for each quart water

Bring the mixture to a boil and pour hot over cucumbers. Seal. This is enough solution for about 2 pints of pickles.
From Mrs. William Ryer Wright, Charlotte, N.C.

Barrows House Mustard Pickle

This "really famous" recipe includes a mustard sauce that may be used in making any mustard pickle.

1 quart small whole onions
1 quart small whole cucumbers
2 heads cauliflower, broken into flowerets
Weak brine to cover vegetables (see brine, page 20)

Let the washed vegetables stand in brine overnight. In the morning boil the vegetables in the same brine. Be sure to use a large kettle. As soon as the contents reach the boiling point, remove from the heat and drain the vegetables.

Make a sauce of the following:

> 2 cups sugar
> 1 cup flour
> 6 tablespoons dry mustard
> 1 tablespoon turmeric
> 2 quarts vinegar

Mix the dry ingredients, adding a little vinegar to blend to a smooth paste. Stir in the remaining vinegar. Place in a large kettle and cook over low heat until the sauce thickens, stirring constantly. Add the drained vegetables to the hot sauce and mix thoroughly. Remove from the heat, and pack immediately into hot sterilized jars. Let stand for several days before using.
From William G. Barrows, Barrows House, Dorset-in-the-Mountains, Vt.

North Carolina Governors' Mustard Pickle

This mixed mustard pickle has been a favorite of a number of the State's governors. It was given to me especially for this book.

> 2 quarts long sour cucumber pickles, diced and drained
>   (see Sour Pickle, page 52)
> 1 quart small white onion sets (seed onions) or small
>   onions
> 4 green sweet peppers, chopped
> 1 red bell pepper, chopped
>   Brine to cover
> 1 large cauliflower, broken into flowerets

On the first day remove seeds and white fibers from peppers. Chop and mix the peppers with the onions. Let stand overnight in a brine made by adding ½ cup of salt to each ½ gallon of water. Next morning combine vegetables and brine in a large kettle and heat to scalding point—but do not boil. Drain the vegetables thoroughly. Boil the cauliflower flowerets in salted water until almost tender. Be careful not to overcook them. Drain. Mix the vegetables and diced pickle in a large kettle.

Make the following sauce:

> 1 tablespoon dry mustard
> 1 ounce turmeric
> 1 cup flour
> 2 cups light brown sugar
> 2 quarts vinegar

Blend the dry ingredients with a little of the vinegar to make a smooth paste. Add remaining vinegar and stir. Boil the sauce until it thickens; then pour it over the vegetables. Heat the vegetable-sauce mixture to scalding, but do not allow it to boil. Seal in sterilized jars. *Never make more than twice this quantity at one time.*

From Miss Laura Reilley, Hostess, Executive Mansion, Raleigh, N.C.

Jane Comer's Mixed Mustard Pickle

This tangy and original recipe is from Jane Comer's copious files of delicious pickles and preserves.

> 1 quart large green cucumbers, sliced crosswise
> 1 quart small green cucumbers, sliced crosswise
> 1 quart small whole button onions, peeled
> 1 quart green tomatoes, sliced
> 1 medium-sized cauliflower, broken into small pieces
> 6 large green sweet peppers, seeded and cut into small pieces
> 1 pint salt
> 2 gallons water

Measure vegetables after slicing. Soak mixed vegetables for 24 hours in a brine made by adding 1 pint of salt to 2 gallons of water. Place vegetables and brine in a large kettle over medium heat. Bring to a rapid boil and remove from the heat immediately. Drain well.

> 6 tablespoons dry mustard
> 1 tablespoon turmeric
> 1 cup flour
> 3 pints vinegar
> 1 cup sugar

Mix the mustard, turmeric, and flour with a little of the vinegar in a saucepan, and blend to a smooth paste. Stir in the remaining vinegar and sugar. Place over medium heat, stirring constantly, until the mixture boils. Remove from heat and pour over the vegetables. Stir the vegetables and sauce together well with a fork, and pack hot into sterilized jars. Seal immediately. Makes about 5 quarts.

From Mrs. Harry F. Comer, Abingdon, Va.

Dutch Salad Pickle

This is a grand mustard pickle for frankfurters, hamburgers, or, indeed, any meat.

> 2 quarts green tomatoes
> 1 quart onions
> 1 quart cabbage
> 3 or 4 green bell peppers, seeded
> 1 quart cucumbers, peeled and chopped (measure after
> preparing)
> ½ cup salt

Grind together all vegetables except the chopped cucumbers, using the coarse blade of the food chopper. Then add salt. Cook over low heat. Let come to a boil, and simmer for about 5 minutes. Watch carefully, since the juice from the tomatoes is the only liquid.

Make a dressing as follows:

> 3 cups sugar
> 1 ounce dry mustard
> 1 cup flour
> 1 tablespoon turmeric
> 2 quarts vinegar

Sift together the dry ingredients. Slowly add 1 quart of the vinegar. Heat the remaining vinegar and add to the first mixture. Stir well to blend. Put the combined mixture in a saucepan over low heat and cook until it has the consistency of starch. Add the vegetable mixture to the sauce, and bring to a boil. Add the chopped cucumbers. Remove immediately from heat. Pack in sterilized jars and seal. Makes about 11 pints.
From Mrs. Tom Hood, in The Delta's Best Cook Book, *American Legion Auxiliary, Greenville, Miss.*

Crisp Garlic Pickle

> 2½ pounds large sour pickles
> 1½ pounds sugar
> 1 teaspoon each black peppercorns and whole allspice
> 1½ teaspoons whole cloves
> 1 tablespoon olive oil
> 2 cloves garlic

Cut pickles into pieces and place in a jar. Add other ingredients and let stand for 4 days. Shake the jar occasionally to mix. After 4 days, seal in sterilized jars.

Stuffed Sweet Pickled Cucumbers

> Cucumbers
> Water
> Salt
> Seedless raisins, washed and drained

Lemons
Whole cloves
Allspice if desired

Soak cucumbers in a good strong brine (1 cup of salt to 1 gal. of water) for 9 days. Then soak in clear water for 48 hours. Slit the cucumbers lengthwise and scoop out seeds. Wipe them dry inside and fill each one with washed raisins (1 to 2 tablespoonfuls for each cucumber), a lengthwise sliver of lemon, and 2 whole cloves. Use a pinch of allspice if desired. Tie or sew up the cucumbers and place them in a stone jar.

Make a syrup of the following:

1 quart vinegar
5 pounds sugar
1 teaspoon each ground cinnamon, cloves, and allspice

Heat syrup and pour boiling hot over the cucumbers. Drain on the following day. Reheat syrup and pour it back over the cucumbers. Repeat this process each day for 3 additional days, until syrup has been reheated and poured again over cucumbers on 5 successive days. Fit the cover on the jar and store.

VARIATION

Cucumbers stuffed with chow-chow (see Chow-chow, page 110) instead of raisins are also very good.

From Mrs. H. F. Shaffer, in Pages from Old Salem Cook Books, *Dorcas Co-Workers of the Salem Home, Winston-Salem, N.C., 1947.*

Toss-in-the-Crock Mustard Pickle

The contributor of this famous recipe does not know how or where the idea originated. But it is a grand way for anyone with— or even without—a garden to maintain a perpetual pickle jar. It is somewhat like a stock-pot—you eat from it and at the same time you add to it.

Use a very large crock—4 to 6 gallons. Choose any assortment of vegetables that take to pickling: cucumber, onion, cabbage, green pepper, hard green tomato, sliced broccoli stems, string beans, cauliflower, root artichokes, carrots, and so on. When the first batch is made, the crock may be almost filled. As some of the contents are taken out, add more vegetables and more sauce to keep the pickle well covered. Do not add more than 1 pound of vegetables a day. Try to use pickle from the bottom of the crock, stirring fresh vegetables well into the sauce near the top.

Wash and dry vegetables. Cut them or leave small ones whole. Pack the vegetables in the crock, and pour over the following sauce to cover the pickle completely:

> 6 quarts vinegar
> 1 pound salt
> 1 ounce each of whole cloves, allspice, ground ginger, black pepper, and celery seed
> 2 ounces white mustard seed
> 2½ pounds brown sugar (or use in the proportion of ¾ brown to ¼ white sugar)
> 1 tablespoon cayenne pepper, *or* 1 ounce each mace, ground nutmeg, and dry horseradish

Boil the vinegar with other ingredients for 8 minutes. Cool. Meanwhile make a paste of:

> 1 pound dry mustard
> 1 ounce turmeric
> Vinegar

Mix mustard and turmeric with a little cold vinegar to make a thin paste. Mix the paste into the vinegar syrup, and blend well. Pour the cold sauce over the vegetables. Close the crock, and leave it undisturbed until vegetables are pickled—they should be ready in a few days. Taste to test. They may be stored at room temperature.

Variation

Try thawed and drained frozen vegetables.
From Mrs. Noel Houston, Chapel Hill, N.C.

Sweet Cucumber-Onion Pickle

Cucumbers, washed and sliced paper-thin, to make 6 quarts
18 small onions, sliced paper-thin
2 green peppers, chopped
½ cup salt
2 dozen ice cubes (or 6 cups ice, cracked into large pieces)
5 cups sugar
1½ teaspoons ground cloves
3 tablespoons celery seed
½ teaspoon ground turmeric
3 tablespoons mustard seed

Mix sliced cucumbers, onions, peppers, and salt in a large crock. Add ice, mixing it thoroughly with the vegetables, and weight down with a heavy cover. Let stand for 3 hours; then drain. Place the vegetable mixture in a large kettle. Combine sugar, spices, and vinegar, and pour the mixture into the vegetables. Heat to the scalding point, but do not boil. Pour immediately into hot sterilized jars, and seal. Makes 7 pints.
From Mrs. Logan Burdette, in What's Dat Cookin'? *St. Monica's Guild, Christ Episcopal Church, Point Pleasant, W. Va.*

French Pickle

4 pounds cucumbers
2 pounds onions
Salt
½ gallon vinegar
1 quart sugar
6 pods red bell peppers, chopped
1 tablespoon celery seed
2 tablespoons mustard seed
1 ounce turmeric
4 tablespoons olive oil or salad oil

Wash, peel, and slice the cucumbers and onions. Mix the vegetables, sprinkle with salt, and let stand for 24 hours. Wash out the salt by running cold water through the vegetables in a colander. Squeeze out all liquid. Put vinegar and other ingredients —except oil—in a large kettle and bring to a boil. Add vegetables and boil for 10 minutes. Set aside to cool. When cold, add the oil. Seal in sterilized jars.

From Miss Betty Allen, in Southern Recipes, *Montgomery Junior League, Montgomery, Ala.*

Curry Cucumber Pickles

      4 pounds medium-sized cucumbers
    ½ cup salt
      Ice water to cover cucumbers
    2 cups cider vinegar
    ½ teaspoon curry powder
    ¾ cup white sugar
    ½ cup brown sugar
    2 tablespoons white mustard seed
    1 tablespoon celery seed
    1 teaspoon ground cloves
    1 red pepper pod, broken in small pieces

Wash cucumbers and cut into 1-inch lengths. Make a brine of ice water and the salt. Let stand 6 hours. Drain and rinse in clear, cold water. Combine the remaining ingredients in a saucepan and bring to the boiling point. Pack cucumbers in hot sterilized jars, and pour the hot syrup over them. Seal at once. Makes about 4 pints.

From Mrs. Kenneth Kay, Leesburg, Fla.

Mary Rutledge's Cucumber Rings

Mrs. Rutledge is widely known in the art of cookery. Her cucumber pickles are highly prized, and her friends all look forward to having them at Christmastime. The pickles are delicious, crisp rings made from commercial pickles.

> ¾ pound sour large pickles, sliced crosswise ¼ to ⅜ inch thick
> ½ pound sugar
> 1 tablespoon whole cloves
> 2 sticks cinnamon

Put pickles in an earthenware, agateware, or glassware container. Sprinkle the sugar and spices over the pickles and stir well. Put aside for 2 days, but stir well and frequently. The pickles will be ready on the third day. They should be brittle and firm. Do not seal in jars or cover tightly. They will keep indefinitely if not eaten. Ha!
From Mrs. Mary Hall Lake Rutledge, Williamsburg, Va.

Lord Higden's Pickle

This is an old English "receipt."

> 3 quarts cucumbers, peeled and chopped
> 4 quarts chopped onions
> 4 quarts green and red sweet peppers, chopped together
> 2 cups salt

Mix vegetables and salt, and put into a stone crock for at least 12 hours. Drain, extracting as much juice as possible.
Have ready a mixture of the following:

> ½ gallon scalding white vinegar
> 4 tablespoons each white mustard seed and ground black pepper
> 1 tablespoon each whole cloves and whole allspice
> 3 tablespoons olive oil

Pack the drained vegetables in a stone crock, and pour the hot vinegar mixture over them until the crock is filled. Weight down the cover. Let stand for 2 weeks, stirring frequently. Pack in sterilized jars.

Barrows House Oil Pickle

Barrows House, in the mountains of Vermont, has for more than fifty years been noted for its fine cuisine, and its pickles are world famous. We are grateful for two of the inn's recipes. (See also Barrows House Mustard Pickle, page 26.)

> 24 cucumbers, about 1 inch in diameter, thinly sliced
> 3 small onions, thinly sliced
> 6 tablespoons salt

Drain the sliced cucumbers. In a jar place alternate layers of cucumbers and onions. Add salt and let stand for 5 hours; then drain.

Make the following sauce:

> 2 quarts vinegar
> ¾ cup white mustard seed
> ½ cup black mustard seed
> 1½ tablespoons celery seed
> ¾ cup olive oil

Heat the vinegar to the boiling point; cool and strain. Add the other ingredients and blend thoroughly. Pour over pickles, completely covering them. Let stand for several days.

VARIATION

To make sweet oil pickles, add 2 cups of brown sugar to the hot vinegar. Strain, cool, and proceed as above. Mixed spices, a hot red pepper pod, and a clove of garlic may be added.

From William G. Barrows, Barrows House, Dorset-in-the-Mountains, Vt.

Nine-Day Sweet Cucumber Pickles

This is a highly prized old Texas recipe.

> 4 quarts fresh cucumbers, cut crosswise into ½-inch
> slices

1st day: Put sliced cucumbers in a brine "strong enough to float
an egg"—4 ounces of salt to 1 quart of water—and let stand
for 3 days.

4th day: Drain cucumbers and put them in clear water for 3 days,
changing the water each day.

7th day: Drain cucumbers and cover with a weak brine (1 tablespoon of salt to 1 quart of water), to which has been added
a piece of alum the size of a marble. Slowly simmer cucumbers in this mixture for 3 hours. Drain.

Make a syrup of the following ingredients:

> 3 pints vinegar
> 3½ pounds sugar
> 1 ounce each whole allspice and stick cinnamon
> ½ ounce celery seed

Let the ingredients come to a boil and pour, while hot, over the
drained cucumbers. Let the mixture stand overnight. On each of
the next 2 days drain off syrup, bring it back to a boil, and pour it
over the cucumbers, letting them stand in the syrup overnight
after each processing.

9th day: Drain off the syrup, heat it to the boiling point, and pour
hot over the cucumbers. Pack the hot pickles in sterilized jars,
cover with the syrup, and seal. Makes 4 quarts pickle.

*From Mrs. Robert Weeren, La Grange, Texas; contributed by
Mrs. F. Burton Jones, Chapel Hill, N.C.*

Airlie Sweet Cucumber Pickles

This grand recipe belonged to Mrs. Goodwin Williams of Airlie
Plantation, Berryville, Va.

    4 pounds cucumbers
    3 quarts fresh water
    1 tablespoon alum
    1 ounce ginger root
    Brine (page 20)

Soak cucumbers in brine for 2 weeks. Drain, and slice crosswise
in ¼-inch slices. Soak slices in cold water until the salt is out.
Put cucumbers in fresh water, add the alum, and boil ½ hour.
Drain, and boil for ½ hour in ginger root tea, which has been
made by using 3 quarts of water for the 1 ounce of ginger root.
    Make a syrup of the following:

    2½ pounds brown sugar
    1 quart vinegar
    1 pint water
    ½ stick cinnamon
    1 teaspoon each whole mace and whole cloves

Put the cucumbers in the syrup and boil all together until the
cucumbers become transparent and the syrup is thick. Seal in
sterilized jars.
From Mrs. Lloyd W. Williams, Spartanburg, S.C.

Icicle Cucumber Pickles

Here is a quick and easy original recipe.

    Cucumbers to fill 3 quart jars
    Ice water to cover cucumbers
    1 quart vinegar
    ½ cup sugar
    ½ cup salt
    1 tablespoon mustard seed

Scrub the cucumbers but do not peel them. Quarter lengthwise and soak in ice water from 3 to 5 hours. Add ice as necessary to keep the water icy cold. Drain and pack cucumber quarters in 3 sterilized quart jars. Combine vinegar, sugar, salt, and mustard seed in a saucepan. Heat to a rolling boil and pour immediately over cucumbers. Seal. They will be ready to serve in 1 month. *From Mrs. Hugh T. Lefler, Chapel Hill, N.C.*

Cucumber-Raisin Pickle

2 quarts brined cucumbers, thinly sliced crosswise
1 pound sugar
1 pint vinegar
1 cup seedless raisins
1 tablespoon each celery seed, mustard seed, and whole allspice

Drain cucumbers, slice, and then measure. Combine the remaining ingredients in an open kettle. Over high heat bring to a boil and boil the syrup rapidly for 5 minutes. Add the cucumbers. Bring the mixture back to boiling. Remove the kettle from the heat. Pack the cucumbers in sterilized jars. Pour over the hot syrup and seal. This makes about 2 quarts of pickles. *From Mrs. Henry Hurdle, Marysville, Calif.*

Mrs. Durant's Crystallized Cucumber Pickle

This is a famous North Carolina recipe.

Medium-sized cucumbers
Brine "strong enough to float an egg" (10 percent brine, page 20)
Solution of half vinegar and half water
3 pounds sugar
1 pint vinegar, and a little extra vinegar
3 tablespoons white mustard seed
2 sticks cinnamon
1 tablespoon chopped ginger root
1 teaspoon alum

Wash the cucumbers. Make a 10 percent brine. Place cucumbers in a large crock, and cover with brine. (The volume of brine necessary to cover any vegetables is about one third the volume of the vegetables to be covered.) Let the mixture stand for 3 days.

Remove the cucumbers from the brine and put them into clear water. Let them stand for 3 days, changing water each day. On the fourth day, remove the cucumbers from the water and cut into 1-inch pieces. Put them in a preserving kettle, and cover with a solution of equal parts of water and vinegar. Place over medium heat, bring to a boil, and boil about 5 minutes or until pieces of cucumber are tender. Remove the kettle from the heat and set it aside. Let the cucumbers stand in the boiled solution for 3 days. Then drain off the liquid and discard it. Pack the cucumbers in sterilized jars.

Combine the remaining ingredients in a saucepan. Bring the syrup to a boil and pour it over the cucumbers. Let the cucumbers and syrup stand in the jars overnight. Then drain off the syrup into a saucepan, return it to the heat, and bring it to a boil. Pour it again over the cucumbers. Repeat this process on 2 more days. On the third day, seal hot. This syrup will make approximately 2 quarts of cucumber pickle.

From Mrs. R. F. Durant, in Soup to Nuts, *Woman's Auxiliary, Church of the Holy Comforter, Burlington, N.C.*

Hot Cucumber Pickles

1 peck small whole cucumbers, washed and dried
1 cup sugar
1 cup black pepper
1 cup salt
1 cup dry mustard
2 quarts cider vinegar

Pack the cucumbers into sterilized jars. Mix sugar, pepper, salt, and mustard with 2 cups of cold vinegar and blend to a paste. Add to the remaining vinegar in a saucepan and bring to a boil.

Cook the sauce until it thickens. Pour the sauce over the packed cucumbers, and seal the jars. Shake the jars frequently or turn them upside down until pickles are well mixed.

From Mrs. D. L. Bost, in The Volunteers Cook Book, *Concord, N.C.*

Holly Hill Pickles

This delicious pickle is made from small commercial brine-proc-essed cucumbers. They are usually sold in bulk, but they can also be processed at home. (See Brined Cucumbers, page 18.)

Take small cucumbers out of brine, and fill a 2-gallon stone crock or jar about four fifths full. Be sure that it has a close-fitting cover. Sprinkle over the cucumbers the following:

> 2 tablespoons olive oil
> 2 tablespoons each white mustard seed, black mustard
>   seed, black peppercorns, and celery seed
> 1 tablespoon whole allspice
> ½ tablespoon whole cloves
> 1 cracked nutmeg, broken into small pieces
> 2 pods red hot pepper
> 1 cup dry horseradish

Boil together:

> 5 pounds sugar
> 3 quarts vinegar

Pour the hot mixture over the pickles. Place a close-fitting cover on the jar or crock, and store. The pickles will be ready in 1 month.

From Mrs. James N. Williamson, Jr., Orlando, Fla., in The Southern Cook Book.

Twenty-Day Cucumber Pickles

This recipe isn't so complicated as it sounds—that is, if you are going to stay at home for 20 days! Make any amount of pickle you want.

1st day: Cut fresh green cucumbers into pieces about ¾ inch in length. Cover them with boiling water and let them stand overnight.

2nd day: Drain. Sprinkle lightly with salt, cover again with boiling water, and let stand overnight.

3rd day: Drain. Sprinkle lightly with powdered alum, cover again with boiling water, and let stand overnight.

4th day: Drain off the alum water. Cover the cucumbers again with boiling water and let stand overnight.

5th day: Drain. Put cucumbers in a pickling crock, cover with boiling vinegar, and let stand overnight.

6th and 7th days: Each day drain off the vinegar. Reboil it and pour it over the cucumbers, adding enough fresh vinegar to cover. Let it stand overnight after each processing.

8th day: Drain off the vinegar and discard it. Pack the cucumbers in quart jars, and add 1 tablespoon of mixed spices and 1 tablespoon of sugar to each jar. Place tops on jars but do not seal. Each day thereafter add an additional tablespoon of sugar to each jar until enough syrup has formed to cover the cucumbers. Then seal the jars. The entire process should take about 20 days.

These pickles have a distinctive flavor and are transparent and crisp.

From Mrs. C. L. Haney, Raleigh, N.C.

Sour Gherkin Pickles

This is a Middle Western recipe that is especially popular around Chicago.

>100 gherkins (tiny cucumbers)
>Ice water to cover gherkins
>Cider vinegar to cover gherkins
>1 ounce dry mustard
>1 cup salt

Wash the cucumbers. Soak them overnight in ice water, dry, and pack in sterilized jars. To determine the required amount of vinegar, place the cucumbers in a large vessel and pour over enough vinegar to cover them well. Drain off the vinegar and blend it with the mustard and salt. Pour the mixture over the packed gherkins and seal.

From Mrs. William Ryer Wright, Charlotte, N.C.

Sweet Gherkin Pickles (Smooth-Skin or Porcupine)

Use smooth-skin or porcupine gherkins that have been processed by the long-fermentation method. Proceed with pickling as for Holly Hill Pickles or pickle by any recipe for sweet cucumber pickles.

Mil McKay's Sweet Cucumber Pickle

This is an old-fashioned, easy, sweet pickle recipe.

>Large cucumbers, cut in strips lengthwise, to fill three
>   quart jars
>Ice water
>Celery stalks
>Sliced onion

Soak the cucumbers in ice water for 5 hours. Remove and dry. Pack upright with a few stalks of celery and onion slices in sterilized jars.

Boil the following together for 5 minutes to make a syrup:

> 1 quart vinegar
> 1 cup sugar
> ½ cup water
> ⅓ cup salt

Pour the syrup over the cucumbers, and seal hot. They will be ready to use in 2 weeks.
From Mrs. H. P. McKay, Onancock, Va.

Elsa Thorley's Mixed Cucumber Pickle

This pickle has a good garlic flavor.

> 4 quarts cucumbers, thinly sliced
> 6 medium-sized onions, thinly sliced
> 1 green pepper, thinly sliced
> 1 red pepper, thinly sliced
> 3 cloves garlic
> ⅓ cup salt
> 2 trays ice cubes
> 3 cups vinegar
> 3 cups sugar (Some persons prefer a little over 2 cups)
> 1½ teaspoons each turmeric and celery seed
> 2 tablespoons mustard seed

To the sliced cucumbers, onions, and peppers add the whole peeled garlic cloves and sprinkle the mixture with salt. Mix the ice cubes into the vegetable mixture and let stand for 3 hours. Drain thoroughly. Put the vegetable mixture into a large kettle. Combine the vinegar, sugar, and spices and pour over the vegetables. Heat just to the boiling point. Pour into sterilized pint jars and seal. Let stand at least 1 month before using. Makes about 8 pints.
From Mrs. Elsa Dodd Thorley, Center Port, N.Y.

Ripe Cucumber Rings

This fine pickle is a Williamsburg favorite.

> Large ripe cucumbers, peeled and sliced in ½-inch rings
> Water
> Salt

Soak the peeled and sliced cucumbers overnight in salt water, using ¼ cup of salt to 1 quart of water. Drain and cook in clear water for 20 minutes. Drain and cover with pickling syrup made of the following:

> 2 cups sugar
> 2 cups vinegar
> 2 cups water
> 1 lemon, thinly sliced
> 2 sticks cinnamon
> 1 tablespoon whole cloves
> 2 teaspoons whole allspice

Simmer the cucumbers in syrup for 15 minutes, or until transparent. Pack the cucumbers in jars, cover with the hot syrup, and seal.

From Mrs. Mary Hall Lake Rutledge, Williamsburg, Va.

Bread-and-Butter Pickle

> 3 quarts medium-sized cucumbers, sliced
> 3 medium-sized onions, sliced
> ½ cup salt
> Water to cover vegetables
> 2 cups vinegar
> ½ cup water
> 2½ cups sugar
> 2 tablespoons mustard seed
> 1 teaspoon each celery seed and turmeric

Combine the vegetables and mix them with the salt. Let stand for 3 hours, and then drain. In a large kettle combine vingear and remaining ingredients and bring to boil. Add vegetables and heat to simmering. Avoid boiling the vegetables, for this makes them soft. Pack while hot in sterilized jars and seal. Makes about 3 quarts.

From Mrs. Henry A. Foscue, High Point, N.C.

Shamrock Inn Sweet, Whole Green-Tomato Pickle

Mary McCrank's "Home-by-the-Side-of-the-Road" inn is famous for good home-made food. We are proud to present her favorite pickle recipe.

> 1 gallon small, whole green tomatoes
> Salt to taste—about 2 tablespoons
> Water to cover
> Whole cloves
> 1 quart vinegar
> 3½ cups granulated sugar
> 3½ cups brown sugar
> 2 or 3 sticks cinnamon

Peel the tomatoes. Put them in a kettle with the water and salt, and boil until tender. Remove the tomatoes from the water, and drain. Stick 2 or 3 cloves in each tomato. Combine vinegar, sugar, and cinnamon in a saucepan, heat to boiling point, and boil until a thick syrup forms. Pour hot over the tomatoes, and let stand overnight. In the morning reheat tomatoes and syrup and pack in sterilized jars. Seal immediately. Makes from 3 to 4 quarts.

From Miss Mary McCrank, Shamrock Inn, Highway 99, Chehalis, Wash.

Champ Clark Green-Tomato Pickle

This is a famous Virginia recipe.

> 3 pints unpeeled green tomatoes, cut into small pieces
> 3 pints cucumber sour pickles, cut into small pieces

3 pints onions, finely chopped
3 pints vinegar
1 stalk celery, finely chopped
3 pounds brown sugar
1 teaspoon each ground cinnamon, whole allspice, and
   ground cloves

Mix all the ingredients in a large kettle, and boil them slowly for 1 hour and 40 minutes. Pour hot into sterilized jars or bottles, and seal.

From Mrs. Harry Gray, in The Suffolk Cook Book, *The Girls' Missionary Society of the Christian Church, Suffolk, Va.*

Crystal Green-Tomato Raisin Pickle

Very elegant is this old recipe of thin crisp tomatoes and raisins.

5 pounds firm uniform tomatoes, sliced crosswise 1/12
   inch thick
1 vial Lilly's lime (purchased at drug or grocery store)
   Water
3 pounds granulated sugar
7 cups cider vinegar
2 tablespoons each whole cloves and allspice
1 teaspoon ginger root
2 sticks cinnamon
1 pound seedless raisins

Place tomatoes in an agateware, porcelain, or stoneware vessel and cover with water mixed with the lime. Let stand for 24 hours. Lift the tomatoes from the lime water, rinse in ice water, and drain. Put the tomatoes in a large kettle and cover with sugar, vinegar, and spices. Bring to a slow boil, and cook until tomatoes are clear and tender. Stir often, but do not break tomatoes. When the tomatoes are transparent, add the raisins. Bring the mixture to a boil, and remove at once from the heat. Seal immediately in hot sterilized jars. Makes from 3 to 4 quarts.

From Comfort, *an old newspaper, c. 1850.*

Old-fashioned Green-Tomato Pickle

This is a special at Thousand Pines Inn, Tryon, N.C.

> 1 peck green tomatoes
> 1 cup salt
> 4 small white onions
> 5 cups brown sugar
> ½ teaspoon ground allspice
> 1 box pickling spices (2 or 3 ounces)
> 4 teaspoons celery seed
> ½ cup mustard seed
> 1 quart vinegar

Slice the tomatoes crosswise as thin as possible. Mix thoroughly with the salt in a china or porcelain vessel and let them stand overnight. Rinse through two clear waters and put in a colander to drain for at least 1 hour. Slice the onions very thin and add to the tomatoes. Stir in the remaining ingredients, and bring to a boil in a large kettle. Cook for 15 minutes, stirring occasionally. Seal hot in sterilized jars. Allow to stand at least 1 month before serving.

From Everyone Eats, *by Selina Lewis, Tryon, N.C.*

Irene's Green-Tomato Pickle

> 1 peck small uniform-sized green tomatoes, unpeeled and sliced
> 1 gallon cabbage, slawed (measure after slawing)
> 2 dozen medium-sized onions, thinly sliced
> 6 to 8 green peppers, chopped
> 1 cup salt
> 2 teaspoons ground cinnamon
> 2 tablespoons turmeric

Mix the above ingredients and let stand overnight. Drain well, and add the following:

2 quarts cider vinegar
3 pounds brown sugar
2 tablespoons celery seed
4 tablespoons mustard seed
2 tablespoons ground mace
2 teaspoons whole cloves

Place the entire mixture in a large kettle and cook for 1½ to 2 hours, or until the vegetables are tender and the mixture thick. Pack immediately in hot sterilized jars. Makes around 12 quarts. *From Mrs. Frederick S. Dixon, Fayetteville, N.C.*

Mary Hopkins's Green-Tomato Layer Pickle

Mrs. Hopkins isn't sure whether she inherited this old recipe from her Middle Western or her Tennessee ancestors. It is unique in that the pickle is processed in layers.

1 peck firm green tomatoes, sliced
Salt
1 ounce white mustard seed
½ ounce each whole cloves, whole allspice, black pepper, ground ginger, and celery seed
1 ounce turmeric
1½ ounces dry mustard
1½ pounds brown sugar
2 dozen medium-sized onions, peeled and sliced
Vinegar

Place the tomatoes in a vessel in layers, sprinkling each layer generously with salt. Let stand overnight. Rinse thoroughly, being careful not to break the tomatoes. In a porcelain kettle, alternate layers of tomatoes, sugar, spices, onions. Cover with vinegar and bring to a slow boil. Simmer until the vegetables are tender. *Do not stir.* Pack in sterilized jars, being careful to lift out vegetables so that there will be an equal amount of onions and tomatoes in each jar. Cover with the hot syrup and seal.
From Mrs. Charles Hopkins, Chapel Hill, N.C.

Airlie Plantation Green-Tomato Pickle

This is a treasured recipe that was originated by Mrs. Goodwin Williams, of Airlie Plantation, near Berryville, Va. It was contributed to this book by her daughter-in-law.

          10 pounds green tomatoes (1 peck)
          2½ pounds onions (¼ peck)
           2 green sweet peppers
           2 red sweet peppers
           ½ cup salt
           2 pounds sugar
           2 ounces each white mustard seed and celery seed
           2 tablespoons turmeric
           2 quarts vinegar

Slice the tomatoes and onions and cut the peppers into strips. Put all together in a kettle and sprinkle with the salt. Let stand overnight. Next day strain through a colander, pressing with the hand so that the salt will come out. Place in a kettle with the remaining ingredients, and boil until the tomatoes are transparent. Seal in sterilized jars. Makes 6 quarts.
From Mrs. Lloyd W. Williams, Spartanburg, S.C.

Valeria's Green-Tomato Pickle

           1 peck green tomatoes, unpeeled
          18 large white onions, peeled
             Approximately 2 cups salt
           4 ounces mustard seed
           3 tablespoons each powdered cloves, ground ginger,
             black pepper, and turmeric
           3 rounded tablespoons ground allspice
           ½ cup dry mustard
           2 quarts vinegar
           2 pounds dark brown sugar

Slice the tomatoes and onions and place in a large pan. Sprinkle with salt. Let stand overnight. Drain off the liquid. Mix the

spices together. In a large kettle pack the tomatoes and onions in layers, sprinkling each layer with the mixed spices. Cover with the vinegar. Place over medium heat and bring to simmering point. Reduce the heat and continue simmering until the tomatoes are transparent. Add the brown sugar and bring back to simmering. Continue simmering until the sugar has melted. Pack in sterilized jars and seal. Makes about 9 quarts.
From Mrs. William De R. Scott, Graham, N.C.

Arkansas Bread-and-Butter Pickle

    4 quarts cucumbers, sliced
    2 quarts onions, peeled and sliced
    ½ cup salt
    2 cups vinegar
    2 cups sugar
    2 tablespoons each mustard seed, celery seed, and
        turmeric

Combine sliced cucumbers and onions and sprinkle with salt. Let stand for 2 hours. In a saucepan combine the vinegar and the remaining ingredients and heat to the boiling point. Drain the vegetables, add them to the boiling vinegar mixture. Boil for 5 minutes, pour into jars, and seal. Makes about 4 quarts.
From Mrs. H. W. Oldham, Eureka Springs, Ark.

Green-Tomato Crisps

Making this delicious pickle is an annual rite with the contributor of this famous recipe.

    7 pounds fully developed green tomatoes, sliced ⅛
        inch thick
    2 gallons limewater (3 cups lime to 2 gallons water)

Soak the tomatoes in limewater 24 hours. Drain and soak for 4 hours in fresh water, changing the water every hour. Make a syrup as follows:

3 pints vinegar

5 pounds sugar

1 teaspoon each whole cloves, powdered ginger, whole allspice, celery seed, ground mace, and ground cinnamon

Bring vinegar, sugar, and spices to a boil. Pour over the tomatoes, and let stand overnight. In the morning, boil for 1 hour. Seal in sterilized jars.

From Mrs. Harry P. Alexander, contributed by Mrs. Willis Slane, High Point, N.C.

Sour Pickle

Cucumbers that have been brined by long fermentation

Stone jar or keg

Vinegar

Remove cucumbers from brine, drain well, pack in a stone jar or wooden keg. Pour over enough vinegar to cover. If a medium sour pickle is desired, use a 45 to 50 grain vinegar. Let stand for about 10 days. Renew the vinegar strength after about two weeks, if this is not done and the pickles are kept in the unsealed container they will spoil. If a very sour pickle is desired, let the cucumbers stand in the 45 to 50 percent vinegar for one week, then drain off solution and pour over a 40 to 45 grain vinegar. Pickles may be removed from jar or keg and sealed in sterilized jars. If sealed they will keep indefinitely.

2. Fruit Pickles

Sweet Pickled Fruit

To PICKLE FRUIT, SUCH AS CHERRIES, DAMSON PLUMS, PEACHES, PEARS, apples, and so on, use an amount of sugar equal to about one half the volume of fruit. The following syrup will pickle approximately 7 pounds of fruit.

> 3 pounds sugar (add 1 cup more for very tart fruit)
> 1 quart vinegar
> 1 stick cinnamon, broken
> ½ ounce whole cloves

Prepare the fruit. Combine the vinegar, sugar, and spices in a saucepan and bring to a full rolling boil. Pour the syrup over the fruit and let the fruit stand in it overnight. Repeat the next day. On the third morning boil fruit and syrup together for about 10 minutes, or until the fruit is tender but not mushy. Pack in sterilized jars and seal according to manufacturer's recommendation.

Pickled Apple Quarters

4 to 6 tart apples of uniform size
2 cups sugar
1 cup cider vinegar
1 stick cinnamon, broken into pieces
1 teaspoon whole cloves
Red food coloring

Pare and quarter apples to make 1 pint of quarters. Combine sugar, vinegar, and spices in a saucepan and boil for 5 minutes. Add apple quarters and cook until tender but not mushy. Add several drops of red food coloring. Pack immediately in hot sterilized jars. Makes about 2 pints.

Pickled Crab Apples

5 pints crab apples of uniform size
1 quart white vinegar
1 cup water
4 cups sugar
4 tablespoons mixed pickling spices tied in cloth bag

Combine vinegar, water, sugar, and spices in a large open kettle. Place over high heat and bring rapidly to a boil. Set the kettle aside and allow the syrup to cool; then add the apples to the cooled syrup. Put back over heat and bring slowly to a boil. Reduce the heat and cook the apples for about 5 minutes. If crab apples are not cooked slowly, the skins will break. Remove the kettle from the heat, remove the spice bag, and let the apples stand in the syrup overnight. Pack apples cold in sterilized jars. Pour over the cold syrup. Seal.

Pickled Blueberries

Elsa Thorley's hobby is raising herbs, and she keeps most of her table space filled with pots of rosemary and tarragon. However, she finds time and space to store this unusual pickle.

1 pint blueberries, not quite ripe
2 tablespoons molasses
1 teaspoon vinegar
½ cup well-packed brown sugar

Wash and pick over the blueberries. Mix berries in the molasses and vinegar. Place alternate layers of the blueberry-molasses-vinegar mixture and the brown sugar in an earthenware crock. Cover and let stand for 3 or 4 days—until the sugar has drawn out enough juice to make the mixture liquid. Pack in hot sterilized jars and seal immediately.
From Mrs. Elsa Dodd Thorley, Center Port, N.Y.

Fresno Stuffed Cantaloupe Pickle

This different and exotic pickle was developed especially for this book. Persian melons are best if they are available, but any small, firm, ripe melon will do nicely.

24 small melons the size of a large orange
½ gallon finely minced cabbage
1 pint finely minced onions
1 pint minced green tomatoes
1 cup salt
   White vinegar
1 cup brown sugar
2 red pepper pods, chopped
3 tablespoons mustard seed, white and yellow mixed
1 teaspoon each ground allspice, turmeric, dry mustard, and whole cloves
½ teaspoon ground ginger
½ pound seedless raisins

Cut section from one side of each melon and save to close the melon later. Remove seeds. Combine minced vegetables in kettle. Cover with 1 cup of salt and let stand for 3 hours. Drain. Discard the liquid. Pack the vegetables lightly in a large preserving kettle and cover with white vinegar, saving a little cold vinegar to mix with the dry ingredients. Blend the dry ingredients and remaining vinegar and add to vegetables. Place the kettle over medium heat and bring to a boil. Cook for 30 minutes. Remove from heat, and drain off the liquid. Save the liquid. Pack the cooked vegetables in the melons. Replace the melon sections and tie with string; then put the melons in a large crock. Cool the syrup and pour over the melons, adding enough vinegar to cover. Weight down the contents with a plate and heavy stone, and close the crock with a tight-fitting cover. Store the crock in a cool, dry place and let stand 3 weeks. Melons may then be removed from crock and packed in large, wide-mouthed sterilized jars.

From Paul Willard, Manager, University-Sequoia and Sunnyside Clubs, Fresno, Calif.

Pickled Cantaloupe

2 pounds peeled, sliced cantaloupe, weighed after preparation
1 pint white vinegar, or enough to cover fruit
1 pound sugar
1 stick cinnamon, broken
2 tablespoons whole mixed pickling spices, or oil of spice to taste

Prepare the melon and marinate in the vinegar overnight. Next morning drain off the vinegar and combine it with other ingredients. Boil the vinegar mixture until it forms a clear syrup. Drop in the melon and cook for about ½ hour, or until the melon is transparent. Pack in hot sterilized jars and seal.

Luta's Brandied Cherries

This is an old-fashioned and grand recipe for brandying cherries.

Red sour cherries
Wine vinegar
Sugar

Pit the cherries and measure them. Mix with an equal quantity of wine vinegar. Place the mixture in a stone crock and cover. Let stand for 48 hours. Drain off the liquid and discard it. Alternate layers of equal parts of cherries and sugar in the stone crock and cover. Stir the mixture once each week. The cherries are ready to serve in 3 months.

From Marjory Hendricks, Normandy Farm, Rockville, Md.

Kümmel Cherries

This is a tasty and potent cherry which may be served as an hors d'oeuvre, with meat and poultry, or in mixed drinks. Our contributor picked up the idea while visiting in Holland.

> 1 pint large black sweet cherries (Bing cherries)
> 4 tablespoons sugar
> Kümmel
> Vinegar

Wash and dry the cherries but do not remove the stems. Pack the cherries into a 1-pint Mason jar and add the sugar. Half-fill the jar with kümmel. Finish filling the jar with vinegar. Seal and set in a dark place. Turn the jar upside down once each day until the sugar is dissolved. The cherries are ready to serve after 1 week. They will keep indefinitely, but they will lose color after 2 or 3 weeks. Chill before serving. Makes 1 pint.

From Dwight Walker, Mebane, N.C.

VARIATION

Substitute Bourbon whiskey for the kümmel and proceed as for Kümmel Cherries.

Spiced Gooseberries

6 cups gooseberries, picked over and washed
6 cups sugar
¼ cup white vinegar
1 teaspoon ground cloves
½ teaspoon each ground cinnamon, and ground allspice
¼ teaspoon ground mace

Mix all ingredients in a kettle and bring to a slow boil, stirring often. Cook until mixture thickens. Pack in hot sterilized jars and seal immediately. Makes about 6 half-pints.

Lemon Pickle

This is an old recipe and is certainly different.

12 large lemons
½ cup salt
8 garlic cloves, peeled
1 tablespoon each ground mace, grated nutmeg, and ground allspice
1 teaspoon red pepper
4 tablespoons dry mustard
½ gallon vinegar

Wash and dry lemons and cut each lengthwise into 8 pieces. Put into an earthenware, enamel, or porcelain pan with the salt, garlic, mace, nutmeg, allspice, red pepper, and mustard. Add the vinegar, and bring the pickle slowly to a boil. Simmer for 30 minutes; then pour into a large stone jar. Stir daily for 1 month; then seal in sterilized glass jars.
From Mrs. William G. Vetterlein, Sedgefield, Greensboro, N.C.

Peach Mangoes

This recipe is from an old newspaper of the mid-nineteenth century. The masthead has been torn away; thus, the locale of the paper and the contributor's residence are not known.

Wash good firm peaches and remove pits. Make a mixture of fresh grated horseradish and mustard seed. Fill one half of peach and fasten halves together with a toothpick. Pack in jars, pour over vinegar prepared as for any spiced fruit. (See Sweet Pickled Fruit, page 53.)

The recipe is different, practical, and delicious.

From Carlyle Haverly, in Comfort, *c. 1900.*

Jessamine Gant's Sweet Peach Pickle

Miss Gant finds that liquid spices give any pickle a rich, clear amber color, especially fruits with delicate meat. This is a famous original recipe.

> 7 pounds firm (clingstone) peaches
> 3 pounds sugar
> 1 pint vinegar
> ½ teaspoon oil of cloves
> ¼ teaspoon oil of cinnamon

Peel the peaches. Make a syrup of sugar, vinegar, and spices and bring to a slow boil. Drop in the fruit, being sure there is enough syrup to cover. Cook slowly for 30 minutes, or until the peaches are tender. Pack fruit in sterilized jars; pour over hot syrup to cover; and seal. (The oils may be bought at drugstores or food markets.)

From Miss Jessamine Gant, Burlington, N.C.

Sweet Seckel-Pear Pickle

Peel firm, ripe Seckel pears, or any small firm pears, leaving the stem on. Drop them into cold water to keep them from turning dark; then blanch by dropping into boiling water. Take out each pear as it rises to the surface. Plunge into cold water and drain. Pack the pears in sterilized jars; and pour over hot syrup in the same proportion as for Sweet Peach Pickle. A drop or two of red or green vegetable coloring may be added to the syrup to give color to the pickle. One tablespoonful of *crème de menthe* added to each pint of pickle gives a refreshing flavor. Add the liqueur after the jars have been packed.

Sweet Pickled Peaches
Made from Canned Peaches

1 No. 3 can peach halves (4 cups)
1 cup vinegar
1 cup water
1 cup sugar, granulated or brown
2 sticks cinnamon, broken
2 teaspoons each whole cloves and whole allspice
1 teaspoon whole mace

Drain peaches and cut halves into smaller pieces (or leave in halves). Discard syrup; combine vinegar, sugar, water, and spices in a saucepan and bring to a rolling boil. Drop the peaches into the syrup and boil gently for 15 minutes, reducing the heat if necessary. Pack the peaches in sterilized jars and cover with the hot syrup. Seal. These pickles may be used immediately if desired. The syrup from the peaches may be used over and over by adding a little vinegar now and then. Makes about 2 pints.
From Mrs. Julia C. Graves, in The Chapel Hill Cook Book, *Women's Auxiliary, Presbyterian Church, Chapel Hill, N.C.*

Cocktail Mélange

Pack sterilized pint jars with pickled cantaloupe (Pickled Cantaloupe, page 56), watermelon rind pickle (Watermelon Rind Pickle, page 63), cucumber rings stuffed with brandied cherries (put 1 cherry in the center of each ring, making a red "eye" in the green cucumber), small, whole sweet gherkins, and either whole or split porcupine gherkins. Alternate pickles so that contrasting colors will make an attractive display. Pour over hot syrup made as for Sweet Peach Pickle. This will be ready after 12 hours. Any desired combination of pickles may be used.

Stone Crock Peach Pickle

This is an easy pickle and can be stored in a crock.

8 pounds peaches
4 pounds sugar
1 quart vinegar
½ ounce each whole cloves and stick cinnamon

Peel the peaches. Put into a stone crock or jar. Pour over them a liquor made of the other ingredients. Let stand overnight. Next day pour off the liquor. Heat it to a boil and pour again over the peaches. Repeat this for 5 days. Then cover the jar tightly. The peaches will keep for a year.

From Mrs. C. B. Pfohl, in Pages from Old Salem Cook Books, *Dorcas Co-Workers of the Salem House, Winston-Salem, N.C., 1947.*

Georgia Peach Pickle

This is a very sweet pickle.

6 pounds whole pared peaches (clingstone)
3 pounds sugar
1 pint vinegar
1 tablespoon whole cloves
1 ounce stick cinnamon

Boil together the sugar, vinegar, and spices for about 5 minutes. Drop in the peaches and cook until the fruit is tender. Seal in sterilized jars. Makes about 6 pints.

From Mrs. James W. Smith, Americus, Ga.

Spiced Plums

7 pounds plums, damson or any other kind
¼ cup each whole allspice and whole cloves
3 pounds sugar
1 cup vinegar

Pit plums or leave in stones as desired. Mix plums with remaining ingredients in a large kettle and cook until the fruit is tender and the syrup has thickened. Pack in hot sterilized jars and seal immediately. Makes 6 to 8 pints.

From Mrs. Harry Robert, Macon, Ga., in Pride of the Kitchen, *Scotland Neck, N.C.*

Ginger Tea Watermelon Rind Pickle

    7 pounds watermelon rind, measured after peeling and
        cutting (one large melon)
    1 vial Lilly's lime
        Water to cover rind
    ½ cup ginger root
        Water to cover rind (for ginger tea)
    ½ cup whole cloves
    2 or 3 sticks cinnamon, broken
    7 pounds sugar
    1 quart vinegar
    2 cups water
        Several drops of green or red food coloring

Prepare rind for pickle by trimming off all the hard, green outside skin of melon and removing any soft red pulp from the inside. Cut the rind in pieces about 1 inch square, or, if desired, cut pieces into fancy shapes with small cookie cutters. Dissolve lime in enough water to cover rind, and soak rind for at least 12 hours. Drain and rinse three times in clear cold water.

Combine the ginger root with enough water to cover the rind and bring to a boil. Add the rind and continue to boil 2 hours. Drain and remove ginger root. Tie cloves and cinnamon in a cloth bag. Make a syrup of sugar, vinegar, and water. Add spice bag and, if desired, vegetable coloring, and bring to a boil. Add rind and cook for 2 hours, or until clear. Remove spice bag. Pack rind in hot sterilized jars and cover with the syrup. Seal the jars. If there is not enough syrup to cover the rind fully, make additional syrup. Makes 7 to 8 pints.

From Mrs. E. H. Morris, Jr., Raleigh, N.C.

Nina Mae's Watermelon Rind Pickle

Peel and cut watermelon rind into convenient pieces. Cover rind with a solution made of:

    1 gallon water
    1 vial Lilly's lime

Soak rind overnight. Remove rind and cover with clear cold water. Boil for 30 minutes in the same water. Remove rind and plunge it into cold water. Make a ginger-root solution by boiling ginger root and water (drinking strength). Boil rind in ginger solution for 30 minutes. Let cold water run down from faucet over this.

For every gallon of rind use:

    2 quarts vinegar
    5 pounds sugar
    1 stick cinnamon
    1 tablespoon each whole allspice and whole cloves

Tie spices in a bag and put in a kettle with the other ingredients. Boil until a thin syrup forms. Drop in rind and boil slowly until transparent—about 3 hours. Seal in jars.

From Nina Mae Shoffner, Burlington, N.C.

Excellent Spiced Pears

    7 pounds pears
    ½ ounce stick cinnamon or cassia buds
    ½ ounce whole cloves
    2 cups vinegar
    6 to 7 cups sugar, according to sweetness of pears
    ½ cup hot water

Peel pears. Leave them whole if they are small, or quarter them if large. Tie the spices in a small cloth bag and put into a large kettle with the vinegar, sugar, and water. Boil syrup for 5 minutes.

Carefully add pears. Reduce the heat and cook slowly—until pears are tender. Pack the fruit in sterilized jars. Remove the spice bag from the syrup and cook the syrup 5 minutes longer. Pour hot over pears. Seal jars. Makes 10 to 12 pints.

From Mrs. L. A. Adams, La Grange, Texas

3. Pickles and Preserves from Frozen Foods

THE QUESTION HAS OFTEN BEEN ASKED ME: "CAN YOU MAKE PICKLES and preserves from frozen vegetables and fruits?" While testing and experimenting with recipes for *Pickles and Preserves*, I found that any food that is quick-frozen may be later utilized in a further preserved form. The discovery is like finding a new star. Anyone who has access to frozen products may make delicious pickles, preserves, jams, and jellies.

It seemed inadvisable to give individual recipes to cover this phase of conserving because the overlapping recipes are numerous. There are a few basic rules that can be given to serve as a guide for the substitution of frozen products for fresh.

1. When making pickle, remember that the vegetables will not be quite as crisp as they would be if fresh vegetables were used.

2. Use only vegetables and fruits that would ordinarily take to pickling: broccoli stalks (save tips for other dishes), lima beans, string beans, cauliflower, Brussels sprouts, corn kernels, carrot strips (or little carrots), melon balls, peaches, berries, and so on.

3. Thaw all vegetables for pickling in water. The ice from the vegetables will keep them crisp.

4. Thaw fruits at room temperature in own juice. Use the juice if the specific recipe calls for it.

5. Do not precook frozen vegetables unless recipe calls for it. If they are precooked, cut the recipe time in half.

6. Frozen products may be bought in 10-pound packages from dealers or in small family packages. Unless a recipe states otherwise, "one package" means the small 10-ounce (approximate) package. (They often vary by an ounce or two.)

7. Frozen fruits are not so high in pectin content as are fresh fruits. Therefore, when making jelly, always test for pectin, or use commercial pectin or lemon. Consult charts that come with the commercial pectin, or see the general instructions for jelly in this book (page 219).

8. Preserves from frozen fruits have a fresh flavor and good color. I always use *the juice from one lemon* to each 10-ounce package of frozen fruit. Use *cup for cup* of sugar and of fruit and its own juice mixed. (See Christmas Strawberry Jam, page 68.)

9. When mixed vegetable pickles are made, use fresh cucumbers, onion, or cabbage to give added flavor.

10. Frozen fruits are especially good for *chutney, fruit butter, fruit honey,* and *paste.* It is never necessary to put cooked frozen fruits through a food mill. Mash with a potato masher.

11. Frozen vegetables may be soaked in limewater for pickle. This will add to the crispness, but they should remain in the lime solution only while thawing.

"Career Girl's" Salad Pickle

I have dedicated this recipe to the busy career girl who has no vegetable garden on her rooftop and only a little time for cooking. It is a combination of frozen vegetables and year-round items that are usually on hand.

> 1 10-ounce package frozen broccoli strips (cut off tips to use later)
> 1 10-ounce package frozen Brussels sprouts
> 1 10-ounce package frozen cauliflowerets
> 2 large unpeeled cucumbers, thinly sliced
> 3 large onions, thinly sliced
> 1 clove garlic, minced
> 1 red bell pepper, cut in strips (or strips of canned pimiento)

Combine frozen and fresh vegetables in a large enamel pan or kettle, and cover them with cold water. When the frozen vegetables have thawed, drain well—first in a colander, then dry on absorbent paper toweling. Meanwhile, make this mustard sauce:

> ½ cup flour
> 4 tablespoons dry mustard
> 1 cup sugar
> 2 tablespoons salt (more, it a saltier pickle is desired)
> 1 quart vinegar
> 1 tablespoon each turmeric, yellow mustard seed, celery seed, and dehydrated horseradish (optional)

Make a paste of flour, mustard, sugar, salt, and a little of the cold vinegar. Combine the remaining vinegar and spices in an enamel, agateware, or porcelain kettle. Be sure to use a kettle large enough to hold both sauce and vegetables. Place the kettle over low heat, stir in the flour paste, and bring slowly to a boil, stirring constantly until the mixture has the consistency of heavy cream sauce (the vegetables will thin the sauce). Add the drained vegetables. Heat thoroughly, but do not boil. Remove from heat and pack at once into sterilized jars. Seal.

Pickle made in the morning may be served for dinner in the evening, but they improve with age.

This is a salad-type pickle, and the vegetables are soft as in bread-and-butter pickle.

VARIATION

Add 3 tablespoons of salt to the water in which the vegetables are thawing. Let them stand for 3 hours, keeping the water cold by adding ice cubes after the frozen vegetables have thawed. The drained vegetables may then be packed in sterilized jars and the thickened hot sauce poured over them. Seal the jars immediately. This will make a crisper pickle, but it should stand at least 2 weeks before being used. Any combination of vegetables may be used. If beans, corn, or other similar vegetables are used, they should be precooked in salted water until almost tender.

Christmas Strawberry Jam

During the Christmas holidays I needed a glass of strawberry jam. There were frozen berries in the locker, and they made a "super" jam. Any berry with high pectin content may be prepared in the same manner. If desired, use commercial pectin according to the manufacturer's chart.

> 2 10-ounce packages frozen strawberries
> Juice of 1 large lemon
> Sugar

Thaw berries at room temperature. Measure berries and the juice together, and for 1 cup of berries and juice use 1 cup of sugar. Mix all ingredients in a wide-mouthed kettle. Stir to dissolve sugar. Bring to a rapid boil and cook rapidly until syrup is thick and responds to the jelly test. Seal in jelly glasses. Makes about 1 pint.

Grape Jelly from Frozen Juice

This is an economical and easy jelly.

2 6-ounce cans frozen grape-juice concentrate
6 cups sugar
3 cups water
1 bottle liquid pectin

Thaw the grape-juice concentrate to room temperature. Mix sugar and water in wide-mouthed kettle until sugar dissolves. Place over high heat and bring rapidly to full rolling boil. Boil for 2 minutes. Remove from heat, add pectin, and stir. Add grape juice and mix well. Skim. Pour immediately into hot sterilized glasses and seal promptly with paraffin. Jelly will jell after it cools in glasses. This makes about 12 jelly glasses full. *Do not make more than this amount at one time.*

Frozen Raspberry Jelly

2 10-ounce packages frozen raspberries
7 cups sugar
1 bottle Certo or other jelly agent

Thaw berries at room temperature. Drain in a colander, saving the juice to make jelly and the berries to use at mealtime. Add water to berry juice to make 4 cups of liquid and pour into saucepan. Stir in sugar and place over medium heat. Boil for 3 minutes. Add Certo (amount according to chart) and boil hard for 1 minute. Pour into jelly glasses and seal. *Do not make more than this amount at one time.*

VARIATIONS

Use frozen strawberries, gooseberries, blackberries, or any high-pectin frozen berries to make jelly as in the recipe above. *Do not make more than the recipe calls for at one time.*
From Mrs. Walter DuBois Brookings, in Alexandria Woman's Club Cook Book, *Alexandria, Va.*

4. *Miscellaneous Pickles*

Pickled (French) Artichokes

The amount of this pickle that you put up should depend entirely upon your needs, your time, the availability of artichokes, and your pocketbook. The work can be reduced by buying artichokes canned in water, ready to pickle right out of the jar or can—but the expense! The smaller the artichokes, the better they are for pickling. You need:

>   24 very small artichokes
>   1 heaping tablespoon mixed spices
>   Olive oil
>   White vinegar
>   Salt
>   Quart jar

Cut off artichoke stems and leaf tips. Remove hard outer leaves, if any, and let the part to be used stand in cold salted water for 1 hour. Drain, saving liquid, and cool under cover (to preserve the color).

Meanwhile, sterilize the jar and put a wooden spoon to soak in the liquid that was saved. When artichokes are cool, fill jar half full with equal parts of oil and vinegar and a sprinkling of mixed spices. Put 5 or 6 artichokes in the jar, adding more spice, and pack down with the wooden spoon (which will not break the artichokes). Continue until all the artichokes have been used. If the jar is not overflowing, add more oil and vinegar mixture. Cover tightly. Store in cool place.

From Italian Cooking for the American Kitchen, *by Garibaldi M. Lapolla, Wilfred Funk, Inc., N.Y.*

Margaret Pruden's Artichoke Pickle

For some years Miss Pruden has made this famous Edenton pickle for special relatives and friends. It has a pungent mustard and red (hot) pepper flavor.

> 1 peck Jerusalem artichokes, scraped or scrubbed
> 3 pounds onions, peeled and sliced
> 3 quarts vinegar
> 5 pounds white sugar
> 2 tablespoons each turmeric, dry mustard, and mustard seed
> ½ cup salt
> Red hot pepper pods to taste

Small uniform artichokes are usually used. If they are large, they should be cut or sliced. Wash scrubbed artichokes and dry thoroughly with a towel—this is the secret of crispness.

Pack alternate layers of artichokes and onions in jars. Combine remaining ingredients in saucepan, place over medium heat, and boil for a few minutes. Pour the hot mixture over the artichokes and onions and let stand overnight. Next day, put tops on jars and seal.

From Margaret H. Pruden, Edenton, N.C.

Mexican Green Chilis

This is a favorite Mexican sauce and is served with every meal in the average Mexican home.

4 green chilis
1 tablespoon minced onion
1 tablespoon minced parsley
4 large green tomatoes
½ cup olive oil
Salt and pepper to taste

Place chilis, onions, parsley, and tomatoes in a covered kettle with water to cover. Bring to a boil. When the vegetables are tender, press through a fine colander, adding salt and pepper. Heat the oil in a frying pan and add the pulp. Fry for 15 minutes. Use at once, or seal in sterilized jars.

From Cooking Round the World and at Home, *Parent-Teacher Association, Eureka, Ark.*

Whole Pickled Beets

3 pints small beets of uniform size
Salt and water
1 quart vinegar
½ cup sugar
2 tablespoons mixed pickling spices
½ cup water
1 teaspoon salt

Wash the beets, but do not skin or trim off the roots. Leave 1 inch of tops so that the beets will not bleed. Put in a large saucepan and cover with salt and water, using 1 tablespoon of salt for each quart of water. Place over medium heat and boil until tender. Drain and cool. Skin beets and trim off roots and top. Combine remaining ingredients in a saucepan. Place over medium heat and boil together for 3 minutes. Pack beets in hot sterilized pint jars. Pour over hot liquid and seal immediately. Makes 3 pints.

Party Sweet Pickled Beets

2 pounds beets of uniform size
4 cups vinegar
2 cups sugar
2 tablespoons mixed pickling spices, tied in cloth bag

Boil the beets until tender. Remove them from heat and peel. Slice in ¼-inch slices; then cut out each slice with a small fancy cookie cutter. Set aside to drain. Put vinegar, sugar, and spice bag in a kettle and boil for a few minutes, or until sugar is well dissolved. Add the beets to the syrup and bring it back to the boiling point. Remove from heat immediately. Pack while hot in sterilized jars and seal. Makes about 2 pints.

Artichoke Pickle

1 gallon Jerusalem artichokes, washed, scraped, left whole
  Sliced onion if desired
3 quarts vinegar
3 pounds sugar
2 tablespoons turmeric
1 tablespoon each mustard seed and celery seed
2 or 3 sticks cinnamon
1 tablespoon ground ginger

Pack artichokes in sterilized jars. Add sliced onion if desired. In a saucepan, combine other ingredients. Cook for ½ hour; then let syrup cool. Pour the cool syrup over the artichokes and seal the jars. If the syrup is hot, the artichokes will shrink.
From Miss Lila Clare Newman, Elon College, N.C.

String Bean Pickle

Either wax or green beans may be used, but the wax beans make a more attractive pickle. Serve as an hors d'oeuvre, as a vegetable with a bowl of mustard sauce, or as a salad.

2 quarts string beans of uniform size
Salt
Water
1 quart cider vinegar
½ cup sugar (omit for sour pickle)
2 tablespoons mixed pickling spices tied in cloth bag
1 clove garlic, peeled

Wash beans and remove strings. Plunge them into cold water and let stand for 30 minutes. Put the beans in a large kettle and cover with a weak brine made by using 1 tablespoon of salt to 1 quart of water. Put over medium heat and bring to a boil. Boil for 20 minutes, or until beans are slightly tender. Do not overcook. Drain and discard the liquid. Put the beans back into the kettle and add the remaining ingredients. Cook over medium heat for 10 minutes. Discard the spice bag. Arrange beans upright in sterilized jars. Pour over the hot syrup and seal immediately.

Brine string beans may be pickled by the same recipe. Do not precook. Put the beans on with the remaining ingredients and cook for 10 minutes. Seal as above. (See also Dill String Beans.) *From Mrs. Stratton Lawerence, Jr., Baton Rouge, La.*

Dill String Beans

1 gallon string beans (wax beans are best)
Water and salt for parboiling beans
2 gallons brine (½ cup salt to 2 gallons water)
3 to 4 stalks dill, fresh or dried
2 tablespoons black peppercorns
3 to 4 bay leaves, broken into small pieces
Fresh grape leaves if possible
1 cup vinegar

Wash beans, remove strings, leaving beans in full le gth. Parboil beans in salted water to cover (1 teaspoon salt to 1 quart water) until beans begin to get tender—do not overcook. Drain off liquid, discard. In a stone crock, pack the beans in alternate layers with sprigs of dill, peppercorns, and pieces of the bay leaves. Cover beans with a generous layer of dill sprigs, then cover all with fresh grape leaves. Combine the salt and the 2 gallons of water; bring to boiling, remove brine from heat and allow it to cool thoroughly. Pour the cool brine over the beans, being sure the beans are well covered. Cover the crock with a clean white cloth; weight down with a plate and a heavy object. Let crock stand in a warm place for 1 week, or until beans stop fermenting. Add the vinegar. Remove crock to a cool place and seal (see general instructions for sealing on page 16), or remove the beans and pack with brine and seasonings in sterilized jars. Seal. Beans are ready to serve in about 1 month. Will make about 4 quarts.

Pickled Cabbage

Any kind of cabbage may be used, but red cabbage is best because of its thicker leaves and stronger flavor. To make "yellow" cabbage, use any white cabbage, and, when boiling, add ½ teaspoon of turmeric to the cooking water.

Salt
1 large cabbage head, quartered
1 tablespoon dry mustard
2 quarts vinegar
1 teaspoon each ground cloves, ground allspice, and whole cloves
½ teaspoon ground cinnamon
1 teaspoon white mustard seed
½ teaspoon celery seed
½ cup brown sugar

Salt the quartered cabbage head, being sure to work the salt down into the leaves. Let it stand overnight. Next day shake the cabbage well to get off excess salt. Put the cabbage into a large kettle. Cover with fresh water and cook until tender. Drain and pack in hot sterilized jars. In a saucepan make a paste of dry mustard and a little vinegar and add the remaining ingredients. Place over medium heat and boil for about 5 minutes, stirring constantly.

Pour the hot liquid over the cabbage in the jars and seal. The cabbage is ready to use at once. Wonderful with corned beef!
From Mrs. H. P. McKay, Onancock, Va.

Cocktail Pickled Carrots

This is an easy and delightful pickle. It gives color to an hors d'oeuvre tray.

> 1 quart small young carrots of uniform size
> 1 quart white vinegar
> 3 tablespoons mixed pickling spices tied in cloth bag
> 2 cups sugar (for more tangy pickle, use only 1 cup sugar)

Wash carrots and remove blemishes and stringy tips. Put in a covered vessel and cook until the skins can be easily slipped off. Do not overcook. Make a syrup by boiling together the remaining ingredients for 10 minutes. Remove the spice bag. Put the carrots in a large bowl or enamel pan and pour over hot syrup. Let them stand overnight in syrup. Next day return carrots and syrup to the cooking kettle. Bring quickly to a boil and continue cooking for about 3 minutes. Pack carrots in sterilized jars and pour over the hot syrup. Seal immediately. Makes about 4 half-pints.

Carrots may be cut into shoestring strips after cooking. If they are cut into strips, do not boil them next day in the syrup. Bring the syrup back to boiling. Pack the strips in jars and pour over the syrup.

Pickled Baby Corn Ears

Use miniature ears of fresh popcorn, not more than 2 to 3 inches in length. Be sure the corn is tender. Bring to a boil enough water to cover the corn well, adding 1 tablespoon of salt to each quart of water. Drop the corn into the boiling water and let stand for 3 minutes. Drain. Pack the corn upright in small jars, and pour over the following hot syrup:

1 quart vinegar
1 tablespoon sugar
2 tablespoons mixed pickling spices

Add ¼ dried red pepper pod to each jar, and seal while hot. Let stand about 2 weeks.

Last-of-the-Garden Pickles

This is a remarkable salad pickle that utilizes the last-of-the-garden vegetables.

3 cups chopped green bell peppers
3 cups chopped red bell peppers
3 cups diced onions
  Salt brine (½ cup salt to 1 quart water)
3 cups diced carrots
3 cups butter beans
3 cups green beans
3 cups cauliflowerets
3 cups diced celery
6 cups vinegar
3 tablespoons mustard seed
6 cups sugar

Allow the combined onions and peppers to stand overnight in salt brine to cover. On the next day, slice and cook the carrots, butter beans, and green beans until they can be pierced with a fork. Do not overcook. In a separate vessel, cook the cauliflower for a short time (until not quite tender enough to pierce with fork). Chop the celery and add it to the cooked vegetables. Drain the liquid from the peppers and onions and add them to the other vegetables. Combine vinegar, mustard seed, and sugar and pour over the vegetable mixture. Boil all together in a large kettle until the mixture comes to a full rolling boil. Pack into sterilized jars at once and seal. Makes about 10 pints.

From Mrs. H. B. Gaston, in The Belmont Book of Recipes, *combiled by the Parent-Teacher Association of Belmont, N.C.*

Pickled Jalapenas

Jalapenas, those wonderful Mexican peppers, make good pickle.

> 1 quart jalapenas, seeded (measure after seeding)
> Brine
> 1 pint vinegar or enough to cover peppers
> 1 teaspoon salt
> 1 teaspoon sugar
> ½ teaspoon sesame seed
> 2 medium-sized onions, sliced
> 2 cloves garlic, peeled
> 1 large bay leaf
> Fresh or dried dill
> Olive oil

Use peppers that have been commercially brined, or soak fresh peppers for 3 to 4 days in a brine made by dissolving 1 cup of salt in 2 quarts of water. Remove peppers. Slit and extract the seeds; discard the seeds. Combine vinegar, salt, sugar, and sesame seed in a kettle. Bring to a rolling boil and add the peppers. Cook until peppers can be pierced with a straw—about 5 minutes. In the bottom of each jar place sliced onion, garlic clove, and pieces of bay leaf. Pack the peppers stem up in the jars, adding a generous sprig of dill to each jar. Fill the jars three quarters full with the hot vinegar syrup and finish filling the jars with olive oil. Seal immediately. Turn the jars often to keep the oil mixed with the pickles.

From Mrs. Vann MacNair, Williamsburg, Va.

Pickled Eggplant

When this book was merely an idea, a friend advised me to get a recipe for pickled eggplant, since it is unusual and good. An alert contributor found this recipe in an old out-of-print cook book. It appears to be of Greek origin and is often served in Greek homes.

   1 large eggplant
   Lemon juice
   1 quart vinegar
   1 cup sugar
   1½ tablespoons mixed pickling spices tied in cloth bag

Wash and peel eggplant. Cut into strips 1 inch thick or into slices and soak for 3 hours in lightly salted water. Drain and let stand in fresh cold water for 3 hours, adding a little lemon juice to prevent discoloration. Pack the eggplant in sterilized jars. Combine the remaining ingredients in a kettle. Bring to a boil and boil for about 5 minutes. Discard the spice. Pour the hot syrup quickly over the eggplant and seal immediately. The eggplant should be ready in 2 weeks.

From Mrs. William G. Vetterlein, Sedgefield, Greensboro, N.C.

Pickled Mushrooms

Pickled mushrooms may be served cold the day they are made, or they may be kept almost indefinitely under refrigeration. They are fine served as part of an antipasto tray (with toothpicks, if eaten with cocktails) or as a condiment with fish or bland meat. To make 2 pints you need:

   3 pounds mushrooms (button variety is best; if larger
      ones are used, cut off ends of stems)
   White vinegar
   Olive oil
   1 tablespoon of mixed pickling spices

Put mushrooms in a large saucepan and wash thoroughly in fairly hot water. Rinse well in a colander under running cold water. Return the mushrooms to the saucepan and cover with a mixture of half vinegar and half hot water. Salt to taste. Boil for 15 minutes. Drain off liquid into another pan, and cool the mushrooms.

   Meanwhile, put a small wooden spoon to soak in the liquid to sterilize it. Mix together equal parts of olive oil and vinegar (less than 2 cups should do) and add spice. Fill a sterilized jar one quarter full with liquid. Add mushrooms, packing them down with the small wooden spoon that has been soaking. (With a wooden spoon, mushrooms will neither be broken nor lose their shape.) Fill jar to overflowing with the remainder of the oil-vinegar mixture. Cover and store in a cool place.

From The Mushroom Cook Book, *by Garibaldi M. Lapolla, copyright, 1953, by Wilfred Funk, Inc., N.Y.*

Pickled Nasturtium Buds

Pickled nasturtium buds were evidently brought to colonial Virginia from England, for E. Smith gave a recipe for the pickle in *The Compleat Housewife,* 1739. The pickled buds have a pungent taste similar to capers and are served in salads and similar dishes.

"Gather your little (nasturtium) knobs quickly after your blossoms are off; put them in cold water and salt for 3 days, shifting them once a day; then make a pickle (but do not boil at all) of some white wine, some white wine vinegar, eschalot (shallots), horseradish, pepper, salt, cloves and mace whole and nutmeg quartered; then put in your seeds and stop them close; they are to be eaten as capers."

From E. Smith's The Compleat Housewife, *London, 1739, in* The Williamsburg Art of Cookery, *by Mrs. Helen Bullock, copyright, 1938, by Colonial Williamsburg, Inc.*

Mock Cocktail Olives

    1 quart plums, full grown but still green or greengages
    Coarse salt
    Brine
    1 clove garlic, peeled

Wash plums and dry but do not remove stones. Make a brine using 1 cup of coarse salt to 1 gallon of water. Heat the brine to the boiling point. Put the plums in a porcelain vessel and pour over hot brine to cover well. Let them stand for 24 hours. Remove the plums and discard the brine. Make a fresh brine of the same proportion and bring to a boil. Drop the plums in and let them stand 1 minute. Remove the plums and pack in a sterilized quart jar. Pour over the hot brine and seal immediately. They will be ready in 1 week.

These plums have the taste and texture of olives and may be served as a substitute for real olives. After processing, the stones may be removed and the "olives" stuffed with pimiento, nuts, cheese, or other filling.

Cocktail Onions

Cocktail onions may be either sweet or sour. To make a sour pickle, omit the sugar from the following recipe. The onions may vary in size from miniature pearl onions to onion sets.

> 5 pounds small pickling onions
> 4 quarts water
> 4 tablespoons salt

Peel off dry skin and soak onions for 2 hours in the water and salt. Peel and discard the tough inner skin. Soak the onions for 48 hours in a brine made of:

> 1½ cups salt
> 4 quarts water

Drain onions and dry well. Heat to the boiling point:

> ½ gallon white vinegar
> 1 cup sugar

Add onions to vinegar mixture and cook for 5 minutes. Pour into sterilized jars. To each jar add:

> 1 red hot pepper pod
> 1 teaspoon each celery seed and white mustard seed
> 4 or 5 whole allspice

Seal the jars immediately.

Mustard Pickled Onions

1 gallon small pickling onions, peeled
Salt water to cover

Let the onions stand overnight in salt water. Next morning pour off the salt water and cover with good cider vinegar. Add:

¼ pound dry mustard
1 teaspoon turmeric
½ teaspoon sugar
3 or 4 small green peppers, ground

Bring the mixture to a boil and thicken with ¾ cup of flour made to a paste with a little cold vinegar. When the mixture has thickened pour into jars and seal. Makes about 4 quarts.

VARIATION

Mustard Cauliflower Pickle

1 gallon broken cauliflower buds

Let the cauliflower stand in salt water for several hours. Drain and add to vinegar mixture made as in onion recipe above, but omitting green peppers. Proceed as in Mustard Pickled Onions.
From Mrs. R. R. Copelen, in How We Cook in El Paso, Texas.

Baked Oranges Whitlock

6 oranges
Water to cover
1 tablespoon salt
2 cups sugar
½ cup light corn syrup
½ cup vinegar
¾ to ⅞ cup extra water
1 teaspoon red food coloring

Cover oranges with water and add salt. Boil for 30 minutes. Drain off the hot water and cover the oranges again with clear water.

Let them stand for 30 minutes. Drain off the liquid and cool the oranges. Boil together the sugar, corn syrup, vinegar, and the ¾ to ⅞ cup of water for 5 minutes. Add the red coloring. Cut each orange into 4 slices. Boil the slices in syrup for 15 minutes; then put orange slices and syrup into a glass baking dish and bake for 1 hour at about 325° F.

These orange slices make an excellent garnish for roast duck or other fowl. Or they may be served as a dessert.

Any left-over red syrup may be saved and used for the next batch of Baked Oranges Whitlock.

If orange slices are not to be used immediately, seal them while hot in sterilized jars. They will keep indefinitely just like any other preserve.

From Hobby Horse Cookery, Favorite Recipes of Marjory Hendricks' Water Gate Inn, Washington, D.C., *compiled by Flora G. Orr, copyright by Flora G. Orr, Washington, D.C., 1950; used by special permission of Marjory Hendricks.*

Stuffed Pepper Mangoes

These are pickled sweet bell peppers and should not be confused with the tropical mango. Green peppers may be used. Try the small "bite" size for hors d'oeuvre. This is a Dutch recipe.

> 1 dozen sweet red bell peppers
> 1 dozen sweet green bell peppers
> 1 quart cabbage (measure after chopping)
> 1 tablespoon salt
> 1 teaspoon each ground cinnamon and ground allspice
> ½ teaspoon ground cloves
> 1 cup brown sugar
> 2 tablespoons white mustard seed
> Cold, strong vinegar

Cut the tops from the peppers and remove seed and white fibers. Save the tops to close the peppers. Stand peppers upright in a pan and soak for 24 hours in a brine made of ½ cup of salt to 1 quart of water. Drain the peppers.

Shred the cabbage as for slaw, shredding thin and rather fine. Mix the cabbage with spices and sugar. Stuff the peppers with the cabbage mixture and put the tops back on the peppers, securing them with toothpicks. Pack upright in wide-mouthed jars, alternating red and green peppers. Pour over cold vinegar to fill the jars and seal. They will be ready to use in about 3 weeks.
From Mrs. Catherine Schoonmaker, Ellenville, N.Y.

VARIATIONS

Use all green peppers if no red ones are available. Red and green peppers mixed make attractive jars. Dwarf peppers are nice for cocktail trays.

Pumpkin Pickle

2½ pounds fresh pumpkin, pared and cut into cubes
  of desired size
1 quart vinegar
2 pounds sugar
1 tablespoon salt
1 teaspoon each whole cloves and whole allspice
1 red pepper pod, broken
1 tablespoon ground cinnamon

Put the pumpkin cubes in a large kettle. In a large saucepan combine vinegar, sugar, salt, and spices. Place over medium heat and boil for 5 minutes. Pour the hot syrup over the pumpkin and place over medium heat. Bring to a boil, reduce heat, and cook slowly until the pumpkin is clear and tender. Lift out the pumpkin and pack into hot sterilized jars. Pour over hot syrup to fill the jars. Seal immediately. Very good. Makes about 2½ pints.
From Miss Miriam LeCompte, Cordon, Iowa.

Pickled Salsify

Salsify was one of the first Colonial vegetables. The white tuber root takes well to pickling.

1 quart salsify strip, measure after preparing
1 pint strong vinegar
2 tablespoons mixed pickling spices tied in cloth bag
1 clove garlic, peeled
1 tablespoon sugar (omit for sour pickle)
2 red pepper pods

Wash and peel the salsify and cut into uniform strips as for French-fried potatoes. Measure. Plunge them at once into cold water and let them stand for 1 hour to crisp; then drain. Pack the strips upright in small jars that are the same height as the strips. Combine the remaining ingredients in an open saucepan. Boil rapidly for 5 minutes. Discard the spice bag. Lift out the peppers. Break them up and put a portion in each jar. Pour the hot syrup over the pickle and seal immediately. Makes about 2 pints.

Pickled Cluster Raisins

A Christmas special for roast fowl.

2 pounds raisins (old fashioned clusters, if possible)
Water
½ cup brown sugar
Cider vinegar
1 tablespoon each whole cloves and whole allspice

Soak the raisins in water to cover until the fruit is plump. Drain and save the juice. Pack the raisins in sterilized jars. Dissolve the sugar in the juice from the raisins. Measure and add an equal amount of vinegar. Mix in the spices. Cover the packed raisins with cold sugar-vinegar liquid. Seal and allow to stand 1 week before using.

From Miss Katie Lea Stewart, New York, N.Y.

Pickled Red Sweet Peppers

1 dozen red sweet peppers
4 cups distilled white vinegar
2 cups sugar

Wash and seed the peppers and cut into ½-inch strips. Boil vinegar and sugar together for 5 minutes. While the vinegar and sugar are boiling, pack the peppers into clean jars that have been dipped in hot water. Cover the peppers with the vinegar solution, filling to within ½ inch of the tops of the jars. Seal according to the type of jar and cover being used. Process immediately in a boiling water bath for 10 minutes. Makes 3 pints.
From Ruth P. Casa-Emellos, Home Economist, The New York Times, New York.

Pickled Turnips

1 quart turnips, peeled and cut into pieces
1 pint vinegar
1 tablespoon mixed whole spices
1 red pepper pod
1 clove garlic, peeled
1 teaspoon salt

Pack the turnips in a sterilized jar. Mix the remaining ingredients and pour cold over the turnips. Seal. Let stand for at least 1 month. Chill thoroughly before serving. Surprisingly good for cocktail hors d'oeuvre.
From Mrs. Kathleen Darlington, Burlington, N.C.

Sauerkraut

Sauerkraut is cabbage pickled in brine and is an economical and wholesome food. If properly pickled, sauerkraut will keep for months. It can be made in small or large quantities.

For making sauerkraut in the home 4- or 6-gallon stone crocks are excellent containers. After fermentation is complete, the sauerkraut may be packed into Mason jars. If larger quantities are made, kegs or barrels may be used.

Only mature, sound heads of cabbage should be used for kraut. Remove all decayed or gritty leaves, quarter the heads, and cut out the core. Shred the cabbage with a hand shredding machine, a slaw cutter, or a large sharp knife.

The cabbage is packed into the container with salt. The fermentation is carried out in a brine made from the juice of the cabbage, which is drawn out by the salt. The salt may be mixed with the cabbage as the container is being packed, or it may be mixed before packing. One pound of salt for every 40 pounds of cabbage makes the proper strength to ensure good sauerkraut. This is about 2 ounces of salt for every 5 pounds of cabbage.

Cabbage should be packed firmly but not pressed down tightly. Fill the crock or keg, cover with a clean cloth, and weight down with a round board or plate.

Keep the sauerkraut container at a temperature of about 86° F. and fermentation will start promptly. A scum will soon form on top of the brine and should be skimmed off frequently. The scum tends to destroy the acidity and may affect the cabbage. If the sauerkraut is kept at 86° F., the fermentation should be completed in about 10 days. (A properly fermented sauerkraut should show a normal acidity of approximately +20, or a lactic acid percentage of 1.8.) (See brines, page 16; see also tests in making fermented pickles, page 20.

When fermentation is complete (the brine will be still), set the sauerkraut in a cool place. If the cabbage is fermented late in the fall, or if it can be put in a cool place, it may be kept in the same container without additional steps to seal the container. The surface of the brine must be kept skimmed.

If the container cannot be kept in a cool place, it should be sealed. One method of sealing is to pour a layer of hot paraffin over the surface, or around the board or plate on top of the container. Another method is to remove the sauerkraut from the container and pack it in sterilized jars, adding enough of the brine to cover. If there is not enough brine, make additional weak brine by using 1 ounce of salt to each quart of water.

If sauerkraut is heated before sealing in sterilized jars, place the jars in a water bath until the center of the sauerkraut is about 160° F., then seal and store in a cool place. It will keep indefinitely.

Technical data are from the U.S. Department of Agriculture, *Farmers' Bulletin* No. 1438, by Edwin LeFevre, Assistant Bacteriologist, Microbiological Laboratory, Bureau of Chemistry.

Odorless Kraut in Jars

Now kraut can be packed in jars just as any pickle.

Cut cabbage as for slaw. Salt it and put it in a stone jar, sprinkling salt on it, then pressing it down until packed. Let it ferment for about 1 week. Put it on the stove in a cooking vessel and let it boil in its own brine for a few minutes. Have sterilized jars ready. Fill the jars with kraut, stuffing well, and seal them tight. Put up in this manner, kraut will keep for years and be perfectly odorless.

From Mrs. R. I. Huettel, La Grange, Texas.

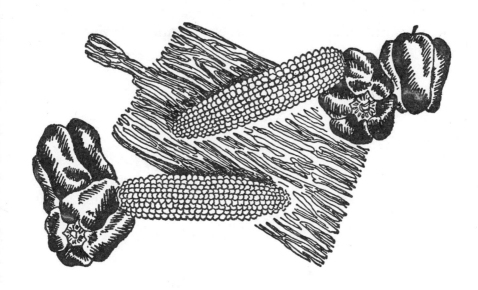

5. Relishes

Relishes, Chutneys, Chowder, Salad, Chow-chow, Piccalilli

Artichoke Relish

This is a grand cold-pack relish of Georgia origin.

    2 quarts Jerusalem artichokes
    1 large head cabbage
    1 dozen green sweet peppers
    1 dozen large onions
    2 cups salt

Scrub artichokes, and cut, shred, or put through a food chopper. Cut, shred, or put other vegetables through food chopper. Mix. Put the vegetables in alternate layers with salt in a large container. Let stand for 12 hours. Drain and cover with weak vinegar-and-water solution, using equal parts of vinegar and water. Let stand for 24 hours. Drain again and cover with following vinegar solution:

> 1 quart vinegar
> 2 pounds sugar
> 1 ounce each celery seed and turmeric
> ½ pound white mustard seed
> 1½ ounces dry mustard

Mix well. Add additional vinegar if needed to cover the vegetables. Pack in sterilized jars, and seal. Pack cold—no cooking. Relish will be ready to use in 1 week.

From Mrs. Harry A. Alexander, High Point, N.C.

Anne Arundel Pickle (Relish)

This is a famous recipe for a ripe-tomato type of relish or soy. It may be bottled or put in jars.

> 12 ripe tomatoes, peeled and cut in pieces
> 4 onions, finely chopped
> 1 small cabbage, shredded
> 6 green peppers, finely chopped
> 2 cucumbers, peeled and sliced
> 1 tablespoon each ground cloves, allspice, and cinnamon
> 1 tablespoon each celery seed and mustard seed
> 8 tablespoons brown sugar
> 3 tablespoons salt
> 4 cups vinegar

Combine all ingredients in a kettle and boil slowly for 2 hours. Bottle and seal. Makes about 3 quarts.

From Mrs. John C. Robertson, in St. Anne's Parish Recipe Book, *Annapolis, Md.*

Apple Relish

Plums, grapes, peaches, mangoes, or any pulpy fruit may be substituted for one half of the apples.

7 pounds unpeeled apples, chopped
2 pounds seedless raisins, chopped
3½ pounds sugar
2 oranges, juice and chopped peel
1 pint vinegar
1 teaspoon powdered cloves
2 teaspoons powdered cinnamon

Put all ingredients into a porcelain kettle. Place over medium heat, and boil for 30 minutes. Pour into hot sterilized jars. Seal. This is excellent with cold meats, especially cold sliced ham.
From Mrs. L. J. Rushworth, in The Episcopal Pantry, *Danville, Va.*

Miss Chloe's Cabbage Pickle (Relish)

This is a fine old South Carolina recipe.

4 quarts chopped cabbage
1 quart chopped onions
2 quarts chopped green tomatoes
Salt
1 cup flour
2 cups brown sugar
2 quarts vinegar
1 teaspoon celery seed
3 tablespoons dry mustard
1 tablespoon turmeric
1 teaspoon each ground cinnamon and allspice

Chop the vegetables—but not too fine. Bite size is best. Place the vegetables in a large vessel and sprinkle well with salt (about 1 cup). Let stand overnight. Next day drain thoroughly. Mix the flour, sugar, and spices with a little of the vinegar to make a smooth paste, and stir paste into remaining vinegar. Put the vinegar mixture into a large kettle and bring to a boil, stirring constantly. Add the drained vegetables and bring back to a boil. Continue cooking slowly for about 20 minutes. Pack in hot sterilized jars and seal. Makes about 9 quarts.

Any combination of crisp vegetables may be used, such as cauliflower, celery, artichokes, red and green sweet peppers. Red peppers make the pickle more colorful.
From Mrs. J. G. Prioleau, Columbia, S.C.

Beet Relish, No. 1

1 quart beets, cooked, skinned, and put through food chopper
1 quart raw cabbage, put through food chopper
2 cups sugar
1 teaspoon salt
1 tablespoon grated horseradish
Vinegar to cover

Measure beets and cabbage after chopping. Add sugar, salt, and horseradish. Cover with vinegar and mix thoroughly. Pack cold in sterilized jars, and seal. Makes about 2 quarts.
From Mrs. H. I. Oswald, in A Book for ye Cooks, *Fredericksburg, Va.*

Beet Relish, No. 2

This is a cooked relish.

1 pound beets
½ pound medium-sized onions, chopped
½ sweet red pepper, chopped
1 tablespoon grated horseradish
¾ cup vinegar
1 tablespoon sugar
¼ teaspoon salt
⅛ teaspoon ground cloves

Trim tops from the beets, leaving about 1 inch, and leave roots on. Wash the beets and place them in a saucepan. Place over medium heat and cook until tender. Drain, cool, and peel the beets; then dice them and mix with all other ingredients in a saucepan. Place over medium heat and cook until thickened. Pack in hot sterilized jars and seal. Makes 1½ pints.

English Chop Pickle

Finely chop 1 large cabbage, ½ gallon of green tomatoes, and ½ gallon of firm cucumbers. Sprinkle with salt and let stand overnight. Next day wash off the salt. Add finely chopped red peppers and finely chopped green peppers, if desired. Mix 4 tablespoons of celery seed, 8 tablespoons of mustard seed, 1 teaspoon each of allspice, ginger, turmeric, cloves, and, if desired, 1 pound of finely chopped raisins and add to vegetables. Heat 4 pounds of brown sugar until dissolved in 3 quarts of good vinegar. While warm—but not hot—pour over the relish, and put it away in a covered stone crock.

From The Williamsburg Art of Cookery, *by Helen Bullock, Copyright, 1938, Colonial Williamsburg, Inc. "An old recipe from Toano, Virginia; Prov'd Travis House 1938."*

Raw Carrot Relish

A can of this relish added to vegetable soup gives the soup a grand flavor.

> 6 cups carrots, peeled and chopped
> 5 cups green sweet peppers, chopped
> 5 cups red sweet peppers, chopped
> 8 cups chopped cabbage (or half cabbage and half cauliflower)
> 3 cups onions, peeled and chopped
> 2 quarts cider vinegar
> 2½ cups sugar
> 6 tablespoons salt
> 2 tablespoons each mustard seed and celery seed

Combine carrots, peppers, cabbage, and onion and mix thoroughly. Pack in sterilized jars. Combine the vinegar with the other ingredients in a saucepan. Place over medium heat and bring to boiling. Pour hot over the packed raw vegetables. Be sure that the vegetables are well covered with vinegar syrup. Seal immediately. Process if desired. If you do so, follow the instruction pamphlet distributed by makers of canning equipment or jars. If the relish is not processed, it should be stored in a cool place.

Celery Relish

1 bunch celery, cut in ½-inch strips
6 green sweet peppers, cut in ½-inch squares
6 red sweet peppers, cut in ½-inch squares
1 pint onions, ground
1 pint vinegar
2 cups sugar
1 tablespoon each mustard seed and celery seed
1 tablespoon salt (or more if desired)

Combine vegetables in a large pan. Cover with boiling water and let stand for 5 minutes; then drain. Repeat the process and let stand for 10 minutes; then drain. Put the vegetables and remaining ingredients in a large open saucepan. Place over medium heat, bring to a boil, and cook for 15 minutes. Pack into hot sterilized jars. Seal immediately.

Corn Salad

This is a delicious old Virginia recipe.

1 small head cabbage, slawed
2½ dozen ears corn (or 9 pints after cutting from cobs)
3 pints vinegar
3 green sweet peppers, ground or chopped
3 red sweet peppers, ground or chopped
4 onions, chopped fine
¼ cup salt
¼ ounce turmeric
½ ounce celery seed
3 pints sugar (6 cups)
2 ounces dry mustard

With a sharp knife cut twice through the grains of corn. Cut the corn from the cob. Mix 1 pint of the vinegar thoroughly with the dry mustard. In a large kettle combine all ingredients and the mustard-vinegar mixture. Place over medium heat and cook for 30 minutes, stirring almost constantly. Pack in hot sterilized jars. Seal immediately.

From Mrs. R. C. Hook, Winchester, Va.

Corn Relish

10 cups corn, cut from cob
10 cups chopped cabbage
12 large onions, chopped
 6 large red bell peppers, chopped
¼ pound dry mustard
½ gallon vinegar
 3 cups brown sugar
 1 small cup salt
 1 tablespoon turmeric

Combine all ingredients in a large kettle and mix well. Place over medium heat, bring to a boil, and cook slowly for 1 hour, stirring frequently to prevent burning. Pack in hot sterilized jars. Remove air bubbles by running a clean silver knife blade down along the side of the filled jar. Withdraw the blade and seal jars airtight immediately.

From Mrs. William Ryer Wright, Charlotte, N.C.

Lillian's Raw Cranberry Relish

1 pound package frozen cranberries or fresh berries
3 small whole oranges
1 cup sugar
½ cup broken pecan meats (more if desired)

Put the frozen berries through a food chopper. If fresh berries are used, wash them and pick off the blossom ends. Cut oranges into quarters and put them through the food chopper. Reserve the juice from berries and oranges. Mix the berries and oranges and stir in the sugar and nuts. Keep refrigerated in a mixing bowl or pack at once into sterilized jars and seal.

Serve this with turkey, chicken, or any other meat. This relish may be made in any season by using frozen berries. Makes about 1½ pints.

From Mrs. Everette Rogers, The National Hotel, Leesburg, Fla.

Spiced Cranberry Relish

2 cups sugar
½ cup vinegar
¾ teaspoon each ground cloves and ground cinnamon
4 cups washed, picked-over cranberries
½ unpeeled orange, finely chopped

Combine sugar, vinegar, and spices in a saucepan, place over medium heat, and bring to a boil. Add the cranberries and finely chopped orange. Cook until all the berries have "popped." Store in covered glass container or sterilized jars. The relish may be used at once. Makes about 2 pints.

Fine Cucumber Relish

This relish has a mustard flavor.

1 dozen large whole cucumbers
2 quarts onions, cut up (measure after cutting up)
3 green peppers
2 tablespoons salt
1 teaspoon turmeric
1 pound sugar
1½ teaspoons mustard seed
1 quart vinegar

Grind vegetables coarsely in a food chopper. Mix with salt in a large mixing bowl and let stand for 1 hour. Drain in a muslin sack or several thicknesses of cheesecloth. In a large kettle combine turmeric, sugar, mustard seed, and vinegar. Place over medium heat and bring to a boil. Add the vegetable mixture all at once and mix well. Reduce heat and cook slowly until the vegetables are tender. Pack in hot sterilized jars and seal immediately. Makes about 4 to 6 pints.

From Mrs. Alfred R. Ehlers, La Grange, Texas.

India Relish

India relish, chow-chow, piccalilli, and pepper hash are very similar. Each recipe calls for a variation in spices and in the combination of vegetables. A somewhat similar relish is known as "Philadelphia Relish." This is a basic relish.

> 2 quarts green unpeeled tomatoes, finely chopped
> 4 quarts cabbage, slawed or chopped
> 6 medium onions, finely chopped
> 3 red sweet peppers, finely chopped
> 2 green sweet peppers, finely chopped
> 6 stalks celery, finely chopped
> 2 tablespoons salt
> 1 horseradish root, grated, or ½ teaspoon dehydrated root, grated
> 1 tablespoon celery seed
> ½ pound white sugar
> ½ pound brown sugar
> 3 pints vinegar
> 1 tablespoon each turmeric and white mustard seed

Mix the chopped vegetables with salt and let stand for 3 or 4 hours. Squeeze out moisture and mix with other ingredients in a kettle. Place over medium heat and boil for 20 to 25 minutes. Pack while hot in jars. Seal immediately. If a sweeter relish is desired, add more sugar. If a sour relish is preferred, add more vinegar and less sugar. Add additional salt and pepper to taste. Makes about 4 quarts.

Good Cucumber Chowder

Chop together:

>   2 quarts cucumbers, peeled and seeded
>   2 quarts cabbage
>   2 onions
>   3 green sweet peppers

Let the mixture stand for 6 hours in a brine made by adding ⅓ cup of salt to 1 quart of water. Drain well.

Make a smooth paste of:

>   ½ cup flour
>   1 tablespoon each turmeric and mustard seed
>   2 tablespoons each celery seed and dry mustard
>   ½ cup vinegar

Heat ½ gallon of vinegar and thicken with the above paste until it comes to a boil. Add the chopped vegetables and bring back to boiling. Seal in sterilized jars. Makes about 2 quarts.

From Mrs. R. H. Melrose, in What's Dat Cookin'? *St. Monica's Guild, Christ Episcopal Church, Point Pleasant, W. Va.*

Gooseberry Relish

Mrs. LeCompte, whose husband is a Congressman from Iowa, spends part of the year in Washington. When Congress convenes, this relish goes to the Capital.

>   4 cups large gooseberries
>   2 medium onions, peeled and sliced
>   1½ cups seedless raisins
>   1 cup brown sugar
>   2½ tablespoons salt
>   ¼ teaspoon cayenne pepper
>   1 teaspoon each ground mustard, ginger, and turmeric
>   1 quart white vinegar

Wash and pick over the gooseberries. Chop berries, onions, and raisins and mix with other ingredients. Place mixture over low heat and bring slowly to boiling. Cook until vegetables and berries are tender. Stir often to keep from scorching. Remove from heat, cool, and rub through a sieve. Return the sieved pulp and juice to the heat, and let it heat thoroughly, but do not boil. Pack hot in sterilized jars. Makes about 2 pints.
From Mrs. Karl M. LeCompte, Cordon, Iowa.

Lime Relish

This is an old recipe. The relish is delicious with sea food or meat.

>   12 thin-skinned limes
>   1 cup vinegar
>   ¼ pint water
>   1½ cups sugar

Wash the limes and soak them in cold water for 24 hours, changing the water several times. Put them in an earthenware dish (or agateware, porcelain, or enamel kettle) and cover with cold water. Place over medium heat and boil until a straw can penetrate them easily. Cool, cut into eighths, and remove seeds. Combine other ingredients in a saucepan and boil together for 20 minutes. Pour the syrup over the limes. Pack in jars and seal immediately.
From Mrs. William G. Vetterlein, Greensboro, N.C.

Loquat Relish

The loquat is a Chinese and Japanese evergreen with fruit about the size of a large gooseberry that has a distinctive apple-like taste. The fruit is used widely in Florida for jelly and relish. The relish is good with game meat.

>   2 cups loquats
>   ¾ pound sugar
>   1½ cups water
>   ½ cup broken pecan meats

Wash fruit and remove blossom ends. Drop the fruit into scalding water and let stand for about 5 minutes. Drain and discard liquid. Skin and seed the loquats, discarding skins and seeds. Combine sugar and water in an open saucepan and bring to a rolling boil. Add the loquats and cook until tender and transparent. Remove from heat and add nuts. Pack in small sterilized jars and seal immediately. Makes about 1 pint.

Mango Relish (Peppers)

4 onions
6 green sweet peppers
6 red sweet peppers
1 cup sugar
2 tablespoons flour
2 tablespoons butter
2 tablespoons dry mustard
1 tablespoon salt
1 cup vinegar

Grind onions and peppers in a food chopper and combine with other ingredients in a saucepan. Cook until thick. Seal hot in sterilized jars. To use as a relish or in sandwiches, combine with mayonnaise.

From Mrs. L. D. Martin, Elon College, N.C.

Mushroom Relish

This relish will keep several weeks under refrigeration and can be served with any dry meat or fish requiring added zest. To make 2 pints:

2½ cups pickled mushrooms (see Pickled Mushrooms, page 79)
½ cup minced green or red raw peppers
½ cup minced green olives
½ cup minced black olives
½ teaspoon each ground nutmeg and ground mace

⅛ teaspoon each ground ginger and freshly ground
   black pepper
1 small sweet gherkin, finely minced
1 small pickled onion, finely minced
2 tablespoons dry sauterne or French vermouth

Combine all the ingredients and fill the jar. Be sure both jar and
cover are sterilized.

From The Mushroom Cook Book, *by Garibaldi M. Lapolla, Copyright, 1953, by Wilfred Funk, Inc., New York.*

Pear Relish

10 pounds firm ripe pears (weighed after peeling)
6 green sweet peppers
6 red sweet peppers
3 small red hot peppers
6 to 8 medium-sized onions
1 tablespoon salt
1 tablespoon each celery seed and mustard seed
2¾ pounds sugar
4 cups vinegar mixed with 1 cup water

Grind the vegetables in a food chopper. Mix thoroughly with the
other ingredients in a large kettle and place it over medium heat.
Bring to a boil and boil for 30 minutes, stirring frequently. Pack
in hot sterilized jars. Seal immediately. Makes about 10 pints.

*From Mrs. Charles H. Robertson, Hillsboro, N.C.; contributed by
her daughter, Mrs. A. M. Carroll, Burlington, N.C.*

Onion Relish

This relish, made with simple ingredients, is very unusual. It has a hot, peppery flavor and is wonderful with fresh vegetables.

14 medium-sized onions, very thinly sliced
6 green bell peppers, seeded and ground
6 fresh long red hot peppers, ground (or 3 dried hot peppers)
1 quart white vinegar
3 cups sugar
2 tablespoons salt

Mix vegetables in a large mixing bowl. Cover with boiling water and let stand for 4 minutes. Drain well in a colander. Return the vegetables to the mixing bowl and cover again with boiling water. Let stand for 4 minutes and then drain as before. Put vinegar, sugar, and salt in a kettle over low heat, stirring until sugar and salt are dissolved. Add the vegetables and bring to a boil. Boil for 15 minutes. Seal hot in sterilized jars.
From Mrs. James M. Edwards, Atlanta, Ga.

Pepper Hash (Relish)

This old recipe dates back to 1864.

12 red bell peppers
12 green bell peppers
12 onions, peeled
Boiling water
1½ pints vinegar
2 cups sugar
2½ tablespoons salt

Seed the peppers. Finely chop peppers and onions together and drain. Put into an enamel vessel. Pour over boiling water to cover

and let stand 5 minutes. Drain off and discard liquid. Combine vinegar, salt, and sugar in a large kettle and heat thoroughly. Add peppers and onions and boil for 10 minutes. Remove from heat. Pack into sterilized jars and seal immediately.
From Mrs. John Woodruff, Mendham, N.J.

Lila's Pepper Relish

Vinegar
½ gallon red sweet peppers
½ gallon green sweet peppers
½ gallon onions
½ gallon green tomatoes
Salt

Grind each vegetable separately in a food chopper. Soak each portion separately in cold water and salt, using enough solution to cover vegetables. To the peppers add ½ cup of salt each; to the onions and tomatoes add ¼ cup of salt each. Soak the vegetables several hours. Drain in a colander and let cold water run through them to take out the free salt. Mix the vegetables together in an enamel kettle and cover with vinegar. Add:

5 to 7 pounds sugar, according to taste
    (This amount of sugar makes a rather sweet, hot relish and may be reduced.)
  1 tablespoon each mustard seed and celery seed
  2 tablespoons turmeric
2½ tablespoons ground ginger
  1 tablespoon each whole cloves and whole allspice (optional)
  2 red hot pepper pods, chopped

Place the mixture over medium heat, bring to a boil, and cook for at least 1 hour, or until the vegetables are transparent and most of the vinegar has cooked out. Pack in sterilized quart or pint jars and seal immediately. Makes 6 to 7 quarts.
From Miss Lila Clare Newman, Elon College, N.C.

Pepper Sauce (a Relish)

    Salt
    1 head cabbage, finely chopped
    3 large green sweet peppers, finely chopped
    2 tablespoons sugar
    2 tablespoons celery seed
    Vinegar

Sprinkle a small handful of salt over the chopped cabbage and let it stand for a few minutes. Squeeze between the hands to get out all the water. Add chopped peppers, sugar, and celery seed and cover with vinegar. Seal cold in sterilized jars.
From Mrs. Ida Genther, in A Book for ye Cooks, *Fredericksburg, Va.*

Piccalilli

Piccalilli is a form of relish or chow-chow in which any assortment of crisp vegetables may be combined with green tomatoes. This is an unusually good hot relish.

    3 pints cabbage, slawed (measured after slawing)
    24 firm green tomatoes, chopped
    24 unpeeled medium-sized cucumbers, chopped
    1 dozen large onions, peeled and chopped
    3 quarts celery, chopped (measured after chopping)
    6 large green sweet peppers, chopped
    4 large red sweet peppers, chopped
    1 cup salt
    1 quart water
    2 quarts vinegar

Combine the chopped vegetables in a large enamel or porcelain pan. Stir in the salt and let stand for about 2 hours; then drain in a colander. Combine the water and vinegar in a large kettle and bring to a boil. Gradually add the chopped vegetables, and let them simmer for 10 minutes. Drain off this liquid by putting vegetables back into the colander. Discard liquid. Pack the vegetables in sterilized jars.

Make a syrup of:

> 1 gallon vinegar
> 3 pounds sugar
> ¼ pound each white mustard seed and yellow mustard seed
> 2 tablespoons dry mustard
> 1 tablespoon each black pepper and cloves
> 3 tablespoons ground cinnamon
> 1 teaspoon cayenne pepper

Combine the vinegar and sugar in a large kettle. Place over high heat and stir until sugar is dissolved. Add spices and bring to full rolling boil. Pour the hot syrup over the vegetables in the jars and seal.

From Mrs. H. P. MacKay, Onancock, Va.

Pineapple Relish

> 1 ripe pineapple, juice
> 1 cup sugar
> 1 cup cider vinegar
> 1 tablespoon cracked cinnamon
> 1 teaspoon each whole cloves and broken ginger root

Peel, core, and remove the eyes from the pineapple. (Save the top and plant it in a flower pot; it makes a nice house plant.) Cut the pineapple into wedges; then chop into coarse pieces. Reserve the juice. In an open kettle combine the fruit juice, sugar, and vinegar, and bring the mixture to a rolling boil. Tie the spices in a muslin cloth bag and drop them into the syrup. Let the spices simmer for about 5 minutes. Add the pineapple and cook for 5 minutes. Discard the spice bag. Cool relish. If it is to be served at once, drain off the juice and save it to pour over baked ham or to make into a dessert sauce. If the relish is to be stored, pack it immediately with the juice in a sterilized jar. Seal immediately. Do not overcook the pineapple; it will turn dark. Makes about 1 pint.

This relish is especially good with cold baked ham.

From Mrs. Everette Rogers, The National Hotel, Leesburg, Fla.

Raw Ripe-Tomato Relish

1 peck ripe red tomatoes (12 to 15 pounds)
1 cup coarse salt
6 medium-sized onions, finely chopped by hand or in food chopper
6 sweet peppers, finely chopped by hand or in food chopper
3 hot peppers, finely chopped by hand or in food chopper
1 cup celery, finely chopped by hand or in food chopper
1 quart cider vinegar
2 pounds brown sugar
2 ounces mustard seed

Scald, peel, and remove all traces of green from the tomatoes. Quarter the tomatoes and put them through a food chopper. Then place them in a large enamel vessel, stir in the salt, and let them stand until the salt is dissolved. Place the salted tomatoes in a colander, jelly bag, or similar container and allow them to drain for several hours until there is nothing left but a mass of pulp.

Put the tomato pulp in a large enamel vessel and add the remaining ingredients. Stir until well blended and the sugar thoroughly dissolved, and then pack at once in sterilized jars and seal immediately.

The relish may be used soon, but it is better if allowed to age for several weeks. It will keep for years if you wish.

The contributor says: "This is a recipe that my family has used for years, and we think it is one of the best relishes we have ever eaten."

From Nellie D. Stewart ("Nancy Nash"), Food Editor, The Nashville Tennessean, Nashville, Tenn.

Apple-Tomato Chutney

4 pounds ripe tomatoes
2 green sweet peppers, minced
2 red sweet peppers, minced
2 cups unpeeled green apples, diced

1 cup chopped celery
1 cup white chopped onions
1½ cups vinegar
1 tablespoon salt
2½ cups sugar
2 tablespoons white mustard seed
⅛ teaspoon cayenne pepper
¼ teaspoon dry mustard
½ teaspoon ground allspice
½ stick cinnamon
1 teaspoon whole cloves (tie with stick cinnamon in cloth bag)

Mix all ingredients except those in the spice bag and place over low heat. Bring to the boiling point, stirring constantly until the sugar dissolves. Add the spice bag and cook slowly for 1 hour, stirring frequently. When thick and clear add:

1 cup seedless raisins
1 tablespoon chopped crystallized ginger

Cook 10 minutes longer. Discard the spice bag. Taste and add more seasoning if desired. Seal while hot in sterilized jars. Makes about 5 pints.

Mango Chutney

This is an authentic tropical recipe, often called "relish."

1 cup red sweet peppers, ground
½ cup green sweet peppers, ground
1 cup white onions, ground
2 whole lemons, ground
1 cup crystallized orange peel, chopped
¼ cup crystallized ginger, chopped
5 cups green mangoes, thinly sliced
1½ cups sugar
3 cups vinegar
½ teaspoon salt
1 tablespoon each mixed ground spices, cloves, allspice, and cinnamon

Combine ground peppers, onion, and lemon in a mixing bowl and mix well. Add sliced mangoes and crystallized fruits. Combine sugar, vinegar, salt, and spices in a large saucepan. Place over medium heat and bring to a slow boil. Reduce the heat. Add mixed vegetables and fruits and cook very slowly until the chutney is thick and the mangoes are transparent. The mangoes should remain in original sliced form.

From Mrs. Everette Rogers, The National Hotel, Leesburg, Fla.

Old English Peach Chutney

The contributor of this recipe says: "This receipt for peach chutney is an old English receipt and is well over one hundred years old. It was taken to South Africa by an English family. The father was later Governor of Cape Town. His daughter became a very close friend of my mother's and gave her this receipt about thirty years ago. To our knowledge this is the only time it has been given outside of the family."

> 6 pounds yellow clingstone peaches, peeled and finely chopped
> 2 quarts vinegar
> 1 pound each white sugar and brown sugar
> ½ pound ginger root, soaked well in water, drained, and chopped
> 1 pound seeded raisins, chopped
> ¼ pound salt
> ¼ pound mustard seed, crushed
> ¼ pound green or red chili or sweet peppers, chopped
> 1 small onion, chopped
> 2 cloves garlic, peeled and chopped

Cook the peaches in 1 quart of the vinegar until soft. Make a syrup of the other quart of vinegar and sugar in another kettle. When syrup is thick, add the peach mixture and other ingredients. Cook for 30 to 40 minutes (stirring frequently), or until the chutney is thick as jam. Seal in sterilized jars.

From Mrs. James L. Robertson, in Recipes from Southern Kitchens, *Junior League of Augusta, Ga.*

Lib Mor's Pear Chutney

5 pounds hard pears, peeled and sliced (weighed after peeling and slicing)
2 pounds brown sugar
3 pints cider vinegar
1 pound seedless raisins
3 cloves garlic, peeled and minced
2 tablespoons mustard seed
6 tablespoons salt
6 fresh red hot pepper pods
16 ounces preserved ginger, with sugar rinsed off, chopped

Mix pears and sugar in a large kettle. Place over low heat and cook slowly until the mixture is thick and smooth, stirring frequently. Add the remaining ingredients and let the mixture come to a boil. Remove the mixture from the heat and let it stand overnight. Return it to medium heat and bring to a boil. Pack while hot in sterilized jars and seal immediately. Mangoes may be used as a substitute for pears. Use green or not quite ripe mangoes.
From Mrs. R. C. Moore, Maplewood Farm, Graham, N.C.

English Mint Chutney

Mint chutney is a delicate condiment to be served with lamb or veal.
1 dozen ripe tomatoes, peeled and chopped
1 pound tart apples, peeled and chopped (weighed after peeling and chopping)
¾ pound raisins, chopped
2 red sweet peppers, chopped
5 large onions, peeled and chopped
1 quart cider vinegar, scalded, then cooled
⅓ cup fresh mint leaves, chopped
1 tablespoon each white mustard seed and yellow mustard seed
2 tablespoons salt
2 cups sugar
½ teaspoon powdered ginger

Scald, peel, and chop tomatoes. Chop the remaining vegetables and fruit coarsely in food chopper or on a chopping block. Scald the vinegar, pour it over mint leaves, and let them steep for 15 minutes. Drain off vinegar and let cool. Discard the mint leaves. Mix all ingredients and place in a stone crock. Cover and store in a cool place for about 10 days, stirring the mixture every day. Seal in sterilized jars.

Rhubarb Chutney

    1 pint vinegar
    2 pounds brown sugar
    2 pounds rhubarb, shredded
    1 pound Sultana raisins, chopped
    2 ounces ginger root or preserved ginger, chopped
    5 cloves garlic, peeled and chopped
    2 lemons, finely chopped
    ½ teaspoon cayenne pepper

Bring vinegar and sugar to a boil in a large saucepan. Add remaining ingredients and cook slowly for about 3 to 4 hours. Place in clean, dry, hot glasses and seal with paraffin. Fills six 8-ounce glasses.

From Mrs. Elsa Dodd Thorley, Center Port, N.Y.

Lazy Day Chow-chow

    1 dozen pickled cucumbers
    1 large onion
    ½ gallon green tomatoes

Finely chop the vegetables. Sprinkle with salt and let stand overnight. Next day squeeze out as dry as possible.
  Combine:

    3 pints vinegar
    ½ pound sugar

1½ tablespoons turmeric

2 tablespoons each dry mustard, mustard seed, and black pepper

3 chopped green peppers

3 chopped red peppers

Mix with other ingredients in a large kettle and place over medium heat. Bring quickly to a boil. Remove from heat and pack in hot sterilized jars. Seal immediately.

From Mrs. W. I. Brooks, in Pages from Old Salem Cook Books, *Dorcas Co-Workers of the Salem House, Winston-Salem, N.C.*

Georgia Chow-chow

This grand family recipe is more than one hundred years old. It was originated by Mrs. Thomas Elder Middlebrooks of Farmington and Athens, Georgia, the grandmother of our contributor's husband.

3 quarts green unpeeled tomatoes (best if gathered after first frost)

1 quart small silver-skinned onions, peeled

6 green hot peppers

1 red sweet pepper (or 3 hot green peppers and 3 hot red peppers)

2 medium-sized heads cabbage

1 quart dill pickle

Vinegar (good quality apple cider)

1 bunch celery

3 cups sugar

2 teaspoons each ground cinnamon and allspice

1 teaspoon each ground cloves and turmeric

½ teaspoon ground mace

½ small bottle dehydrated horseradish

Chop tomatoes, onions, peppers, and cabbage into small pieces but not fine as for relish. Soak overnight in a weak salt brine. Chop dill pickles a little smaller than gum drops. Place pickles in a porcelain (glass or pottery) bowl and cover with vinegar. Let stand overnight. Next day put tomato, onion, pepper, and cabbage mixture into a bag and squeeze out well, discarding the liquid. Place vegetables in a large enamel kettle. Add the vinegar strained from the dill pickles and enough extra vinegar to make 1 quart. (Do not add the dill pickles at this time.) Place over medium heat and cook until the vegetables are barely tender. Remove from heat and cool. Place in a bag and squeeze out again, discarding the liquid. Return to the kettle.

Chop the celery and put it into a separate saucepan. Cover with a mixture of vinegar and water and place over medium heat. Bring to a boil and boil for 15 minutes. Drain. Add celery, sugar, ground spices, and dill pickles to tomato mixture. Cover well with vinegar. Place over low heat and bring to a boil. Cook slowly for about 1 hour, or until tender, stirring often. Just before removing from the heat, add horseradish. Stir well. Pack hot in hot sterilized jars. Seal immediately.

From Mrs. Thomas C. Beusse, Athens, Ga.

Carolina Chow-chow

    4 quarts green tomatoes
    2 quarts onions
    6 pounds cabbage
    6 hot peppers
   12 green sweet peppers
 1½ cups salt
    2 quarts vinegar
    5 pounds sugar
    5 tablespoons dry mustard
    6 tablespoons flour
    1 teaspoon turmeric
    1 cup water
      Spices
      Mustard seed
      Celery seed

Grind the tomatoes, onions, cabbage, and peppers in a food chopper. Put together in a large vessel, add the salt, and cover with cold water. Let stand overnight. Next day drain thoroughly, pressing out all liquid. Make a dressing by mixing the flour, turmeric, and mustard together and blending to a smooth paste with the cup of water. Bring the vinegar to the boiling point and stir in the paste, stirring constantly. When the sauce begins to thicken, add half of the sugar and cook for several minutes. Place the well-drained vegetables in a large kettle, and pour the hot sauce over them. Add the remainder of the sugar and season to taste with mixed spices, mustard seed, and celery seed. Reheat the chow-chow but do not boil. Pack hot in pint jars and seal immediately. Makes 14 pints.

From Mrs. E. W. Harvey, Greenville, N.C.

Emma Pollard's Chow-chow

Good and unusually spicy! Colorful in jars.

> 1 gallon cabbage, chopped
> ½ gallon green tomatoes, chopped
> 4 large green sweet peppers, chopped
> 2 pods red hot peppers, chopped
> 2 pounds dark brown sugar
> 1 quart onions, chopped
> 4 tablespoons ground mustard
> 2 tablespoons ground ginger
> 1 tablespoon each ground cinnamon and ground cloves
> 2 tablespoons turmeric
> 1 tablespoon celery seed
> 2 tablespoons salt
> ½ gallon vinegar

Mix all the ingredients in a large kettle. Place over medium heat, bring to boil, and boil for 40 minutes. Cool. Pour into sterilized jars. Seal.

From Mrs. Frank Pollard, Burlington, N.C.

6. Bottled Foods

Catchups, Chili Sauces, Sauces, Fruit Nectars, Juices, and Syrups

WHEN A RECIPE CALLS FOR FOOD TO BE BOTTLED, AIRTIGHT JARS may almost always be substituted. Bottles, however, are more practical for any liquid: catchups, sauces, fruit and vegetable juices, and so on. Liquids may be served more conveniently from bottles, and they will not turn dark so quickly as in wide-mouthed jars.

The basic rules for bottling are the same as for any canned food. The containers and caps must be sterilized before using and sealed after being filled. (See General Instructions, page 5.)

There are two methods of sealing bottles: one is to use caps and a capping machine; the other is to use corks. When corks are used, the tops are sealed with wax, paraffin, or resin. To cork bottles, fill the container to the neck, insert the cork tightly into the neck (or follow individual recipe), and cut it off level with the mouth of the bottle. Melt sealing wax for one bottle at a time, and

114

cover the cork, letting the wax run down over the bottle top to form an airtight cap. To seal with paraffin, melt the paraffin in a metal vessel, and dip the top of the bottle into the hot paraffin. Cool and repeat the process until a thick coating seals the top.

Thorley's Chili Sauce

2 quarts ripe tomatoes, peeled and quartered
2 green peppers, cleaned and cut up
2 onions, cut up
1 pint vinegar
1 tablespoon salt
½ cup brown sugar
1 teaspoon each ground cloves and ground allspice
1 teaspoon black pepper

Combine ingredients and cook until very thick, stirring frequently. Cooking will take at least 4 hours. Pour into hot sterilized jars and seal. Makes 4 pints.
From Mrs. Elsa Dodd Thorley, Center Port, N.Y.

Canned Tomato Chili Sauce

Home-canned or commercial tomatoes may be used to make this good chili.

3 No. 2½ cans tomatoes, chopped (save juice)
3 green peppers, seeded and chopped
3 large onions, ground
3 stalks celery, ground
1 tablespoon salt
1¼ cups vinegar
1½ tablespoons sugar
½ cup mixed pickling spices (tied in cloth bag)

Mix all ingredients in large kettle. Bring to a slow boil and simmer for 3 to 4 hours, or until thick. Stir often to keep sauce from sticking. Discard the spice bag. Seal the sauce in hot sterilized bottles or jars. Makes about 2 pints.

New York Chili Sauce

This is a grand chili sauce.

> 1 gallon ripe tomatoes, peeled and chopped (measured after peeling and chopping)
> 2 cups red sweet peppers, chopped (measured after chopping)
> 2 cups onions, chopped (measured after chopping)
> 1 pod red hot pepper
> 1 cup sugar
> 3 tablespoons salt
> 1 tablespoon each mustard seed and celery seed
> 3 tablespoons mixed pickling spices
> 2½ cups vinegar

Mix the measured vegetables in a large kettle and add pepper, sugar, and salt. Place over low heat to cook. Tie the spices in a bag and add to the vegetables after they have cooked 30 minutes. Continue cooking until sauce is very thick. Then add vinegar and boil until there seems to be no more "free" liquid. Taste, and add more seasoning if desired. Pour while boiling hot into hot sterilized jars. Seal immediately.
From Mrs. Catherine H. Schoonmaker, Ellenville, N.Y.

Iowa Cranberry Catchup

This is a grand catchup for turkey.

> 1 quart fresh raw cranberries, washed and picked over
> 1 cup strong vinegar
> 2 cups brown sugar
> 1 teaspoon salt
> 1½ cups water
> 1 teaspoon each ground cloves, ground allspice, and ground cinnamon
> ½ teaspoon ground mace

Combine cranberries with vinegar, water, and spices, and cook slowly until the berries are soft. Rub through a fine sieve and discard skins and seeds. To the sieved pulp, add the sugar and salt. Cook slowly until the mixture thickens. Seal immediately in sterilized jars or bottles. Makes about 1 quart.
From Miss Miriam LeCompte, Cordon, Iowa.

Bandon Plantation Cucumber Catchup

Inglis Fletcher, North Carolina's noted historical novelist, gives us this old Chapman family recipe. It is a favorite meat sauce at Bandon. It requires no cooking.

    4 large cucumbers, peeled and sliced
    6 onions, peeled and sliced
    ½ cup each white mustard seed and black mustard seed
    1 teaspoon ground cloves
    1 tablespoon ground black pepper
    2 tablespoons ground cinnamon
    1 tablespoon ground mace
      Vinegar

Let cucumbers and onions stand overnight in a colander covered by a plate and pressed down with a weight, such as an old flat iron. In the morning drain off the liquid, and discard it. Finely mince cucumbers and onions with a knife and drain again until quite dry, discarding the liquid. Mix with spices and add vinegar to cover cucumber-onion mixture. Put into sterilized bottles or jars. Seal and store in a cool place.
From Inglis Fletcher, Bandon Plantation, Edenton, N.C.

Ivy House Cocktail Sauce

On the Richmond Road, just outside Williamsburg, is the charming Ivy House, famous for the hospitality and original dishes of the owners, the Rutledges. Ivy House blended sauces are much in demand. For this book the Rutledges have given two of their favorites.

>1 bottle chili sauce (14 ounces), commercial or home-
>   made
>1 bottle horseradish (3 to 4 ounces, or more, if desired)
>1 tablespoon any good hot sauce
>½ tablespoon Worcestershire sauce
>½ tablespoon A-1 sauce

Blend the ingredients in the order given. Mix well and chill. If the sauce is to be kept more than a few days, pour it into sterilized jars and seal. Keep refrigerated. This is a very hot sauce, perfect with shrimp or other seafood.

From Mr. and Mrs. John David Rutledge, Ivy House, Williamsburg, Va.

Grape-Apple Catchup

Fruit catchup is served just as vegetable catchup is. Fruit catchups are sweet-sour, like chutney, and are excellent with lamb, veal, pork, and other meats. They are also good served as pudding sauces. Cranberries, plums, peaches, apples, lemons, and other fruits may be used.

>2 pounds tart apples
>2 pounds Concord grapes or any tangy grape
>2 cups mild white vinegar
>3 cups sugar
>½ teaspoon salt
>4 tablespoons mixed spices, tied in cloth bag

Peel, core, and dice the apples. Wash the grapes, and remove the stems. Mix the fruits, and put them in a covered pan with no water. Steam on slow heat until the fruit is soft. Press the fruit through a sieve or food mill. Add vinegar and sugar to juice and whatever pulp is pressed through the sieve. (Discard the pulp left in the sieve.) Put the vinegar-fruit mixture in a saucepan and add the salt and spice bag. Simmer for 20 minutes. Discard the spice bag. Bottle the sauce while hot and seal immediately. Makes about 4 pints.

Black Pepper Cucumber Catchup

3 dozen cucumbers, peeled and finely chopped
8 onions, peeled and finely chopped
½ pint salt
1 cup black pepper
Vinegar

Sprinkle the cucumbers and onions with salt, and let them drain for 8 hours. Add the pepper to the cucumber and onion pulp. Mix well and pack in sterilized jars. Cover with vinegar and seal. Keep in a cool place.
From Mrs. R. W. Shields, in Pride of the Kitchen, *Scotland Neck, N.C.*

Grape Catchup (Relish)

Concord grapes to make 8 cups pulp
6 cups sugar
1 teaspoon cinnamon
1 teaspoon each ground cloves and ground allspice
1 cup vinegar

Heat the grapes slowly until the skins come off. Put through a sieve and measure. There should be 8 cups of pulp for the ingredients listed above. Add the other ingredients and cook until the mixture has the thickness of catchup. Delicious with meat. Makes about 6 pints.
From Mrs. A. E. Nelson, in The Bergen Cook Book, *Roland, Iowa.*

Plum Sauce

½ gallon firm plums
2 pounds sugar
½ teacup good apple vinegar
½ teaspoon each extract of clove and extract of ginger

Wash the plums. Put them into a saucepan and cover with water. Boil for 15 minutes. Pour off the water and add the sugar and vinegar. Boil for 30 minutes. Mix the clove and ginger extracts with a little water and add to the plum mixture. Boil for a few minutes. Pour into sterilized jars and seal.

From Mrs. F. H. Marshall, in Southern Recipes, *compiled by the Montgomery Junior League, Montgomery, Ala.*

Home-made Catchup

        10 pounds unpeeled ripe tomatoes, cut up
         2 pounds onions, peeled and chopped
         2 tablespoons mixed pickling spices
         2 cloves garlic, peeled and chopped
         2 cups sugar
        ¼ cup salt
         1 tablespoon Tabasco sauce
        1½ cups vinegar

Combine tomatoes, onions, spices, and garlic in a kettle. Place over medium heat and bring to a boil. Let the mixture cook slowly for 2½ to 3 hours. Strain, saving the juice. To the juice add sugar, salt, Tabasco, and vinegar. Return the mixture to medium heat, and cook it until thick enough to bottle. Seal immediately.

From The Ideal Cook Book, *La Grange, Texas.*

Fresh Horseradish Sauce

Fresh horseradish has a pungency unlike that of processed horse-radish and is a delicious condiment to keep on hand. The root is easy to grow and simple to process. When grating the root, it is advisable to work out of doors, since the aroma stings the eyes.

         1 pound horseradish root
         2 tablespoons sugar
           White vinegar
         2 drops garlic or onion juice (optional)

Scrub the root, and peel off the outer thick skin. Grate the root on a fine bread grater. Mix with sugar and garlic or onion juice, if desired. Cover with vinegar. Let the mixture set, adding vinegar until the root will not absorb any more. Seal in small airtight jars. Do not use large jars, since the root turns dark quickly after the jar is opened.

"Old Sour"

In Key West, "Old Sour" is standard household "equipment" and is used on all kinds of seafood, in salads, and in other dishes.

> 1 pint fresh lime juice, strained
> 1 tablespoon salt

Mix, bottle, and cork. Store until the juice ferments.
From The Key West Cook Book, *Key West Woman's Club, Key West, Fla.*

Strawberry or Raspberry Shrub (Vinegar)

Fruit shrub has long been a favorite "cooler." The art of making this beverage has been neglected since commercial beverages came into prominence. For those who have the makings, here is a good old recipe.

> 12 pounds ripe strawberries (or raspberries), "nicely dressed"
> 3 quarts best vinegar
> Sugar
> Brandy

Cover 4 pounds of strawberries with the vinegar and let stand for 3 days. Drain off the juice through a jelly bag and pour the liquid over the same amount of fresh berries. Let these stand for 3 days. Repeat the process once again. Finally, drain, and to the liquid add 1 pound of white sugar for each quart. Boil the sugar and liquid together for a few minutes. Add 1 gill (¼ pint) of brandy to each quart of the liquid. When cool, bottle and cork or seal. When serving, use 1 part liquor to 2 parts ice and water.

Currant Shrub

1 pint currant juice
1 pound sugar
Brandy

Boil together the sugar and juice for 10 minutes. To each pint of shrub, add 1 gill (¼ pint) of brandy. Seal in bottles. Serve like strawberry shrub.

From Excellent Receipts, *St. Thaddeus Church Fair, Aiken, S.C. (1874).*

Hoskins Barbecue Sauce

This recipe was originated to baste a green pork shoulder, but it is an excellent sauce for any barbecue meat or fowl.

1 medium onion, peeled and minced
1 clove garlic, peeled and minced
¼ pound butter
Juice of ½ lemon
Peel of the lemon cut into slivers (use only the yellow rind)
1 cup brown sugar
1 cup vinegar and water, mixed (about ½ cup each, depending on taste)
1 cup tomato catchup
2 tablespoons Worcestershire sauce
1 teaspoon Tabasco sauce
½ teaspoon chili powder

Put the minced onion and garlic into a skillet with the butter and allow to cook slowly until onion and garlic brown slightly. Mix all other ingredients together and add to the butter sauce. Return the skillet to the heat and heat mixture thoroughly, but do not boil. Use at once or pour into sterilized jars or bottles and seal.

From W. Cramey Hoskins, Louisville, Ky.; supplied by Cissy Gregg, Home Consultant, The Courier-Journal, Louisville, Ky.

Mushroom Catchup

This catchup is expensive, but delicious. It makes a wonderful steak sauce or seasoning for gravy.

        4 quarts fresh mushrooms
        1 cup water
        1½ cups white vinegar
        1 tablespoon salt
        ½ teaspoon each ground allspice and ground cloves
        ¼ teaspoon mace
        ⅛ teaspoon red pepper
        1 tablespoon dry mustard
        ¼ teaspoon onion juice

Clean, skin, and wash mushrooms. Cut off the fibrous parts of the stems. Put the mushrooms and 1 cup of water in a covered saucepan. Place over high heat and bring to the boiling point. Reduce the heat to low and simmer until mushrooms are tender. Press through a sieve, saving all pulp and juice that comes through the sieve. Add the remaining ingredients to the mushroom mixture, and return it to the heat. Boil for about 30 minutes. Pour into hot sterilized bottles or jars. Seal immediately. About 5 pints.

Tomato Juice Cocktail

        1 peck ripe unpeeled tomatoes, cut into pieces
        1 cup sugar
        4 tablespoons salt
        ⅛ teaspoon each red pepper, black pepper, ground cinnamon, and nutmeg
        4 tablespoons vinegar

Cook and strain tomatoes. This should yield about 1 gallon of juice. Add the other ingredients and bring to a hard boil. Pour into hot sterilized jars or bottles and seal. Chill before serving. Garnish each glass with lemon, if desired.
From Mrs. John W. Aldrich, in Alexandria Woman's Club Cook Book, *Alexandria, Va.*

Pepper Sauce

     12 onions
     12 sharp red hot peppers
     24 red sweet peppers
      4 tablespoons salt
      2 cups water
      2 pounds brown sugar
      1 quart vinegar
      2 tablespoons mustard seed
      4 tablespoons horseradish

Grind onions and peppers in a food grinder and put into a large kettle with the remaining ingredients—except the horseradish. Place over low heat and cook for 1 hour. Add the horseradish and continue cooking for 10 minutes. Pour into hot sterilized jars and seal immediately.

From Mrs. Peyton B. Winfree, in Favorite Foods of Virginians, *Church Service League, St. Paul's Episcopal Church, Lynchburg, Va.*

Red Wine Tomato Catchup

This catchup is extra hot and very different.

         1 bushel ripe unpeeled tomatoes, washed and chopped
      1½ quarts cider vinegar
         1 pint good red wine (or ½ pint red wine vinegar)
         2 tablespoons dehydrated horseradish mixed in 1 table-
             spoon cold water
         2 tablespoons cracked peppercorns
         2 tablespoons ground allspice
       ½ teaspoon ground cloves
       ¼ teaspoon ground cinnamon
       ½ ounce ground mace or nutmeg
         2 cups brown sugar

Boil the tomatoes in their own juice until soft. Strain, saving the juice. This should yield about 2 quarts. Mix this tomato juice with

the remaining ingredients in a large kettle and boil until reduced
to about one third of the original volume. Taste and correct
seasoning for sugar and salt. Bottle while hot and seal immediately.

Spaghetti Sauce to Be Frozen or Canned

This is a basic sauce which may be stored indefinitely. The seasoning may be corrected according to taste.

> 2½ tablespoons olive oil or salad oil
> 3 large white onions, peeled and minced
> 2 cloves garlic, peeled and minced
> ¾ pound ground beef (stew beef or chuck)
> ¼ pound ground lean pork
> 1 No. 2 can tomatoes or 1 quart home-canned tomatoes
> 1 can tomato paste (standard size), or 1 can con-
> densed tomato soup
> ½ cup minced celery, measure after mincing
> ½ cup minced green pepper, measure after mincing
> 1 tablespoon black pepper
> 1 tablespoon Worcestershire sauce
> 1 teaspoon each whole cloves and whole allspice
> 1 bay leaf
> 1 tablespoon sweet pickle vinegar (drained from any
> pickle)
> Salt to taste

Use a large saucepan with a cover. Place pan on medium heat and
pour in olive oil. Let the oil heat. Add the onion and garlic and
cook on medium heat until tender but not brown, stirring constantly. Stir in ground beef and pork. Increase the heat and cook
the meat until it is deep gray in color, stirring constantly. Add
tomatoes, tomato paste (or soup), celery, green pepper, black
pepper and Worcestershire sauce. Cover the saucepan and let
the mixture come to a boil. Reduce the heat and simmer 1 hour,
stirring often. Tie spices and bay leaf in a cloth bag and add to
sauce. Add vinegar and salt to taste. Remove the cover from the

saucepan and simmer the sauce in open pan until the mixture is thick and deep red in color.

This sauce may be used at once over cooked spaghetti. If it is to be stored in food freezer, allow it to cool; then pour into standard round pint cartons with tops. Fill the cartons and adjust the tops. Set upright in the freezer until the sauce freezes. If it is to be canned, pour the hot sauce into sterilized pint jars and seal airtight immediately, according to type of jars used. Makes about 3 pints.

Ivy House Tartar Sauce

This fine sauce has a very distinctive flavor.

> 1 clove garlic, peeled
> 1 cup mayonnaise
> 1½ tablespoons imported capers, finely ground
> 1½ tablespoons onion, finely ground
> 1½ tablespoons onion juice
> 1½ tablespoons sweet pickle relish

Rub a chilled mixing bowl with garlic. Add mayonnaise and stir thoroughly so that the garlic essence completely envelops the mayonnaise. Add the finely ground capers and their juice and the finely ground onion and onion juice. Last, add pickle relish. Blend well, chill, and serve. If the sauce is to be kept, pour it into sterilized jars and refrigerate. This is perfect with any seafood, but it also makes a tasty relish to accompany many other foods. *From Mr. and Mrs. John David Rutledge, Ivy House, Williamsburg, Va.*

Green Tomato Sauce (Pickle)

> 30 medium-sized green tomatoes
> 3 large onions, peeled
> 3 bell peppers
> 1 tablespoon each whole allspice and cloves
> 1 tablespoon ground cinnamon

    1 teaspoon celery seed
    2 tablespoons salt
    1 quart vinegar
    2 cups sugar

Chop the vegetables and drain them in a colander. Combine the
vegetables and remaining ingredients in a large kettle and cook
slowly for 1 hour.
From Mrs. John Woodruff, Mendham, N.J. (c. 1864)

Tomato Catchup

    1 peck ripe unpeeled tomatoes, cut up
    6 medium onions, peeled and sliced
    2 cloves garlic, peeled and minced
    2 red sweet peppers, seeded and chopped
    1 red hot pepper pod
    1 bay leaf
    1 tablespoon each whole allspice, celery seed, and mus-
        tard seed
    1 stick cinnamon
    1 tablespoon salt
    ½ teaspoon white pepper
    ½ cup white sugar
    ½ cup brown sugar
    2 cups strong vinegar

Combine tomatoes, onions, garlic, and sweet peppers in a large,
wide kettle and cover with water. Cook over medium heat until
soft. Strain through a fine sieve or cheesecloth. Tie red pepper
pod, bay leaf, allspice, celery seed, mustard seed, and stick cinnamon in a bag and add, with salt and pepper, to the tomato juice.
Return the juice to the heat and boil, stirring often, until the
mixture has been reduced by one half. Add the white and brown
sugar and vinegar and cook 10 to 15 minutes longer. This catchup
should be sufficiently thickened to bottle, but if a thicker consistency is desired, make a paste of 1 tablespoon of flour with a
little cold vinegar and add to the catchup, stirring until it thickens.

Pour into hot sterilized jars or bottles and seal immediately.
Makes 5 to 6 quarts.

Canned Tomato Soy

2 No. 2½ cans tomatoes
½ pint sour pickles, finely chopped
8 medium-sized onions, peeled and finely chopped
2 pounds sugar
1 tablespoon each black pepper and dry mustard
1 teaspoon ground cinnamon
2 tablespoons Worcestershire sauce
1 teaspoon ground cloves
1½ tablespoons salt
1 pint vinegar

Combine all ingredients in a large kettle. Bring to a boil and
cook slowly for about 2 hours, or until thickened. Stir frequently
to prevent scorching. Pour into hot sterilized bottle or jars and
seal immediately.

Green Tomato Soy

Soy is a pungent cooked relish of thick consistency. It is usually
made of green or ripe tomatoes.

2 gallons green tomatoes, thinly sliced
12 good-sized onions, peeled and thinly sliced
2 quarts vinegar
1 quart sugar
2 tablespoons each dry mustard, black pepper, and salt
1 tablespoon each ground allspice and ground cloves

Combine all the ingredients in a large kettle. Place over low heat
and simmer slowly until the vegetables are tender, stirring frequently to prevent scorching. Pour into hot sterilized jars or bottles
and seal immediately. Makes about 4 to 5 quarts.
From Mrs. Lyman Jones, in The Suffolk Cook Book, The Girls'
Missionary Society, Christian Church, Suffolk, Va.

Uncooked Tomato Catchup (Relish)

This is a refreshing catchup or relish. It is good added to soups, green salads, and other foods. Any amount you wish may be made.

    1 peck firm ripe tomatoes, peeled
    5 green peppers, finely chopped or ground
    6 onions, ground
    2 cups celery, finely ground or finely chopped
    5 cups vinegar
    1 pound brown sugar
    3 tablespoons salt
    2 ounces white mustard seed

Chop the tomatoes and drain through a colander, saving the juice. Combine all other ingredients with the juice and mix thoroughly. Pack in sterilized bottles or jars and store in a cool place. Do not keep more than a few days without refrigeration.
From Mrs. William Walter Brown, II, Burlington, N.C.

VARIATION

Horseradish Catchup

To make an extra-hot catchup, add 2 tablespoons of dehydrated horseradish mixed with 1 tablespoon of cold water or 1 cup fresh grated horseradish.

Fresh Vegetable Relish

    1 pound tomatoes, peeled and diced
    2 medium-sized onions, peeled and minced
    2 tablespoons minced fresh parsley
      Juice of 1 lemon
      Salt and pepper

Combine tomatoes, onions, parsley, lemon juice, salt, and pepper, mixing well. Use at once or pack in sterilized jars. Store as for Uncooked Tomato Catchup.

Pickling English Walnuts

"The walnuts should be gathered when the nut is so young that you can run a pin into it easily; pour boiling salt and water (brine) on, and let them be covered with it nine days, changing it every third day—take them out, and put them on dishes in the air for a few minutes, taking care to turn them over; this will make them black much sooner—put them in a pot, strew over some whole (black peppercorns) pepper, cloves, a little garlic, mustard-seed, and horse-radish scraped and dried; cover them with strong, cold vinegar." (Pack in jars and seal.)

Mrs. Mary Randolph's Virginia Housewife, *1831, in* The Williamsburg Art of Cookery, *by Mrs. Helen Bullock, copyright, 1938, Colonial Williamsburg, Inc.*

Making Walnut Catchup

"Gather the walnuts as for pickling (while young enough that you can run a pin into the nut easily), and keep them in salt water the same time (9 days, changing the water every third day); then pound them in a marble mortar—to every dozen walnuts, put a quart of vinegar; stir them well every day for a week, then put them in a bag and press all the liquor through; to each quart (liquor), put a teaspoon of pounded cloves, and one of mace and six cloves of garlic—boil it fifteen or twenty minutes, and bottle it."

Mrs. Mary Randolph's Virginia Housewife, *1831, in* The Williamsburg Art of Cookery, *by Mrs. Helen Bullock, copyright, 1938, Colonial Williamsburg, Inc.*

Bottling Fresh Fruit

This is an old way to conserve fresh fruit uncooked.

Fresh fruit, such as currants, raspberries, cherries, plums, gooseberries, damson plums, and the like, may be bottled. Use wide-mouthed glass bottles and new corks that fit tightly. (See bottling instructions, pages 6–7.) Let the fruit be full grown, but not too ripe, and gathered in dry weather. Pick them off the stalks without bruising or breaking the skin and reject any that are at all blemished. If the fruit are gathered in damp weather, or if the skins are cut at all, the fruit will mold.

Have ready some perfectly dry bottles and some new dry corks or bungs. Burn a match in each bottle to exhaust the air, and quickly put in the fruit to be preserved. Gently cork the bottles, and put them in a very cool oven. Leave them there until the fruit has been reduced by one fourth. Then take the bottles out—but do not open them—and immediately beat the corks in tight. Cut off the tops of the corks, and seal them with resin. If kept in a *dry* place, the fruit will remain good for months. It is on this principle that the success of the preparation depends, for if the fruit is stored in a place that is even slightly damp, it will soon spoil.

From The Everyday Cook Book, *by Miss E. Neil, (c. 1875).*

Apricot Nectar

  2 pounds ripe apricots
  2 cups water
    Sugar

Wash, stone, and slice the fruit. Place the apricots and water in a saucepan and heat slowly to the simmering point. Remove from heat and press through a colander; then through a sieve. Measure the juice into a saucepan, and bring it to the slow simmering point. For 1 cup of juice stir in ⅓ cup of sugar. Stir until the sugar is dissolved and the mixture is thoroughly heated. Bring back to the slow simmering point. Remove from heat and pour at once into sterilized jars. Seal immediately. Process in a hot-water bath according to the chart furnished by the jar manufacturer.

Peach Nectar

Use the same proportions and the same procedure as in Apricot Nectar. If the peaches are not very sweet, use ½ cup of sugar instead of ⅓ cup.

Fruit and Berry Nectar

Nectar from fruit—berries, grapes, plums, and the like—makes a refreshing syrup that may be used in cold drinks or served over desserts.

> 1 quart vinegar
> 12 pounds very ripe fruit, crushed
> Sugar

Pour the vinegar over the crushed berries and set them aside for about 1½ days in a graniteware or porcelain container with a cover or with a cloth tied over the container. Strain first through a thin cloth; then though a thick one. (Or use cloth bags.) Measure the juice and add an equal measure of sugar, stirring until dissolved. Place over medium heat, bring to a boil, and boil for 5 minutes, counting the time after the syrup begins to boil. Remove immediately and seal in sterilized jars or bottles. No processing is needed. To serve as a beverage, use 4 tablespoons of syrup to an iced-tea glass of crushed ice. For a smaller glass, use 3 tablespoons of syrup.

From Mrs. J. S. Howle, in The Pee Dee Pepper Pot, *Darlington, S.C.*

Fruit Juices

Canned fruit juices have many uses; they may be served as a beverage, made into jelly, used to flavor desserts, to make syrups, and so on.

The juice from such fruits as blackberries, cherries, currants, grapes, pineapples, raspberries, strawberries, cranberries, loganberries, and elderberries may be treated in this way.

To obtain the best flavor, the fruit must be cooked and the juice pressed out. Use only sound, ripe fruit. Wash and crush the fruit, adding a small amount of water. Heat slowly to the simmering point, and cook until the fruit is soft. Strain through cheesecloth. Retain the juice and discard the pulp. The juice may be canned with or without sugar. If sugar is added, use about 1 cup of sugar to 1 gallon of juice, or more if desired. Put the sugar and juice in an open saucepan. Bring to the slow simmering point and pour at once into sterilized jars, filling jars to within ½ inch of the top. Process according to individual recipe instructions or according to the chart furnished by the jar manufacturer.

Fruit Syrups

After the juice has been extracted, as for Fruit Juices, measure the juice. For 1 cup of juice add 1 cup of sugar. Place juice and sugar in an open saucepan and bring to the boiling point. Pour immediately into sterilized jars. Seal immediately.

Blackberry Cordial

Ripe blackberries
Sugar
2 teaspoons grated nutmeg
1 tablespoon each cracked stick cinnamon and whole cloves
1 teaspoon each whole allspice and broken ginger root
3 tablespoons vanilla

Mash the ripe blackberries and strain them through cheesecloth. Save the juice and discard the pulp. To 1 pint of juice add 1 pint of sugar. Tie the spices in a cloth bag. In an enamel pan mix the juice and sugar and add the spice bag. Place over medium heat and bring to a boil. Reduce heat to low and continue cooking slowly for 25 minutes. Remove the spice bag and add vanilla. Pour into sterilized jars to within ½ inch of the top. Seal immediately.

Pure Blackberry Syrup

Over vanilla ice cream this is heavenly.
6 quarts ripe blackberries, washed and stemmed
2½ quarts water
5 cups sugar

Crush the berries and add the water. Bring to a rapid boil and boil rapidly for 10 minutes. Reduce the heat and simmer for 5 minutes longer. Strain the juice through a jelly bag. There should be about 6 cups of juice. To each 6 cups of juice add 5 cups of sugar. If there is less juice, reduce the sugar proportionately. Boil the juice and sugar rapidly for 10 to 15 minutes, or until the syrup begins to thicken slightly. Do not overcook, for, if you do, the syrup will begin to jell. Bottle at once, cork, and seal.

Orange or Lemon Syrup

This is a grand old recipe for making a delicious syrup.

Combine a pound and a half of white sugar with each pint of juice from fresh oranges or lemons or from a combination of the two. Add some of the peel cut into slivers and boil all together for 10 minutes. Then strain, bottle, and cork. Mixed with ice water, it makes a fine beverage. It is also useful to flavor pies and puddings.

From Excellent Receipts, *published for the benefit of St. Thaddeus Church Fair, Aiken, S.C. (1874).*

Muscadine Grape Juice (Syrup)

This grand grape juice is actually a heavy rich syrup that is a favorite nectar at the North Carolina Executive Mansion. It may be diluted and served as a beverage, or it may be used over desserts and for flavoring.

> 15 quarts muscadine grapes, washed and stemmed
> 5 quarts water
> 9 cups sugar

Combine the grapes and water and bring to a boil. Boil on high heat for 20 minutes. Reduce the heat to low and boil for 10 minutes longer. Drain off the juice through a colander, and then strain it through cheesecloth. Halve the juice and the sugar. Mix each portion of sugar and juice in a separate container and boil

rapidly for 10 minutes. (By dividing the syrup, the mixtures reduce to proper strength.) Pour the syrup into Mason jars with rubber collars. Fill to overflowing—let the juice run out onto the rubber collars so that jars will be completely filled. Seal as tightly as possible. The caps must be airtight.
From Miss Laura H. Reilley, Hostess, The Executive Mansion, Raleigh, N.C.

Pineapple Syrup

This is a rich syrup made from fresh pineapple. It is not so sweet as canned pineapple juice.

> 3 pounds fresh pineapple, weighed after peeling and chopping
> 1 quart water
> Sugar

Boil the pineapple and water together until the fruit is soft. Mash the fruit well with a potato masher and strain off the juice. Measure the juice, and to each pint add 1 pound of sugar. Boil sugar and juice together until the syrup is heavy and amber-colored. Seal in bottles. Use over desserts or as flavoring for beverages and in cakes. When making a coconut cake, for example, spread this syrup over the layers, and then sprinkle with fresh grated coconut. Delicious!
From Mrs. A. G. Lea, St. Petersburg, Fla.

Pomegranate Syrup

> 6 cups pomegranate pulp
> 7 cups sugar

Put fruit pulp and sugar in a saucepan and mix thoroughly. Let the mixture stand for 24 hours. Place the pan on medium heat and bring quickly to a rapid boil. Strain and discard pulp. Pour the syrup into sterilized jars or bottles and seal immediately.

Roselle Syrup

4 cups roselle calyces ("Florida cranberries")
8 cups water
Sugar

Put calyces and water in an open kettle over low heat. Bring to a boil and cook until the calyces are tender and the liquid has been reduced to about one half. Strain through a jelly bag. Discard pulp and save juice. To 1 cup of juice add 1 cup of sugar. Put sugar and juice in a wide-mouthed kettle. Place over medium heat and bring to a boil. Let it boil up three times. Remove from heat. Pour into sterilized bottles and seal. This syrup is good for flavoring cakes and desserts.

The calyx of any fragrant rose, quince, hawthorn, or primrose may be substituted for the roselle calyx.

Mint Sauce

This is a grand sauce for lamb or veal.

1 cup water
1 cup vinegar
2 cups sugar
1 cup mint leaves

Combine the water, vinegar, and sugar in a saucepan and boil 2 or 3 minutes, or until syrupy. Wash and stem fresh mint leaves and pack tightly into cup to measure. Grind the mint leaves and stir into the hot syrup. Pour into bottles and cork or cap. It is not necessary to seal the bottles airtight, since this sauce will keep indefinitely without refrigeration. Makes about 1 pint.
From Mrs. L. A. Patterson, Edenton, N.C.

Conserving Apple Cider

Use only fresh cider made from sound apples. Pour the cider into an enamel or agateware kettle. Place over medium heat and heat to boiling point—but do not boil. Fill sterilized jars to within an inch of the top. Process in hot-water bath according to the chart furnished by the manufacturer of the jars used.

7. Brandied Fruits and Syrups

BRANDIED FRUITS AND MELLOW SYRUP CAME INTO BEING LONG BEFORE Benjamin Appert and the Mason jar gave the world a safe steam-pressure way to preserve food. The first products were perhaps primitive when compared with the rich *mélange* of today, but there were vinegar, spices, a type of wine, honey, and at last sugar to bring the art to its highest development.

A century ago the custom of brandying fruits flourished on the Continent and at home. Every complete cellar had, along with its rows of preserves, jams, pickles, marmalades, and relishes, a crock or two of brandied fruits mellowing in the dry, cool darkness. The alcoholic abstainer—and the more energetic cook—often buried jars of fruits and sugar in the ground, thus letting time and nature distil their own special brand of liqueur. The brandy "graves" were marked with as much caution as a gold prospector used in marking his claim. The clink of a shovel against clod and stone on a dark wintry night led, often, not to some secret mortal grave, but to an embarrassed host, frantically digging out a pudding topping for a waiting guest.

Our puddings, ice creams, and other desserts wilted somewhat during our period of drought. Happily, brandy is again available, and the discriminating and wise host has turned his thoughts once more to this elegant mode of food preservation.

The true brandied fruit will always be a mixture of fruit, sugar, and brandy. From the first strawberry in the spring through the last fox grape of autumn, fruits may be stored by this simple and economical method. Raspberries, blackberries, blueberries, gooseberries, peaches, plums, figs, citrus fruits, cherries, grapes, apricots, pineapples, and bananas are some of the more common fruits that take well to brandying.

The essentials for brandying are fresh ripe fruit in perfect condition, sugar, spices, brandy, sterilized jars or crocks, and a gourmet's taste and imagination.

An old way to prepare a crock for use is to pour in a few spoons of brandy, ignite it, and swirl the liquid fire around the sides. Immediately thereafter pour in the base and cover the jar. This is dangerous unless the utmost precaution is taken. The safest way is to sterilize the jar with boiling water, turn it upside down, and let it dry thoroughly.

Each fruit may be brandied separately, but combinations, known as *mélanges*, are superb. The syrup from the *mélange* is richer than that from a single fruit and therefore more highly prized. (See Brandied Fruit Mélange, page 143.)

Brandied fruits should "ripen" for several months.

Apricots in Brandy

    3 pounds freshly gathered not too ripe apricots, peeled
    1½ pounds sugar
      Water
      French brandy

Place the apricots in a preserving kettle, and add sugar and just enough water to cover. Take out the apricots, and bring the sugar and water to a boil. Add the apricots and cook them for

5 to 6 minutes. Lift the apricots out of the syrup and lay them in a dish. Boil the syrup until it is reduced one half. When the apricots have cooled, put them in sterilized jars and cover them with a mixture of half syrup and half French brandy. Seal. If the apricots are clingstone, they should remain in the syrup about 10 minutes.

Condensed from Mrs. Mary Randolph's Virginia Housewife, *1831.*

Brandied Apple Sauce

This may be served at once or sealed and kept for future use.

>   1 quart ripe apples, peeled and quartered
>   1 orange, peeled and sliced
>   1 cup sugar
>   1 teaspoon ground cloves, or cinnamon, or mixed spices
>   ½ cup peach brandy
>   2 cups water

Mix the apples and orange, cover with water, and simmer in a covered saucepan until the fruit is reduced to pulp. Drain, press through a sieve, and add the remaining ingredients. Continue simmering until mixture thickens. Pour into sterilized jars and seal.

Brandied Cherries

>   1½ quarts cherries, washed and drained (any variety)
>   ½ cup sugar
>   French brandy

Cut stems of cherries so that each one will have about 1 inch of stem. Pack cherries and sugar in alternate layers in sterilized jars, filling the jars to within 1 inch of the top. Add enough good brandy to fill the jars and seal. Let stand at least 30 days. Turn the jars upside down each day for 1 week so that the sugar and brandy will mix. Store in a cool dark place. Makes about 1¼ pints.

Cherries in Brandy

Use the short-stemmed bright red cherries in bunches. Make a syrup with equal quantities of sugar and cherries. Measure the cherries in a cup, and use the same number of cups of sugar. Add ¼ cup of water for each cup of sugar and boil together for 5 to 8 minutes, or until the syrup spins a thread. Scald the cherries, but do not let the skins crack, which they will do if the fruit is too ripe. Put the cherries in bottles, and cover them with equal quantities of syrup and French brandy.
From Mrs. Mary Randolph's Virginia Housewife, *1831.*

Cherries in Kirsch Syrup

Serve these piled high and dripping with syrup over ice cream, cake, pudding, and other desserts, or strain off the syrup and bottle it and make tarts with the cherries.

    4 pounds sour red cherries, pitted
    3 pounds sugar
    1 pint white grape juice
    3 tablespoons kirsch liqueur (kirschwasser)

Wash cherries and remove stems and stones. Bring sugar and grape juice to a boil, add the cherries, and cook until the syrup is thick and the fruit is transparent. Just before removing from the heat, add the kirsch. Pour into sterilized bottles or jars and seal.

Wild Cherries in Syrup

Wild cherries are so small that the stones must be left in. Wash the cherries and cut off the stems. Cover with water and simmer for 30 minutes. Strain off the juice. To each cup of juice add 1 cup of sugar. Bring the juice to a boil, add the cherries, and cook until the syrup thickens. Add kirsch if desired, but wild cherries have a strong flavor, and may not need it. Seal in bottles or jars.
From Mrs. Vann MacNair, Williamsburg, Va.

Black Cherries in Syrup

Using same amounts of cherries, juice, and kirsch, process as for cherries in kirsch syrup, but with 2½ pounds sugar, as black cherries are sweet. Use red currant juice for grape juice if possible.

Brandied Grapes, No. 1

Use clusters of grapes that are not quite ripe. Wash and pack lightly in jars. Into each quart jar add ½ cup sugar and 6 whole allspice. Fill jar with brandy. Let stand for a month in sealed jars.

Use to garnish cocktails, meat, or poultry. With cheese and crackers, they make a nice dessert.

Brandied Grapes, No. 2

Snip the grapes from the cluster, but leave a tiny stem on each. Wash and dry. Place in a sterilized quart jar, add ½ cup sugar, and cover with brandy or whisky. Seal. Ready to use after 36 hours.

Brandied Fig Preserves

    2 pounds figs, weighed after preparation
    2 pounds sugar
      Brandy

Pare the outer skin off the figs and drop them into clear, cold water to keep them white. Take up in a colander and weigh. Put the sugar in a preserving kettle with just enough water to dissolve the sugar. Bring the syrup to a boil and drop in the figs. Bring again to a good boil. Skim out the figs with a strainer and lay them in the sunshine for 20 minutes to dry. Meanwhile, boil the syrup and skim. Drop the figs again in boiling syrup. Do this three times. When the syrup has become quite thick, pack the preserves into sterilized jars. On top of the preserves lay a piece of brandy-soaked paper cut round to fit inside of the jar. Seal. Makes about 2 pints.

From Mrs. L. McLemore, in The Galveston Souvenir Cook Book, *Galveston, Texas.*

Brandied Fruit Mélange

To the French belongs credit for the brandied *mélange*—a rich mixture of fruits, spices, sugar, and brandy (or other spirituous liquors if desired). It is made in a crock and may be stored in sterilized jars. Any combination of fruits may be used. It is well, however, to consider the flavor and the color of the syrup before adding the fruits. If an amber syrup is desired, use only light fruits; if a dark syrup, use dark fruits, such as dark berries, plums, black cherries, and so on. Since only fresh fruits as they ripen should be used, it is wise to make a schedule of the fruits that will be on the market in your part of the country. The first fruit is universally the strawberry, which is usually included in the brandy base. Raspberries, cherries, peaches, plums, and so on, come along in succession or at slightly overlapping intervals.

The Creoles have built quite a ceremony around the annual *mélange,* so they serve it during the Christmas holidays and during the Mardi Gras. This recipe is a refinement of a *mélange* recipe given me in New Orleans several years ago. (See Brandied Fruits, page 139, for detailed instructions.)

> 4- to 6-gallon crock, sterilized and having a close-fitting cover
> 1 pint French brandy
> 1 pint kirsch
> 1 pint sherry wine
> 6 cups ripe firm strawberries, washed, capped, and drained
> 6 cups sugar
> 1 tablespoon each grated lemon rind, grated orange rind, whole cloves, and allspice
> 2 sticks cinnamon
> 1 tablespoon green ginger root, broken

The above ingredients are the base for the *mélange.* First put the spirituous liquors, spices, and grated rind into the crock. Crush the strawberries and simmer in their own juice until the fruit is tender. Drip through a jelly bag, discarding the pulp. To the hot juice add the sugar and stir until it is dissolved. Cool the syrup and add it to the other ingredients in the crock. Stir; then cover the crock. Let the mixture stand for at least 1 week.

As fruits are available, add equal quantities of fresh fruits and sugar, stirring after each addition. Never add more than 2 quarts of fruit at one time. If a rich red syrup is desired, use red cherries, red raspberries, red plums, peaches, and so on. Two or three kinds of fruit may be added at the same time. For each 2 quarts of fruit and sugar, add an additional pint of brandy. More spices also may be added. Continue this process until the crock is filled. Put the cover on the crock and tie a cloth over it. Let it stand without disturbing for 2 to 3 months. Seal the *mélange* in sterilized jars and store them in a cool, dark place to ensure perfect color and mellowness. There will be extra syrup which may be separated from the fruit and bottled.

Creole Brandied Peaches

6 pounds firm ripe peaches
3 pounds sugar
1½ pints good brandy or whisky.

Peel the peaches and leave them whole. Cover them with sugar and let them stand for 3 hours. Turn fruit and sugar into a saucepan and bring to a slow boil. Simmer the peaches until they are tender when pierced with a straw. Remove the peaches and cool them in a dish. Boil the syrup until thick. Pack the peaches in cold sterilized jars and cover with a mixture of half syrup and half brandy or whisky.

VARIATION

White Brandied Peaches

Use the recipe for Creole Brandied Peaches. Add a white brandy instead of an amber-colored brandy.

Old-Fashioned Buried Brandied Peaches

This old-fashioned dish is made with sugar and peaches. They may be stored in a cool place instead of in the ground.

> Clingstone peaches, peeled
> Sugar

Pack the peaces in sterilized quart jars. Fill the jars with granulated sugar. Strike each jar lightly against the table so that the sugar will sift well into the spaces between the peaches. Repeat until sugar has completely settled. Fill the jars to the top. Screw the tops on the jars, and set them away in a cool, dark place for 24 hours. Reopen each jar and force in one or more additional peaches until the jar is firmly packed. Seal the jars airtight. Wrap them in heavy paper and bury them in a hole at least 1 foot deep. Cover with soil. Be sure to mark the spot where the jars are buried! Leave the fruit there until the sugar has formed a clear syrup—about one month. If the peaches are not buried, they should be stored where the temperature is not below 45°. *Do not let them freeze.*

Orange Brandy

This brandy is often poured over fruit cakes and desserts. It is also used as a flavoring and as a beverage.

> 2 cups fresh orange juice
> Peel of 7 or 8 oranges, cut in very thin slivers
> 2 quarts best French brandy
> 1½ pounds of sugar (3 cups)

Mix orange juice, peel, and brandy in a large jar or crock. Let the mixture stand not sealed but well covered for 4 days. Add the sugar, and let it stand for another 24 hours. Strain and bottle. Cork and seal. Do not use for 30 days.

Brandied Peaches

   Peaches
   Water
1 pound sugar
½ pint peach water
½ pint white brandy

Pare the peaches and put into a kettle as many as will fill a 2-quart jar. Pour over them enough water to almost cover them. Boil until they are heated through. Skim them out and put into jar, saving the juice that the peaches were boiled in. Keep the peaches near the fire while you boil the sugar and ½ pint of the peach juice that the fruit was boiled in. When syrup is thick, add .the brandy. Pour hot over the peaches and seal. After cooking this quantity will fill a quart jar.
From Sadie L. Motter (Mrs. Robert L.), in The DAR Cook Book, compiled by the Valley Forge Committee, copyright, 1949, by Aileen Lewers Langston.

Brandied Plums

2 quarts ripe plums (greengages are best for this)
1 cup sugar
   Brandy

Select ripe plums that are firm and perfect. Wash well and drain. Pack in quart jars in alternate layers with the sugar, filling the jars to within 1 inch of the top. Fill with brandy and seal. Store in a cool, dark place for 1 month. Turn the jars upside down once each week. The longer they stand the better. Makes about 2 pints.

Brandied Prunes

1 cup prunes
1 cup sugar
½ lemon, sliced paper-thin

        French brandy
¼ teaspoon salt
5 whole cloves

Wash the prunes and soak them in enough water to cover for 12 hours. Put the prunes and the water they were soaked in into a saucepan and add the sugar, lemon, spices, and salt. Boil the prunes until they are tender. Remove them from the syrup and pack them in hot sterilized jars. Reduce the syrup to one half. Pour over brandy to fill ¼ jar. Then fill the jars with syrup. Seal.

The prunes may be stuffed after they have been in the brandy for 2 weeks. To stuff, slit the prunes and remove the stones. Fill with nuts, cheese, or chopped crystallized fruits.
From Mrs. Kenneth Kay, Leesburg, Fla.

"Peris in Syrippe (and Wyne)"

It is interesting to note that as early as the middle of the fifteenth century, cook-book writers were giving recipes for the preservation of fruits in sugar and wine. They appear to have been meticulous in the preparation of these foods. The fruits most commonly used were apples, pears (wardon), quinces, pomegranates, prunes, and dates, and the chefs were overgenerous with spices and wines. Jelly (gely), preserves, a sauce similar to apple butter called "mush," marmalade, and fruits in syrup were apparently popular fare.

The following recipe, from an old French-English book in my collection, gives evidence that many of the recipes of the fourteenth and fifteenth centuries have undergone few changes and lends authenticity to Lucy Street's modern version of Pears in Red Wine (see page 148).

"Take wardon and cast hem in a fair potte. And boile hem til hei ben tendre; and take hem vppe, and pare hem in ij. or in iij. And take powder of canell, a good quantite, and cast hit in gode red wyne, and cast sugur thereto, and put hit in an earthen potte, And let hit boile; And then cast the peris thereto, And late hem boile togidre awhile; take powder of gingre, and a litell saffron to colloure hit with, and loke that hit be poyante and also Doucet."

My own rather free translation: "Take pears (or quinces) and put them in a clean pot and boil (with water) until they are tender. Take them up and cut into two or three pieces. Mix a good quantity of cinnamon with sugar and red wine. Put the mixture into an earthenware pot and let it boil. Add the pears, and let all boil together for a few minutes. Add powdered ginger and a little saffron for color. See that the syrup is pungent and clear."

From Two Fifteenth-Century Cookery-Books, *ed., Thomas Austin, London, 1864, from Harleian Ms., c. 1430, and Ashmole and Douce Mss., c. 1429, published for the Early English Text Society, 1864–1871, Oxford University Press, New York.*

Lucy Street's Pears in Red Wine

Very elegant are these pears which Lucy and James Street served hot or cold. They are good with chicken or turkey, or they may be served as a dessert with a scoop of vanilla ice cream and pear syrup poured over all.

     1 cup sugar
     ½ cup red wine (any kind)
     1 piece stick cinnamon, 1 inch long
     1 slice lemon
     6 pears, peeled and cored (if small, leave whole)

Combine sugar, wine, cinnamon, and lemon in a saucepan. Place over medium heat and bring to a boil. Drop in small whole pears or halves of large pears. Cook over medium heat until the fruit is tender. Remove the pears and discard the cinnamon stick. Continue cooking syrup until reduced to one half the original amount. Serve the pears at once, if desired, or pack them in a sterilized jar, cover with syrup, and seal.

From Mrs. James Street, Chapel Hill, N.C.

Figs in Wine

Outside my bedroom window is a huge fig tree which bears two crops each year—one in June and the other in late fall. The first figs are large, juicy, and too heavenly to preserve or store for long. Since they have a tendency to spoil very quickly, I conserve most of the first crop by immersing them in cold wine. They may be stored in any wine, but since I have grapes, I usually put the figs in scuppernong wine. Red wine is used if the grape wine is running low. Here is the way to do it:

Wash the figs and dry them carefully and tenderly—they bruise easily. Roll them in a blend of ground cloves, mace, allspice, and cinnamon, using equal quantities of each. Pack the figs in sterilized Mason jars and pour over wine to cover well. Seal and store in the refrigerator or in a cold, dark place. They may be served within 12 hours, but they will keep for several weeks.

For a delightful dessert, serve these figs in little baked tart shells with whipped-cream topping. They are also delicious with cheese and crackers.

8. Preserves

THE TERM "PRESERVES" IS GENERALLY ASSOCIATED WITH FRUIT OR a combination of fruits cooked with equal parts (or less) of sugar —or such sugar substitutes as white corn syrup and honey—until the fruit is clear and the syrup reaches a thick and jellylike consistency. However, preserves may be made of many other items; nuts, roots (ginger root), flowers, citrus peel, vegetables with a high sugar content, and so on.

Only whole, small, perfect fruit or large perfect fruit cut into pieces should be used to make preserves. Good fruit that is imperfect may be cut or mashed and made into palatable by-products, such as jam, fruit butter, fruit catchup, fruit paste, fruit cheese, relish, marmalade, jelly, fruit juice, fruit syrup, and so on, for which recipes will be given in later chapters.

Each preserve recipe gives specific instructions, but here are a few general rules that should be observed.

1. Unless otherwise stated in a recipe, the produce should be washed and drained thoroughly. If soft fruit, such as berries, are being used, they should be picked over, the blossom ends removed, and dropped—a few at a time—into cold water. Rinse

gently and skim quickly out of the water. Combine fruit with sugar as soon as possible.

2. Measure or weigh produce after preparation. As a rule, a good preserve consists of equal parts of sugar and fruit (1 cup of sugar to 1 cup of fruit, or 1 pound of sugar to 1 pound of fruit). In some instances only three quarters of the amount of sugar may be used.

3. If white corn syrup or honey is substituted for sugar, it is advisable to use equal parts of the substitute and sugar. For example, if a recipe calls for 1 cup of sugar, use ½ cup syrup or honey and ½ cup of sugar.

4. Unless a recipe states otherwise, preserves should be carefully placed in the cooking vessel. Arrange alternate layers of sugar and fruit, using sugar for the bottom layer. Bring the mixture to a slow boil by placing the kettle first over low or medium heat to draw out the fruit juice. Continue cooking at a high temperature and stir frequently to prevent the preserves from sticking or scorching. As preserves begin to boil, a scum will form on the surface. This should be skimmed off as it forms, since it is simpler to skim it off when the whole mass is boiling. A little butter added to the mixture when preserves are put on to cook will eliminate much of the scum (see Kay Houston's Strawberry Preserves, page 177). When the syrup in preserves has reached the jelly stage, the preserves are ready to remove from the heat.

5. It is important to know the pectin content of fruit juice in order to determine the amount of sugar needed to make the jelly. There are many ways to test jelly. Each person has her own. The most scientific method is to test with Epsom salts, sugar, and juice extracted from the cooked fruit. Use 1 tablespoon of juice, ½ tablespoon of sugar, and ½ teaspoon of Epsom salts. Stir until sugar and salts have dissolved. Then set aside for 5 minutes without stirring. If the mass has set in a firm jelly by the end of that time, the fruit has ample pectin for good jelly. In that case use 1 cup of sugar to each cup of juice. If the salts mixture is still soft at the end of 5 minutes, use only ½ to ⅔ cup of sugar for each cup of juice. If the mixture fails to set at all, use commercial

pectin or add a juice rich in pectin, such as apple, currant, or lemon.

6. A few old-wives' ways to test jelly are:

a. Hold a spoonful of jelly up over the boiling syrup. If the mixture "sheets off" in flakes or in a mass, the jelly is ready to remove from the heat.

b. Put a teaspoonful of syrup in a cold saucer and set it in the ice box for 5 minutes. If it jells, the syrup is ready.

c. Dip a silver fork in the syrup, remove, and hold up to cool. If the syrup jells between the fork tines, it is ready.

d. Drop a few drops of syrup on a cold surface. If it does not spread, the jelly is ready.

7. When the jelly is ready, remove it at once from the heat, and pour it immediately into sterilized jelly glasses; cover with a thin coating of melted paraffin (see General Instructions).

Miss Nellie's Preserved Apples

Miss Nellie, the heroine of William Meade Prince's *The Southern Side of Heaven*, preserves foods in the grand manner of her Southern ancestors. This recipe is from her files.

> Any amount of apples
> An equal amount of sugar
> Water
> Lemon
> Cinnamon

Peel, core, and quarter apples; then weigh. Weigh enough sugar to equal the weight of the apples. In a kettle make a heavy syrup of sugar and water, using ½ cup of water for each pound of sugar. Place over medium heat and bring to a boil. Flavor with lemon or cinnamon to taste. (Grated lemon rind, slices of lemon, or broken pieces of ginger root are good for flavoring apples.) Drop in the apples and simmer until the fruit is transparent. Take care not to cook until the apples break. Pack the hot apples into hot sterilized jars, cover with syrup, and seal.
From Miss Nellie Roberson, Chapel Hill, N.C.

Apple-Ginger Preserves

2 pounds hard apples
4 cups sugar
3 cups water
1 ounce candied ginger cut into small pieces

Peel and core apples and cut into pieces. Drop into cold water. Combine sugar and 3 cups of water in a saucepan. Heat to boiling and cook until a rich syrup forms. Add the ginger. Drain apples thoroughly and drop into boiling syrup. Cook until clear but not mushy. Pour into sterilized jars and seal immediately. Makes 2 pints.

Whole Crab-Apple Preserves

6 pounds washed crab apples
3 pounds sugar
1 pint water

Combine sugar and water in a large saucepan. Heat to the boiling point and boil for 2 minutes. Drop the apples into the syrup and cook for 5 minutes. (They cook quickly.) Fill hot sterilized jars with apples and pour the hot syrup over them. Seal immediately.

Apricot-Pineapple Preserves

½ pound dried apricots
2 cups diced or crushed pineapple
3 cups water
3 cups sugar
¼ cup lemon juice

Soak the apricots until soft; drain. Mix apricots and pineapple with the water and cook slowly in a covered saucepan for 25 minutes. Mash thoroughly and add sugar and lemon juice. Cook until the mixture thickens. Pour into hot sterilized jars. When cool, cover with melted paraffin. Makes about 1½ pints.
From Mrs. I. J. Wicks, in The Bergen Cook Book, *Roland, Iowa.*

Old-Fashioned Blackberry Preserves

4 quarts firm blackberries, ripe but not too soft
8 cups sugar

Wash and pick over berries. Then put them in a colander and pour boiling water over them. Place the drained berries in a saucepan over low heat to draw out the juice. Bring to a boil and cook for 20 minutes. Add sugar and bring back to boiling. Continue cooking for 15 minutes. Cool and then seal in hot sterilized jars. Makes 8 pints.

VARIATION

Dewberry Preserves

Dewberry preserves may be made by the same recipe as that for Old-Fashioned Blackberry Preserves.

Carrot Preserves

Juice and ground rind of 2 lemons
Juice and ground rind of 3 oranges
4 pounds sliced raw carrots
4 pounds sugar

Grind oranges and lemons, save juice. Scrape carrots and slice in thin slices. Put carrots in covered saucepan with just enough water to cover. Steam until carrots are tender. Drain off liquid. Add ground lemons, oranges, and juice. Add sugar. Cook in open kettle until mixture is thick. Pack into hot sterilized jars and seal at once. Makes about 4 pints.

Cherry Preserves 1947

In 1947 our contributor made a cherry preserve that pleased her so much that she affectionately added the date to the name.

After pitting cherries (red, sour), lift them out of the juice and measure them. Place not more than 4 cups of fruit in a wide-mouthed kettle. Add one half as much sugar as cherries and bring slowly to a boil. Cook until the syrup is thickening and "slipping" from the spoon—about 20 to 25 minutes or to 222° F. if a candy and preserving thermometer is available. Pour immediately into glasses. When cool, seal with wax or paraffin.

These preserves are ruby red. The cherries taste fresh and the syrup jells. The juice which was discarded when the cherries were pitted may be made into syrup and used in drinks, sauces, and so on.

From Mrs. D. E. McConnell, Gastonia, N.C., in The Southern Cook Book.

French Preserved Chestnuts (Marrons Glacés)

Preserved chestnuts in French brandy are an elegant addition to the pantry shelf. Italian chestnuts are recommended.

   2 quarts chestnuts, measured after peeling
   3 cups sugar
   3 cups water
   ⅛ teaspoon salt
   1 tablespoon vanilla
   3 tablespoons French brandy

Put whole chestnuts into a large saucepan. Cover with water, heat to boiling, and cook for 30 minutes. Drain, cool, and peel the chestnuts. Combine sugar, water, and salt in a large saucepan, heat to boiling, and cook together for 6 minutes. Add peeled chestnuts and cook slowly for 30 minutes or until the nuts look transparent. Remove from the heat and let stand in the syrup overnight.

Next day return the mixture to heat and bring to a boil. Cook for 6 minutes. Add vanilla and brandy, and bring quickly to a boil. Remove from heat, pour into hot sterilized jars, and seal. Other nuts may be preserved in the same manner: pecans, English walnuts, black walnuts, or mixed nuts. Already dried or processed nuts should not be parboiled. Add less salt if the nuts have been salted. Makes about 3 quarts.

Preserved Citron

1 cup water
4 pounds citron
4 pounds sugar (8 cups)
1 lemon, thinly sliced
1 teaspoon broken ginger root

Peel and cut citron into strips, the full length of the fruit. Remove seed; then weigh the fruit. Combine sugar and water in saucepan, heat to boiling, and boil gently for 20 minutes. Add citron and continue to boil for 1 hour, or until the fruit is tender. Do not stir while boiling. Add lemon and ginger root and boil for only 1 minute. Remove immediately from heat. Pour into sterilized jars and seal.
From The Everyday Cook Book, *by Miss E. Neil (c. 1875).*

Baked Damson Preserves

2½ pounds damson plums
2½ pounds sugar
1 lemon, thinly sliced

Wash plums, cut into halves, and remove stones. Alternate layers of plums, sugar, and lemon in a large baking dish. Cover and bake at 350° F. for 3 hours. Remove and pack in sterilized jelly glasses. Let cool and cover with paraffin. Pears, peaches, and other pulpy fruit may be preserved by this method. Makes 2½ pints.

Black Fig Preserves

3 pounds black figs, peeled and cut into quarters
1 lemon, juice and grated rind
4½ pounds sugar
2 cups water

Combine all the ingredients and cook until the figs are transparent and syrup is thick. Seal in sterilized jars. The fruit may also be left whole. To make a good conserve, add chopped nuts several minutes before removing the fruit from the heat.

Thousand Pines Inn Fig Preserves

Thousand Pines Inn is a charming Southern establishment at Tryon, N.C., presided over by its owner, Selina Lewis. Miss Lewis not only loves to cook, but also likes to write about cooking. The following is from her own cook book based on her favorite Thousand Pines recipes.

For best results you should use the small delicate figs grown in the South, called "celestial figs"—perhaps because they will not keep! They must be soft but not mushy. Be most careful to see that they have not soured. They should be preserved almost as soon as they are picked. With a sharp knife snip off the blossom end and the stem; then weigh, using the following measurements for a gauge:

> 6 pounds prepared figs
> 4½ pounds sugar
> Juice of 2 lemons
> Rind of 1 whole lemon, sliced into thin strips
> 4 pieces of ginger root

Put the fruit into a large preserving kettle. Pour over the sugar and lemon juice and allow to stand for 1 hour. Then bring to a boil, stirring gently from the bottom and always being careful not to break the fruit. Fig preserves have a very bad habit of scorching and boiling over. Boil for 10 minutes. Remove from fire and add lemon rind and ginger root. Let cool for 1 hour or longer. Bring to a boil again and cook for 5 minutes. Remove from heat and cool overnight. Next morning, slowly bring to a boil over a very low heat, stirring constantly. Cook 5 minutes and then remove the ginger root. Put in sterilized jars. Cover with paraffin, seal, and watch with a shotgun!
From Everyone Eats, by Selina Lewis, Tyron, N.C.

Green Grape Preserves

This is best when made from green mustang grapes from Texas. It has a grand and different flavor.

Pick the grapes when they are the size of buckshot or small peas—before the seeds have formed. Stem, wash, and weigh the grapes. Then take pound for pound of sugar and grapes. Add just enough water to dissolve the sugar and boil to a thin syrup. Add the grapes and cook them slowly until the syrup turns to a dark red and the grapes are almost black. Seal.

From Mrs. F. Burton Jones, Chapel Hill, N.C.

Greengage Preserves

4 pounds greengage plums
4 pounds white sugar
1 pint water
Kernels from the plums

Wash and dry plums. Split them lengthwise and remove kernels, putting both aside. Combine the sugar and water in an open kettle. Place over medium heat and boil for 10 minutes. Drop in the plums, and simmer them until they are almost tender. Take them from the heat and pour into another open kettle. Let them stand overnight. Meanwhile, blanch the kernels by pouring boiling water over them. Let them stand for 20 minutes; then skin them. Next morning add the kernels to the plum-syrup mixture. Place over medium heat, bring to a boil, and cook for 10 minutes. Let the preserves cool for about 10 minutes; then skim out the plums and pack them into ½-pint jars. Pour over the syrup and kernels. Seal the preserves when they are thoroughly cooled. Makes about eight half-pints.

From The Everyday Cook Book, *by Miss E. Neil (c. 1875)*

Preserved Ginger Root

1 pound ginger root, scraped, then weighed
1 pound sugar
1 cup water
½ teaspoon cream of tartar

Scrape the dried roots with a sharp knife, removing the thin out-side dry bark. Boil the roots in water to cover for about 10 minutes, or until tender. Drain. Mix sugar and water and cook to form a medium-thick syrup. Add the ginger root and cream of tartar. Bring back to boiling and cook for 2 minutes. Remove from the heat and pour into sterilized jars. Seal. Makes about 1 pint.

Whole Kumquat Preserves

The bitter-sweet kumquat is a native of China, where it has long been known as the "gold orange," and is one of our most decora-tive citrus fruits. Small, almost pear-shaped, with tender skin and pungent seeds, the whole kumquat is edible and makes delicious preserves, marmalade, jelly, and other dishes. Tropical-fruit packers use the kumquats to fill in or decorate crates of oranges and grape-fruit and also ship them separately to other markets.

> 1 quart kumquats
> 1 tablespoon baking soda
>   Water
>   Sugar

Scrub the kumquats with a soft brush in clear water. Rinse and discard the water. Put the kumquats in a colander and sprinkle with the soda, setting the colander in a pan. Pour over enough boiling water to cover the fruit. Turn the fruit into the pan and let stand 10 minutes. Drain the kumquats in a colander. Discard the soda water, and let cold water run over the kumquats for several minutes. Slit each kumquat. Place them in a kettle and cover with clear cold water. Place over medium heat and boil for about 10 minutes. Drain. Make a syrup by combining 2 cups of sugar to 2 cups of water. Let the syrup boil for 1 minute. Drop in the kumquats. Boil slowly until the fruit is transparent and the syrup begins to jell. Pack the kumquats in small jars. Pour in the hot syrup within about ½ inch of the top of the jar and partly seal. Process in a hot-water bath for 5 minutes. Seal. Makes about 3½ pints.

Ogeechee Lime Preserves

This recipe can bear frequent repetition. It is reprinted from Harriet Ross Colquitt's *The Savannah Cook Book*, Savannah, Ga.

"The Ogeechee lime, a Spanish type . . . , found along the banks of the Ogeechee River, is very scarce now and is considered a great delicacy when preserved, to be served with meat or game. It is often found by the Negroes of that section and brought into the city markets.

"Cut blossom end off limes and soak them in alum solution (1 tablespoon alum to 2 gallons water) for 24 hours. Take out of alum solution and boil in clear water. Drain and put in a syrup made of 1 cup of sugar to 1 cup of water; 1 pound of sugar being allowed for 1 pound of fruit. Cook slowly until limes are transparent. Seal in sterile jars."

The Mango

The exotic and luscious mango was originally produced in the Orient and is thought to have been first cultivated about four thousand years ago. Down through centuries writers and poets have praised it as "the pride of the garden," "the choicest fruit of Hindustain," more delicious than "the apples of Hesperides," and so on. The fruit is large and meaty, with a flavor somewhat like a peach "sweet and pleasant," and the tree foliage is dense, brilliant, and lovely. The Portuguese are credited with having brought the mango to America sometime during the middle of the eighteenth century. It now thrives in almost all tropical sections of the Americas. The fruit is usable, whether green or ripe. The green fruit is used more often for pickles, preserves, chutneys, and relishes. The ripe fruit is served raw or cooked. Even the inside kernel is eaten, as are other nuts. The poorer varieties of the fruit are very juicy and the flesh is mushy. The finer varieties are firm, like a fine peach or melon.

In all pickles, preserves, marmalades, and other recipes in this book—unless otherwise stated—the green mango is used. The fruit is peeled, stoned, and prepared according to individual recipes.

Mango Preserves

2 quarts ripe mangoes, peeled and sliced (measured after
    slicing)
2 quarts sugar, measured in same container as fruit
1 teaspoon chopped crystallized ginger
2 tablespoons water

Mix sugar and ginger with the mangoes and add water. Put into
a large saucepan, and heat to a slow boil, stirring frequently. Cook
slowly until the mixture is thick and the fruit is transparent. Seal
while hot in sterilized jars. Makes about 3 pints.

Mango Chips

4 pounds mango chips
4 lemons
4 pounds sugar
¼ pound ginger root

Peel and slice green mangoes into thin slices or chips. Cut the
lemons into small pieces. Mix all ingredients in a large kettle and
cook slowly until the fruits are tender. Pack in sterilized jars and
seal.
From The Puerto Rican Cookbook, *copyright, 1948, by Eliza B. K.
Dooley, San Juan, Puerto Rico, Dietz Press, Richmond, Va.*

My Own Preserved Stuffed Oranges

4 small uniform oranges
Sugar
Nuts
Dates or other processed fruits
Water

Soak oranges overnight in cold water. Drain and dry. With a sharp
knife cut out a round conical section from the stem end of the
oranges, cutting down to the center. Save the section. Scoop out
seeds and as much hard fiber from the core as possible. Soak the

oranges in fresh water for 3 hours, using enough water to cover. Drain the liquid from the oranges. Measure and put into a saucepan, and for each cup of juice add 1 cup of sugar. Meanwhile, chop dates or other processed fruits (figs, raisins, and the like) and nuts, using equal quantities of each. Mix the nuts and fruits and fill the cavities of the oranges. Cut out the pulp from the section cut from the stem of the oranges and fit it back into the top. Fasten the tops with toothpicks, or tie the oranges with twine so that the top section will be held in place.

Bring sugar and orange-water mixture to a boil, and let it boil for 5 minutes. Drop the oranges into the syrup and simmer them until the skins look transparent. Press the oranges down into the syrup frequently, using a wooden spoon, so that they are completely covered with syrup. Pack the oranges into low, squatty, wide-mouthed Mason jars, and pour over the hot syrup. Be sure that each jar is tightly packed; otherwise the oranges will float to the top. Let the jars stand for several days before opening. Chill, slice, or cut the oranges into quarters and use to garnish meat or fowl. I serve these every Christmas with roast goose.

Papaya Preserves

The papaya is one of our most delicious and beneficial tropical fruits. The meat in flavor is a cross between a cantaloupe and a peach and is served both raw and cooked. It makes a nice salad and is used in candy, preserves, and chutney. For centuries the natives of the tropics knew that the leaves and juice of the papaya had a tenderizing effect upon meat. These properties have in recent years been utilized by commercial food industries. The fruit has a high pepsin content and in powdered form is used as a digestant.

> 1 medium-sized papaya, prepared and then measured
> 2 cups water
> 2 cups sugar
> 1 large lime (sometimes called "Key lime"), juice and
>   rind
> 1 stick cinnamon

Peel the papaya, take out the seeds, and cut the meat into pieces. Measure enough to fill 2 cups. Combine other ingredients in an open saucepan. Bring the syrup to a boil and drop in the fruit. Cook slowly until the papaya is transparent. Seal immediately in sterilized jars. Will make about 2½ pints.

The pawpaw, or papaw, a similar fruit of North American origin, can be used equally well in this recipe.

Peach Chips

4 pounds firm ripe peaches
2 pounds sugar
Powdered sugar

Peel the peaches and slice very thin, then weigh. Place alternate layers of peaches and granulated sugar in a wide-mouthed saucepan. Set aside for 2 hours. Place over low heat to draw out juice. Bring to a boil and boil until the peaches are clear but not mushy. Spread out the peach slices on flat platters or on a pane of glass and put them in the sunshine to dry. Turn them frequently, so that they will dry on both sides. When the slices are dry, lift them up and pack them in thin layers in a wide-mouthed jar, sprinkling powdered sugar over each layer. Fill the jar and seal. These are delicious and make an attractive garnish for meat— especially for baked ham.

Good Plain Peach Preserves

5 pounds peaches (firm clingstones make the best preserves)
5 pounds sugar

Peel the fruit and cut into halves or quarters. As they are peeled, drop them into cold water. Drain. In a porcelain container put alternate layers of peaches and sugar, adding a few peach stones for an almondlike flavor. Let the fruit and sugar stand overnight. Drain off the juice, and boil it until it begins to thicken. Add the peaches and cook until they are transparent and tender and the syrup is thick. Skim. Remove peaches and pack in sterilized jars. Pour over the hot syrup to fill the jars. Seal.

If firm preserves are desired, lift the peaches out of the syrup when they become clear and spread on platters in the sun for 20 minutes. Cook the syrup down until thick. Return the peaches to the syrup and proceed as above.

Peach-Cantaloupe Preserves

6 peaches, peeled, stoned, cut into bite-sized pieces
½ cantaloupe, peeled, seeded, cut into bite-sized pieces
2 small oranges, peeled, sectioned, seeded
Sugar

Measure the fruit and add ⅔ cup of sugar to each cup of fruit. Let stand several hours. Place fruit and sugar mixture in a preserving saucepan and cook, stirring frequently, until the fruit is transparent and tender and the syrup is thick. Pour into hot, sterilized jars and seal immediately. Makes approximately 3 half-pints.
From R. W. Voorhees, Brooklyn, N.Y.

Muskmelon (Cantaloupe) Preserves

This is an old and excellent recipe.

Take green melons that are fully grown but not ripe. Pare and cut them in shapes to suit your taste. In the evening put them in a weak brine and leave them until the next day at noon. Then wash in fresh water. Place in a kettle in enough water to cover them and add a piece of alum the size of a hickory nut. Cover with grape leaves and scald. Then take them up and drain. Add 1 pound of sugar to 1½ pounds of melon. Season with sliced lemon and ginger according to the amount of preserves. Cook until the mixture is thick and the melon is transparent. Seal.
From Mrs. M. L. Chesley, in A Book for ye Cooks, *Fredericksburg, Va.*

Martha Washington's Pear Preserves

This famous recipe was contributed to the *Old North State Cook Book*, Charlotte, N.C., by Mrs. W. Frank Sample.

"Here is a dish from Mount Vernon which brings to mind George Washington's visit to Charlotte, in 1791. He entered the city on North Tryon Street, riding in 'a snow white coach with gilded springs, with his crest emblazoned upon the door.' Four horses drew this elegant vehicle, and his entourage included, besides the coachman and postillion, his valet de chambre, 2 footmen, 4 riding horses, and a baggage wagon."

> Pears
> Brandy
> ½ pound sugar for each pound fruit

The pears should be very fresh. Wash them and put them into boiling lye for 1 minute (or peel the pears, Introduction, page 5). Remove them from the lye and put them into cold water. Next, put them into a prepared syrup of sugar and water, using just enough water to dissolve the sugar. Cook them for 15 minutes. Take out the pears and put them on plates to cool. Boil the syrup down to one half the original quantity. Put the pears and syrup in jars and add some brandy to each jar. Seal while hot.
From The Southern Cook Book.

Easy Pear Preserves

> 2 quarts firm ripe pears, peeled and cut into desired pieces (leave small Seckel pears whole)
> ¾ quart cold water
> 5 cups sugar

After peeling, drop pears into cold water to keep them from turning dark. Put them in a colander and pour boiling water over them. Drain. Next put the pears in a large saucepan and add ¾ quart of cold water. Place over medium heat, bring to a boil, and cook for 20 minutes. Add sugar and continue cooking for 20 minutes more, or until syrup is thickened. If desired, add 1 tablespoon of chopped candied ginger. Pour into hot sterilized jars and seal immediately.

Pear Chips

    4 pounds sugar
    4 cups water
    2 lemons, sliced paper-thin
    ¼ cup chopped crystallized ginger
    6 whole allspice
    4 pounds firm, ripe pears, peeled and sliced very thin
        or ground

Combine sugar and water in a large saucepan. Place over medium heat and bring to a boil. Add all the other ingredients and boil until the pears are transparent and tender and the syrup thickens. Pour into sterilized jelly glasses and seal.
From Mrs. W. H. May, Jr., Burlington, N.C.

Peach-Pear Preserves

    1 pound firm, ripe pears, peeled and cut into pieces
    1 pound peaches, peeled and cut into pieces
    1½ pounds sugar

Combine fruits and sugar and let stand 12 hours. Bring to a very slow boil, stirring often; then boil rapidly until the fruit is transparent. Pour at once into sterilized jars and seal. Candied ginger, lemon, or orange may be added.

Lemon-Ginger Pear Preserves

    6 pounds pears
    4 pounds sugar
    1 cup water
    3 lemons, juice and peel
    1¼ pounds ginger root (or less according to taste)

If ripe pears are used, peel and cut into pieces. If hard, green pears are used, parboil them for 20 minutes; then peel and cut into pieces. Weigh. Squeeze out lemon juice and cut rind into pieces. Put the water into a large kettle over medium heat. Add the sugar, fruit, lemon peel, and ginger gradually, stirring constantly to prevent burning. Continue cooking. When you can pierce the pears with a broom straw, they are done. Remove the kettle from the heat and add lemon juice. Fill sterilized jars and seal.

From Miss Sarah Berry, in Saint Anne's Parish Recipe Book, *Annapolis, Md.*

Pineapple Preserves

    3 cups ripe pineapple, cut into pieces
1½ cups sugar
    Water

Peel and remove eyes and core of fresh, ripe pineapple. Cut into pieces; then measure. Put the pineapple and sugar in an open kettle and add just enough water to dampen the sugar. Bring to a slow boil and cook for 15 minutes. Remove from the heat and let stand until cool. Pour into sterilized jars and seal.

Preserving Purple Plums (using brown sugar)

    2 pounds brown sugar
    2 cups water
    2 pounds purple plums, picked over and washed

Combine sugar and water in a saucepan (the same amount of white sugar may be substituted if desired). Place over medium heat and cook until the syrup is perfectly clear. Pour the boiling hot syrup over the plums and let them remain in the syrup for 2 days. Drain the syrup into a saucepan and return it to the heat. Bring to a boil and skim. Pour the syrup over the plums and let stand for 2 days. Put syrup and plums together in a saucepan. Place over low heat and simmer gently until the syrup is thick and reduced. Pour into sterilized glasses and seal with paraffin.

Small damson plums, cherries, or other fruits are excellent when prepared in this way. When preserving greengage plums, use only white sugar.

To preserve plums without skins, pour boiling water over the fruit and let stand until the water cools. Then pull off the skins.
From The Everyday Cook Book, *by Miss E. Neil (c. 1875)*

Pumpkin Chips

This is an old preserve, one of the first made by the early American settlers.

> 1 pound pumpkin chips
> 1 pound sugar
> Juice of 2 lemons and grated peel
> ¼ cup chopped crystallized ginger

Pare fresh pumpkin and slice it into paper-thin chips, as for potato chips, using the chipping side of a grater if possible. Mix all ingredients in a saucepan. Place over low heat, bring very slowly to a boil, and cook until pumpkin is transparent. Lift out the chips and pack in glass jars. Continue boiling the syrup until it is thick. Spoon the syrup over the chips, being sure to fill the jars with syrup. Seal hot.
From an old cook book owned by Mrs. Norman Riddle, Burlington, N.C.

Pure Raspberry Preserves

> 4 cups raspberries
> 4 cups sugar

Wash the berries and pick off the blossom ends, being careful not to crush the berries. Place berries and sugar in alternate layers in an ópen saucepan. Let them stand overnight to draw out the juice. Next day place over low heat and bring slowly to a boil. Continue boiling on medium heat until the syrup is thick. Pour hot into sterilized glasses or small jars. Makes about 4 half-pint jars or glasses of preserve.

Cherries and other berries may also be preserved according to the preceding basic recipe.

Quince Preserves

> 3 pounds pared quinces
> 3 pounds sugar
> 1 pint water

Wash and pare quinces and cut them into quarters (if large cut into eighths). Take out the cores and the hard places around them. Boil the fruit in clear water until tender; then spread it on a towel to dry. For 1 pound of fruit allow 1 pound of sugar and 1 pint of water for each 3 pounds of sugar. Combine the sugar and water in a preserving kettle and bring it to the boiling point. Put in the fruit and cook it slowly. Put it on the back of the stove so that it hardly cooks at all, and keep it on for 1 hour or more without the fruit's cooking to pieces (the longer it cooks, the brighter red it will be). Skim out fruit and pack it into sterilized jars. Strain the hot syrup over the fruit and seal.

From Miss Parloa's New Cook Book and Marketing Guide, *c. 1880–1890.*

Kay Houston's Strawberry Preserves

This original recipe has two distinguishing features: the addition of a little vinegar to preserve the red color of the berries and the addition of butter to make skimming unnecessary.

> 2 quarts strawberries
> 6 cups sugar
> ½ cup water
> 1½ teaspoons vinegar
> 2 teaspoons butter

Wash, drain, and stem the berries and measure. You should have a little more than 6 cups. Place sugar, water, vinegar, and butter in a large preserving kettle and cook, stirring constantly, until the mixture turns to syrup. Add the berries, stirring well. Bring to a boil and boil rapidly for 10 minutes. The syrup should fulfill the jelly test by dropping in heavy drops from a silver spoon. Pour into shallow platters and let stand overnight. Pour into sterilized jars and seal.

From Mrs. Noel Houston, Chapel Hill, N.C.

Mrs. Holt's Strawberry Preserves

This is a perfect recipe for strawberry preserves, worked out after many seasons of trial and error.

> 4 cups fresh strawberries
> 5 cups sugar
> 3 tablespoons lemon juice, or ¼ teaspoon cream of tartar

Place alternate layers of berries and sugar in a large kettle. Be sure to have sugar as the first layer in the kettle. Bring slowly to a boil. When the whole mass is boiling, cook for 9 minutes. Remove from heat and add the lemon juice or the ¼ teaspoon of cream of tartar. Let stand overnight. On the second day, boil for 9 minutes. Allow to cool, and place in glasses. Seal with wax or paraffin. Cooked this way the preserves are beautiful, and tender jelly surrounds the plump bright berries. Makes four half-pints.

From Mrs. Don S. Holt, Concord, N.C., in The Southern Cook Book.

Scotch Preserves

This is a "Scotch" way to save small left-over quantities of preserves and to produce a surprise as well.

As you make each variety of preserve, put any small left-over amount into a sterilized quart jar. Cover and refrigerate. Before adding an additional layer of preserves, add 1 teaspoon good brandy. When the jar is filled, stir once or twice to swirl the mixture. Seal in the same jar. The preserves may be peach, pear, fig, mango, strawberry, raspberry, or any other combination.

Wild Strawberry Preserves

Wild strawberries make delicious preserves, as they have a delicate flavor and are firmer than cultivated berries. Make as for Mrs. Holt's Strawberry Preserves.

Sun-Cooked Strawberry Preserves

This is an ante bellum elegance that lost its charm when there were no longer any little "shoo-fly" boys to stand watch while the berries basked in the sun. For those who have time, this is a grand recipe.

> 3 pounds perfect, ripe strawberries
> 3 pounds granulated sugar
> 2 cups boiling water

Hull the berries, being careful not to crush them. Wash and drain. Mix sugar and boiling water and cook until syrup spins a thread (232° F.). Do not stir the syrup after it begins to boil. Add the berries and bring back to a boil. Cook for 15 minutes. Pour out onto large china steak platters and cover with netting or clear panes of glass. Set the platters out in the hot sunshine for 2 days. (Bring them in each night.) Stir occasionally. When syrup is thick, pour the preserves into hot sterilized jars and seal.
From Comfort, *an old newspaper, c. 1850.*

Squash Preserves

Here is something new to do with squash—and surprisingly good.

> 1 gallon hard yellow or white squash (summer squash),
>   cut up
> ½ gallon sugar (measure in same container as squash)
> 1 lemon, thinly sliced
> 1 pint water
> 1 small can crushed pineapple

Wash and cut squash into pieces and mix with the other ingredients. Put in a large bowl or crock and let stand overnight. Next day put on to cook in a large preserving kettle. Cook until the squash is transparent and the syrup thick. Pour into sterilized jars and seal.

From The Ideal Cook Book, *La Grange,. Texas.*

Red Tomato Preserves

5 pounds ripe red tomatoes
8 cups sugar
2 lemons, thinly sliced

Skin the tomatoes by scalding them in hot water for 2 to 3 minutes, then plunging them into cold water. Slip the skins off by hand. Cut the tomatoes into quarters. Mix sugar with tomatoes, and let the mixture stand in a large bowl overnight. Drain off the juice into a saucepan and cook until the syrup spins a thread. Add tomatoes and lemons and cook over low heat until the tomatoes are transparent. Seal.

From Mrs. Christy Johnson, in The Bergen Cook Book, *Roland, Iowa.*

Fruit Preserved in Sand

What a wonderful occasion it was—years ago—when my father opened the apple or pear box! That was, of course, before the magic of temperature control was available to all packers. The tantalizing smell of the fruit and the excitement of digging for it in the cool clean sand played an important part in our Thanksgiving and Christmas celebrations.

To preserve fruit in sand, select from the late crop perfect fruit—apples, pears, or any firm meaty fruit. Do not wash or polish, but carefully brush off dirt and insects. Prepare a wooden box with lid. (An old trunk is excellent.) First, put in a deep layer of sand, then a layer of fruit, settling the fruit down into the sand so that they cannot touch the sides of the box. Alternate with layers of sand and fruit until the box is filled, being careful not to let the fruit touch one another. The last layer should be a thick layer of sand. Close the box and store in a cool, dry place. Packed this way, fruit will keep for months and will be mellow and juicy.

Kay Houston's Yellow Pear Tomato Preserves

Mrs. Houston adds a little butter to all of her preserves to eliminate tedious skimming.

> 3 to 4 pounds yellow pear tomatoes
> 3 to 4 pounds sugar
> 1 lemon, very thinly sliced
> Few pieces ginger root, or ½ teaspoon ground ginger
> 1 teaspoon butter

Cover the tomatoes with boiling water and let stand for 2 minutes. Drain and cover with cold water. Slip skins from tomatoes, and, taking one tomato at a time, squeeze out by hand much of the seeds and juice. Discard seeds and juice. Measure the tomatoes, and use pound for pound of sugar. Mix. Put tomatoes, sugar, and other ingredients into preserving kettle and bring slowly to a boil, stirring constantly. Boil gently until the syrup is quite thick and tomatoes are transparent. Seal at once in sterilized jars. Wonderful with chicken or veal.
From Mrs. Noel Houston, Chapel Hill, N.C.

Watermelon ("Sweetmeat") Preserves

> 6 cups watermelon rind
> 7½ cups sugar
> 2½ cups water
> 1 lemon, thinly sliced
> ½ ounce ginger root, broken up

Prepare rind by cutting off hard green outside skin and the soft pink inside pulp. Cut the rind into pieces. Cover with water and boil for 2 hours, or until tender. Cool in the water. Drain and measure to make 6 cups. Boil together the other ingredients for 10 minutes. Add the rind and cook for about 1 hour, or until the rind is transparent. Always keep the rind covered with syrup while cooking. If the syrup is too thin, add additional sugar; if too thick, add water. Remove from heat. Seal hot in sterilized jars.
From Mrs. William Ryer Wright, Charlotte, N.C.

Ripe Tamarind Preserves

Place ripe, uncooked, shelled tamarinds in a jar. Cover with a good simple syrup. Cover tightly (seal) and store for at least 3 months before using.

From The Key West Cook Book, *Key West Woman's Club, Key West, Fla.*

9. Conserves

CONSERVE DIFFERS FROM PRESERVES AND JAM IN THAT IT IS A combination of fruits, sugar, and nuts. Often raisins or other processed fruits are added. The mixture is cooked in an open kettle (according to individual recipes) and must be stirred frequently. In conserve the syrup is not so thick as that for jam, and the fruits should be transparent in appearance.

Conserve is served in the same way as any other preserve and is often used to garnish desserts. It is sealed just as preserves are.

Apricot Conserve

1 pound ripe apricots
1 cup shredded canned pineapple
1 unpeeled orange, seeded
1 cup chopped black walnut meats (or other nuts)
Sugar

Peel the apricots, remove the seeds, and cut the fruit into slivers. Mix fruits and nuts and measure into a large saucepan. Add 1 cup of sugar for each cup of fruit and nuts. Place over low heat and cook slowly, stirring constantly, until mixture thickens and fruit is transparent. Pack into sterilized jelly glasses or jars. Seal. Makes 2 to 2½ pints.
From Mrs. Angus Craft, St. Petersburg, Fla.

Beet Preserves (Conserve)

For many years I tried to find a recipe for these fine beet (Russia) preserves or conserve. Now, at last, here it is.

> 2 pounds raw beets, peeled and cut into thin strips
> 3 pounds sugar
> ½ cup water
> 3 lemons, thinly sliced
> 2 cups chopped pecans
> Crystallized ginger to taste

Mix all the ingredients but the nuts and ginger. Cook very slowly, stirring frequently. When the syrup begins to thicken, add the nuts and chopped ginger to taste. Cook until the mixture is thick. Seal in small glasses or jars.
From Mrs. Max A. Sarsohn, Ensley, Ala., from What's Cookin' in Birmingham? *Birmingham, Ala., in* The Southern Cook Book.

Bing Cherry Conserve

> 2½ pounds Bing cherries (or black sweet cherries)
> ¾ pound processed dates
> ¼ pound processed figs
> ¼ pound seedless raisins
> ¼ pound pecan meats
> ¼ teaspoon each ground cloves and cinnamon

Wash and pit the cherries. Drain off the juice and save in a large saucepan. Chop the remaining fruits and nuts. Add sugar to cherry juice and boil until the syrup spins a thread. Add the cherries and cook for 5 minutes. Add the remaining ingredients and cook slowly until the mixture thickens. Seal in sterilized jelly glasses. This is a rich conserve.

From Mrs. Charles Mason Crowson, Columbia, S.C.

Grape Conserve

    5 pounds grapes, any variety
    4 pounds sugar
    2 pounds raisins
    ½ pound English walnut meats, broken into pieces

Skin the grapes and save the skins. Stew the skinned grapes until tender. Put through a sieve into the same vessel with the skins, discard the seeds. Turn the grape pulp and skins into a kettle and cook over low heat for about ¾ hour, stirring frequently to prevent sticking. (Grape conserve is likely to stick unless watched closely. An asbestos mat will help prevent sticking.) Add sugar and raisins and cook until the mixture is thick. About 20 minutes before taking the conserve from the heat, add the walnuts. Pour into hot sterilized jelly glasses and cover. When cold, seal with paraffin.

From Mrs. A. E. Nelson in The Bergen Cook Book, *Roland, Iowa.*

Conserve Mélange

    3 pounds Concord (or any purple) grapes, stemmed
        and mashed
    1½ pounds unpeeled red apples (Winesaps), chopped
    ½ unpeeled grapefruit, chopped
    1 unpeeled lemon, chopped
      Water
      Sugar
    ½ teaspoon each ground cloves, allspice, and cinnamon

Mix the fruits and put them in a covered kettle. Cover with cold water and simmer until reduced to a soft pulp. Run the mixture through a food mill or fine sieve. To each cup of refined pulp add

1 cup of sugar, and add spices. Cook slowly, stirring frequently, until the mixture is stiff and clear and there is no "free" liquid. Seal in sterilized jelly glasses.

From Miss Miriam Le Compte, Cordon, Iowa.

Mango-Pineapple Conserve

4 cups mango pulp
2 cups shredded pineapple
2 cups preserved figs
4 oranges
2 lemons, sliced, with rind grated
Sugar

Cut the mangoes in thin slices. Drain the pineapple. Remove syrup from figs and chop. Grind or slice oranges. Combine fruit and weigh. For 1 pound of fruit add 1 pound of sugar. Put all ingredients in a saucepan and cook slowly until the mixture jells. Pour into sterilized jars and seal.

From Mrs. H. C. Fisher, in Katch's Kitchen, *Compiled by the Department of Applied Education of the Women's Club, West Palm Beach, Fla., 1938.*

Pear Conserve

3½ pounds pears
2 pounds sugar
½ box seedless raisins
1 cup chopped pecans
1 orange, thinly sliced

Grind the pears and raisins. Cook the pears and sugar together slowly until the mixture begins to thicken. Add the other ingredients and cook until the mixture becomes thick and has a deep reddish color. Seal in sterilized jars.

From Mrs. David Verner, Charleston, S.C.

Peach-Raisin Conserve

Hudson Valley peaches are used in this conserve from one of Jane Nickerson's New York *Times* columns. But any peach may be used.

>   4 pounds peaches, peeled, pitted, and sliced
>   3 cups water
>   6 cups sugar
>   2 cups seedless raisins
>   1½ cups chopped nuts

Cook the peaches, water, and sugar together for about 15 minutes. Add raisins and cook until the mixture thickens. Add nuts and cook 5 minutes longer. Pour into hot sterilized jars and seal while hot. Makes about 7 pints.

From Jane Nickerson, Food News Editor, The New York Times, *New York.*

Plum Conserve

>   4 pounds Italian plums (those great purple ones)
>   2 oranges
>   1 lemon
>   1 pound seedless raisins
>   1 cup broken nut meats
>   ½ cup hot water
>   3 pounds sugar

Wash the plums, cut into halves, and remove the stems. Squeeze the juice from the oranges and lemon, and put the peels through a food chopper. Mix the plums and hot water in a kettle, cover, and bring to the boiling point. Add the sugar, peel, juice, and raisins. Cook slowly until the plums are transparent. Add the nuts and cook 10 minutes longer. Pour into small jars and seal with paraffin.

From Mrs. Marvin Varney, Williamson, W. Va., in What's Dat Cookin'? *St. Monica's Guild, Christ Episcopal Church, Point Pleasant, W. Va.*

Raspberry-Cherry Conserve

1 cup red cherries, pitted
1 cup raspberries (any variety)
1 whole orange, chopped
1 cup broken walnut meats
2½ cups sugar

Wash and prepare the fruit. Crush the cherries and cook in their own juice until tender. Add a little water if there is not enough juice. Add raspberries and simmer until the mixture begins to thicken; then add sugar, nuts, and orange, and cook until thick. Pour into sterilized jars and seal. Makes about 3 half-pint jars of conserve.

Rhubarb (Pie Plant) Conserve

1 whole orange
1 whole lemon
4 cups chopped rhubarb
4 cups sugar
1 teaspoon cinnamon
1 cup chopped nut meats
1 cup seedless raisins (if desired)

Chop the oranges and lemons and put all ingredients—except the nuts—in a large kettle. Set on warm stove or low heat until the sugar is melted. Bring to a slow boil and cook until the mixture begins to thicken. Let cool. Add nuts. Seal in sterilized glasses with paraffin. If raisins are used, add them with the fruits.
From Mrs. T. I. Sampson, in The Bergen Cook Book, *Roland, Iowa.*

Mrs. Gant's Tomato Conserve

2 lemons, thinly sliced
1 quart ripe tomatoes, peeled and diced
1 pint tart apples, peeled and diced
1 cup shredded pineapple
4 cups sugar

Cover the sliced lemon with water and cook until tender. Add the other ingredients and cook until thick and transparent. Seal in sterilized glasses.

From Mrs. Roger Gant, in The Southern Cook Book.

10. Jams

JAM, LIKE PRESERVES, IS A COMBINATION OF ONE FRUIT AND SUGAR or a combination of several fruits and sugar. It differs from preserves in that in jam the fruit is crushed and the finished product is of a thicker consistency and texture. It is a good way to use fruit that is not perfect enough in form to be made into preserves, and it has a rich flavor. The fruit may be precooked and sugar added. The last cooking—if done on the top of the stove—should be in an open kettle and should be stirred almost constantly to prevent scorching.

An easy and safe way to make jam is to bake it in the oven. If jam is baked, the cooking may be started on top of the stove in an open kettle, then finished in an earthenware casserole or baking dish. If the entire process is carried out in the oven, begin cooking at around 200° F. to 250° F., and hold the temperature there until the sugar dissolves. Increase the heat to around 325° F. to finish cooking. (See Baked Pear Marmalade, page 202.) Oven-cooked jam should be stirred occasionally so that the top fruit will not become dry.

The usual proportion for making jam is 1 cup of sugar to 1 cup of crushed fruit. This will make about ½ pint of jam.

Jam is packed and sealed just as preserves are. It is best to use half-pint or pint jars or jelly glasses.

Dried-Apricot or Dried-Peach Jam

    2 pounds dried apricots or dried peaches
    2 quarts cold water
    2½ pounds sugar

Wash fruit thoroughly and drain. Soak for 3 days in cold water. Bring to a boil in the water that the fruit was soaked in. Add the sugar and boil slowly for 1½ hours. Stir often. Seal in sterilized jars.

Use half dried apples and half dried peaches for a variation.

Peach Jam

    4 cups cooked peach pulp (measure after cooking)
    4 cups sugar

Use ripe peaches. Wash, pare, and cut into small pieces. Put the fruit in a covered saucepan and simmer in their own juice (no water added) until the fruit is tender. Mash with a potato masher. Measure the pulp into another saucepan and add the sugar. Return to heat and cook slowly until the mixture is thick and the fruit looks transparent. Stir frequently to prevent scorching. Pour into hot sterilized jelly glasses or jars and seal. Makes about 2 pints.

Carissa (Natal Plum) Jam

The "Carissa," or natal plum, is a tropical fruit used widely to make jelly, jam, conserve, and so on.

    Plums   Lime juice
    Water   Sugar

Cut the plums in half, remove the stones, and cut into smaller pieces. Barely cover with water and steam gently in a covered saucepan until the fruit is very tender. Mash well with a potato masher. For every 3 cups or less of pulp and juice add ½ cup of lime juice. Bring to a boil, and add cup for cup of sugar. Cook, stirring constantly, until 2 drops form slowly on the side of a spoon. Drop a little onto a cold saucer. When this forms a light "skin," the jam is cooked. Place in sterilized jars and seal. If pectin is used, follow instructions for Cherry Jam as given in the chart accompanying bottled pectin.

From Mrs. Carl Hilton, in The Key West Cook Book, *Key West Woman's Club, Key West, Fla.*

Purefoy Blackberry Jam

Among the South's best hotels is the Purefoy, which has long been noted for real home-cooked Southern food. Most of the pickles, relishes, and preserves served there are made in the hotel's own kitchen from Mrs. Purefoy's tried and tested recipes. This jam is pure, seedless, and delicious.

> 1 pound ripe blackberries
> 1 pound sugar

Wash and pick over the berries. Run them through a sieve. Weigh the berries and juice. Boil rapidly without sugar for 30 minutes, stirring frequently and skimming. Add the sugar and boil for 10 minutes. Remove from heat. Take out ½ cup of jam and set on ice to test for consistency. If it is too thin, boil it a little longer. Seal hot. Makes about 2 pints.

From The Purefoy Hotel Cook Book, *copyright, 1941, by Eva B. Purefoy, Talladega, Ala.*

Carrot Jam

4 cups chopped raw carrots
3 cups sugar
Juice and grated rind of 2 lemons
½ teaspoon each ground cloves, ground allspice, and
    ground cinnamon

Combine all ingredients. Bring to a slow boil, reduce heat, and simmer, stirring constantly, until thick. Seal as any jam. This is excellent with meats or game fowl.

Red Cherry Jam

4 cups ripe, red, sour cherries, pitted and crushed
1 tablespoon water
6½ cups sugar

Put the cherries, juice, and water into a preserving kettle. Bring to a slow boil, stirring constantly. Cover and simmer for 15 minutes, or until the cherries are tender. Add the sugar and stir well to mix. Bring to a full boil and cook until the syrup jells. Remove from heat and seal in jelly glasses.
From Mrs. Frank Hall, Reidsville, N.C.

Cranberry Jam

2 pounds raw cranberries
1 cup raisins
2 oranges
3 cups sugar
¼ teaspoon salt
1 pint water

Pick over the berries, and wash both berries and raisins. Peel the oranges and remove the seeds. Combine the fruits and chop. Add the other ingredients and cook for about 30 minutes, or until thick, stirring often. Pour into sterilized jars and cover with paraffin.

Black-Currant Jam

1 pound fresh black currants
1 pound sugar
½ cup white grape juice or water

Pick over the currants carefully and wash thoroughly, since they are usually gritty. Mix the sugar and currants and add grape juice or water. Bring to a boil and cook for 20 minutes. Remove from heat and let stand for 1 minute. Skim and seal in jelly glasses.

Red-Currant Jam

Follow the recipe for Black-Currant Jam, but use ¾ pound of sugar to each 1 pound of fruit.

Ginger-Fig Jam

5 pounds fresh figs, peeled and cut into pieces
1 lemon, chopped, discarding seeds
    Water
4 pounds sugar
1 teaspoon salt
½ cup ginger root, soaked and scraped

Combine the figs, lemon, and enough water to cover. Put in a preserving kettle and cook for 1 hour. Add the sugar, salt, and ginger, and cook until the figs are clear and the syrup is thick. Pour into hot sterilized glasses and seal.

Gooseberry Jam

4 pounds gooseberries, red or yellow
4 pounds sugar
¼ teaspoon salt

Remove the stems from the gooseberries. Wash the berries and crush, saving the juice. Boil the crushed berries and juice slowly until the berries are tender. Add sugar and salt and cook until thick. Pour into hot sterilized glasses and seal as any jelly or jam.

Kumquat Jam

4 pounds unpeeled kumquats, thinly sliced
8 cups sugar

As the kumquats are being sliced, save all the juice. Discard seeds and fibers. Put the fruit and juice in a large kettle and simmer uncovered for 1 hour, or until the fruit is very tender. Add the sugar and mix thoroughly. Pour into a baking dish, and bake in a moderately hot oven (375°–400° F.) for 30 minutes, or until the fruit is transparent and the syrup is thick. Pour into sterilized glasses and seal. Makes 7 pints.

Kumquat Conserve

Follow the recipe for Kumquat Jam, and add 1 cup of chopped nuts and 1 cup of chopped dates to the cooked kumquat mixture. Then add sugar and proceed as for jam.

Muscadine Grape Jam

4 pounds grapes
Water
2½ pounds sugar

Skin the grapes, saving skins and pulp in separate containers. Combine pulp and water in a large kettle and cook for 15 minutes. Put the pulp through a sieve to remove seeds. Save the pulp and juice and discard the seeds. Meanwhile, mix the pulp and skins. Add the sugar and cook slowly until thick. Spices may be added if desired. Let the jam stand until slightly cooled. Pour into sterilized glasses and seal.

Scuppernong Grape Jam

Scuppernong grape jam may be made by the same method and using the same proportions.

Mango Jam

1 pound ripe mangoes, peeled
Water
¾ pound sugar

Slice mangoes into a saucepan. Add water to cover and cook for 10 minutes, or until tender. Drain the liquid from mangoes and save fruit and juice. Combine sugar and juice and bring to a rapid boil, boiling until the mixture is moderately thick. Return the mangoes to the syrup and cook until the mixture is thick. Seal in sterilized glasses.

From Mrs. Mary Nesbit, Tampa, Fla.

Pumpkin Jam

This is a rare old Virginia recipe.

5 pounds fresh or canned pumpkin
1 pound dried apricots
1 pound seedless raisins
2½ pounds sugar
2 tablespoons lemon juice
2 tablespoons chopped crystallized ginger

If fresh pumpkin is used, peel, remove seeds, and cut into cubes. Mix in sugar and let stand for 12 hours. Wash and cut apricots into pieces and add to the pumpkin. Add raisins, lemon juice, and ginger. Cook slowly until the pumpkin is transparent and tender. Seal as any jam.

From Mrs. R. D. Lea, Sr., Petersburg, Va.

Pure Raspberry Jam

4 cups raspberries, red or black or mixed
4 cups sugar

Wash and mash berries. Cook in their own juice for 30 minutes, stirring often. Add 1 cup of the sugar and bring slowly to a boil.

Boil for 5 minutes. Then gradually add the remaining sugar, bringing the syrup back to the boil after each addition. When the jam is thick, remove it from the heat and pour hot into jelly glasses. Seal with paraffin. Makes 4 jelly glasses of jam.

Any berry jam is good made by this same recipe.

Raspberry-Cherry Jam

> 3 cups red sour cherries, pitted
> 3 cups red raspberries, hulled and washed
> 6 cups sugar

Pit the cherries and mash. Cook in their own juice until the cherry skins are tender. Mash the raspberries and add to cherries. Cook the fruit mixture until it thickens. Add sugar, bring the mixture back slowly to boiling, and cook rapidly until it has thick jam consistency. Cool in the pan for 5 minutes. Seal in sterilized jelly glasses.

Eight-Minute Strawberry Jam

> 1 quart ripe strawberries
> 4 cups heated sugar

Crush washed, hulled strawberries in a saucepan and bring to the boiling point in their own juice. When boiling over the entire surface, begin timing. Boil hard for 5 minutes for a medium thick jam; for heavier jam boil 7 minutes. Stir in the heated sugar, and when it is dissolved bring the mixture to a good boil and boil for 3 minutes. Pour the jam into hot sterilized glasses and cover at once with melted paraffin. Let the paraffin cool and add a second layer of melted paraffin. Cover, label, and store in a cool, dark place.

From Mrs. R. C. Moneymaker, Alleghany County, in Recipes from Old Virginia, *compiled by The Virginia Federation of Home Demonstration Clubs, copyright, 1946, by The Federation of Home Demonstration Clubs, The Dietz Press, Inc., Richmond, Va.*

Tomato Jam

> 6 pounds ripe tomatoes, scalded and peeled
> 1 pound raisins, chopped fine
> 3 pounds brown sugar
> 1 pint vinegar
> 2 tablespoons ground cinnamon
> 1 tablespoon ground cloves
> 1 nutmeg, grated
> ½ teaspoon black pepper
> 1 tablespoon salt

Cut the peeled tomatoes into eighths and put into a large kettle. Add all the other ingredients and cook slowly for 2 hours. Seal in sterilized jars.

From Lilian Dickinson, in Pride of the Kitchen, Scotland Neck, N.C.

Mrs. Green's Uncooked Jam

> 1 pound ripe raspberries or strawberries
> 1¼ pounds sugar

Combine sugar and berries and crush with a potato masher. Each berry must be thoroughly mashed. Put the fruit mixture in a cool place for 24 hours, stirring occasionally. When all the sugar is dissolved in the juice, fill sterilized jars, seal, and store in a cool, dark place.

From Mrs. Paul Green, in The Chapel Hill Cook Book, The Woman's Auxiliary, Presbyterian Church, Chapel Hill, N.C.

Mango Honey

> 3 cups cooked mango pulp
> Water
> 3 cups sugar

Peel ripe mangoes and cut into pieces. Barely cover with water. Simmer the fruit until it is tender and the water is reduced to a thick juice. Put through a sieve or food mill. Measure. Add sugar and cook until thick like jam. Seal in small sterilized glasses. Strained honey may be used instead of sugar. Makes 1 pint.

VARIATION

Peach Honey

Make peach honey by the same recipe, using the same proportion of sugar and fruit.

Purefoy Pear Honey

> 7 pounds pears
> 5 pounds sugar
> Juice of 3 lemons
> 2 cups canned crushed pineapple

Peel and core the pears and grind in a food chopper, using the fine blade. Put the pears in a large kettle and add sugar and lemon juice. Place over medium heat and cook until the mixture has the consistency of apple butter. Add pineapple 15 minutes before removing from heat. Seal hot in sterilized glasses. Makes about 7 pints.

From The Purefoy Hotel Cook Book, *by Eva B. Purefoy, Taladega, Ala.*

Damson–Fox Grape "Cheese"

This "cheese" is similar to fruit paste or very thick, concentrated jam.

> 3 pounds damson plums, mashed (leave stones with mixture)
> 1 pound fox grapes (or any tangy wild grapes), mashed
> 1 orange, finely chopped
> Sugar
> 1 pound black currants, fresh or processed

Mix the damsons, grapes, and orange in a large saucepan. Place the fruit over medium heat and simmer in their own juice until tender. Sieve to remove all fibers, seeds, and skins. Measure pulp. For each cup of pulp, add 1 cup of sugar. Wash and pick over the currants. If processed currants are used, pour boiling water over them and drain. Add the currants to the pulp and sugar mixture. Place over low heat and cook slowly until a thick, almost stiff, consistency is reached. Pour into sterilized jelly glasses and seal. Makes about 2½ pints.

From Mrs. H. P. McKay, Onancock, Va.

Guava Paste

Guava paste, which is actually a "brick" preserve, has the consistency of thick, firm fudge. It is packed commercially in small flat Cellophane-lined wooden boxes. At home it may be packed in any box that is not airtight.

> 3 pounds guavas
> Water
> Sugar

Cut the guavas in pieces. Put in a saucepan, cover with water, and cook until the fruit is tender. Remove the fruit from the heat and mash to a soft pulp. Strain through a fine sieve or jelly bag. Save pulp and juice. Place the pulp in the top of a double boiler and cook until it has become a thick mass. Measure the juice. Place the juice in a saucepan, and for each cup of juice add ¾ cup of sugar. Bring juice and sugar slowly to the boiling point, stirring to dissolve the sugar. Add the guava pulp to the syrup, and continue cooking slowly until the mixture will form a soft ball in cold water. Allow it to cool slightly. Pour into Cellophane-lined boxes. Dust the top of the paste with powdered sugar to protect it against mold. Fold the Cellophane securely over the paste and close the boxes. The paste will keep indefinitely if stored in a dry, cool place.

Quince Paste

The quince, once known as a "wardon" or "pere," is one of the oldest fruits preserved in sugar by the English and the French (see Peris in Syrippe, page 147). This recipe is similar to Quince Marmalade (page 203), which seems to have been popular in the fourteenth and fifteenth centuries, according to *Two Fifteenth-Century Cookery-Books*.

Cut the quinces into quarters and remove cores and seeds. (Quince peel has a high pectin content; the core and seeds are unpleasant to taste.) Cook unpeeled until tender. Lift the peel off the fruit. Press through a fine sieve. To each pound of pulp add 1 pound of sugar. Stir until sugar is completely mixed with the fruit. Place over heat and bring to a slow boil. Simmer for 15 minutes. Spread out on platters for 5 to 6 days. Each day sprinkle on a thin coating of granulated sugar; next day, turn and sprinkle sugar on the other side. When the mixture has thickened to a paste, pack it into jars and seal. This may be packed in small boxes lined with wax paper (or aluminum foil) and kept in a cool place indefinitely. Cover the boxes. Occasionally sprinkle powdered sugar over the top of the paste.

From The Everyday Cook Book, *by Miss E. Neil (c. 1875).*

11. Marmalades

MARMALADE IS A POPULAR BREAKFAST PRESERVE AND SHOULD HAVE A tangy or piquant taste. The best-known marmalades contain citrus fruits, but many excellent marmalades are made from other fruits and combinations of fruits.

In a good marmalade the fruit appears to be suspended in clear jelly syrup. To obtain the best results, do the final cooking in an open kettle on high heat. Test as for jelly (see page 152). Let the marmalade stand until almost cold before pouring it into the jars. Stir to mix the fruit with the jelly so that the fruit will be well distributed. Seal as for jelly.

Apricot-Raspberry Marmalade

2 pounds fresh, ripe apricots
2 cups raspberries (red or black)
2¼ pounds sugar
¼ cup water

Wash, peel, and pit the apricots and wash the raspberries. Mix the fruits and add sugar and water. Cook slowly until thick. Test by putting a little on a cold plate. When the syrup stiffens as soon as it is cool, it is done. Pour into sterilized glasses and seal with paraffin.

From E. H. Matthew, in Maryland Cooking, *Maryland Home Economics Association, Baltimore, Md.* (May be obtained from Mrs. Elizabeth Reitze, 106 Forest Drive, Catonsville 28, Md.)

Apricot-Date Marmalade

> 1 cup dried apricots
> 4 cups water
> 1½ cups pasteurized dates
> ½ cup nut meats, chopped
> 1 cup sugar
> Juice of 1 lemon

Soak the apricots in 2 cups of water overnight. Chop the dates and add them to the apricots. Add the remaining 2 cups of water. Place the fruit mixture over low heat and cook slowly until the fruits are soft. Add sugar and lemon juice. Cook slowly until the mixture thickens to the same consistency as jam. Add chopped nuts and cook 5 minutes. Pour into sterilized glasses and seal with paraffin. Makes about two 6-ounce glasses.

This makes a rich filling for party sandwiches.

From Mrs. Amos O. Jacobson, in The Bergen Cook Book, *Roland, Iowa.*

Apricot-Pineapple Marmalade

> 1 pound dried apricots
> 9 cups water
> 1 cup pineapple juice
> 6 cups sugar
> 1 cup crushed pineapple

Wash the apricots, add water, and soak for 2 days. Add pineapple juice. Bring the mixture to a boil and simmer for 1 hour. Add sugar and pineapple and boil, stirring frequently, until the mixture jells, or until it reaches 220° F. Pour into hot sterilized glasses. Cool and cover with paraffin.

From Mrs. L. D. Martin, Elon College, N.C.

Crab-Apple Marmalade

6 pounds crab apples
6 pounds sugar
2 pounds raisins
2 teaspoons each ground cloves and ground cinnamon
2 oranges
1 pint vinegar

Cut the raisins and apples quite fine. Peel and skin oranges and finely chop the peel. Put spices in a small bag. Put all together in a kettle, cover, and cook until tender. When the mixture is thick and the fruit is tender, take out the spice bag. Seal while hot. Makes 6 pints.

From Mrs. Goddard, in The Galveston Souvenir Cook Book, *Galveston, Texas.*

Calamondin Marmalade

The calamondin is a tropical citrus fruit that looks like a small tangerine but has the bitter-sweet taste of the kumquat. The ripe fruit is edible, and its juice adds a piquant flavor to any beverage calling for orange or lemon juice. It makes good preserves, jellies, and marmalades. The tree is decorative and prized as an evergreen.

Calamondins
Soda
Boiling water
Cold water
Sugar

Wash the calamondins and sprinkle generously with soda. Cover with boiling water and let stand for 10 minutes. Drain, remove seeds, and slice into thin slices. Put the fruit in a kettle and cover with cold water. Bring to a boil and boil until the fruit is tender. Remove from the heat and measure into another kettle. Add an equal measure of sugar for fruit mixture. Return to the heat and boil rapidly until the syrup reaches the jelly stage. Pour into sterilized jelly glasses and seal with paraffin.

The contributor of this recipe has a large calamondin tree in her garden and each year makes many jars of this fine marmalade.

From Mrs. Sarah Stoner, St. Petersburg, Fla.

Fig Marmalade

  5 pounds figs (weigh after peeling and draining)
2½ pounds sugar
  2 sticks cinnamon
  2 lemons, sliced

Drop peeled figs into cold water. Drain and combine with other ingredients in a kettle. Place over low heat and bring slowly to a boil. Simmer for 2 to 3 hours. Pour into hot jelly glasses and seal as for jam or jelly.

Greengage-Plum Marmalade

4 cups greengage plums, washed and cut into pieces then weighed
  Water
3 cups sugar

Use firm ripe plums. Remove the stones, but do not peel the plums. Put the fruit into a kettle and barely cover with cold water. Bring to a boil and simmer until the plums are tender and the water has almost cooked out. Add sugar and cook until the mixture is thick, stirring often. Pack into sterilized jelly glasses and seal. Makes 4 to 5 jelly glasses of marmalade.

Lime Marmalade

6 large (Key) limes, if possible, or 12 ordinary limes
2 lemons
  Sugar

Wash the fruit and slice very thin, discarding seeds and white fiber. Place in a preserving kettle and cover with water. Cook, covered, for 20 minutes. Measure the fruit and water mixture and add 1 cup of sugar for each cup of fruit mixture. Place over medium heat and bring to a boil. Cook rapidly until the syrup jells. Seal in hot sterilized jelly glasses.
From Mrs. Everette Rogers, The National Hotel, Leesburg, Fla.

Kumquat Marmalade

3 pounds kumquats
  Water
  Sugar

Weigh the fruit before preparation. Remove skins from kumquats and save both pulp and skins. Cover the pulp with 3 cups of water and simmer for 30 minutes. Strain and to the juice add 3 cups of water. Discard the pulp. Cover the kumquat skins with fresh water and cook separately until tender, draining them several times if the bitter taste is disliked. Grind or cut the skins into fine slivers. Measure the pulp juice and add ¾ cup of sugar for each cup of juice. Add the kumquat skins and bring the mixture to a boil, cooking until the syrup jells. Cool for several minutes. Pour into hot sterilized glasses. Makes about 3 pints.
From Mrs. Trevor Bevan, St. Petersburg, Fla.

Normandy Farm Caramelized Citrus Marmalade

Normandy Farm, a charming authentically French Provincial restaurant, was once the old Riverside Riding Academy and became an institution in Washington social life in 1931. In 1942, Mrs. Marjory Hendricks remodeled the Academy into a war-

needed restaurant. It was decorated by her sister, Genevieve Hendricks, a noted interior decorator. While its owner served overseas with the Red Cross, Normandy Farm was closed. It was reopened in 1947. This unusual and simple marmalade is one of Marjory Hendricks' specialties.

1 gallon sugar
1 gallon water
1 gallon mixed citrus peel: orange, lemon, grapefruit, finely sliced

Pour the sugar into a heavy preserving kettle and caramelize it over very low heat, stirring almost constantly. When sugar becomes a thick amber syrup, add the water and stir. Add the citrus peel. Cook slowly until the peel is transparent. Pour into sterilized jars and seal.
From Marjory Hendricks, Normandy Farm, Rockville, Md.

Papaya-Pineapple Marmalade

1 ripe papaya, put through coarse food chopper
1 ripe pineapple, peeled, put through coarse food chopper
1 teaspoon green ginger, shaved fine, to each cup of mixed fruits
1 cup sugar for each cup mixed fruits (if pineapple is very sweet, use slightly less sugar)

Combine the fruits and ginger and boil gently for 10 minutes. Add the sugar and cook until the fruit is transparent and thick. Pour piping hot into hot sterilized jars and seal at once.
From The Fruitful Papaya, *by Isabelle E. Thursby, for University of Florida Extension Service and U.S. Department of Agriculture.*

Pear-Pineapple Marmalade

2 quarts pears, peeled
1 9-ounce can crushed pineapple
5 cups sugar
Grated rind of 1 orange

Peel the pears and drop into cold water. Drain. Put the pears in a colander and pour boiling water over them. Drain. Grind the pears, saving all juice. Measure pears and juice. Cook the pears in their own juice for 15 minutes, stirring often. Add the other ingredients, and cook until the mixture thickens and the fruit is transparent. Seal in sterilized glasses.

From Mrs. Harrison T. Nicholas, Huntington, W. Va.

Scotch Orange Marmalade

True Scotch marmalade is world famous and is made with the slightly bitter and tangy Seville orange. The Seville orange, deriving its name from the district in Spain to which it was introduced by the Moors, was brought to America by Columbus and carried through all Spanish America by early explorers. It is thought to have originated in China and Japan.

> Oranges
> Water
> Sugar

Wash the oranges and remove the peel. Discard two thirds of the peel, saving only the best part. Cut the peel into thin slivers. Measure the peel and put in a kettle, and add four times as much water as peel. Boil for 10 minutes and then drain. Repeat this process until the peel is very tender but not mushy. Measure the pulp of the oranges and discard the seeds. Put in an open kettle and cover with water. Boil until the fruit becomes soft and mushy. Remove from heat. With a wooden spoon press the fruit down to extract as much juice as possible from it. Strain through a jelly bag and discard the residue.

Measure the juice. Combine the orange juice with the cooked peel in an open kettle. To 1 pint of mixture add 1¼ pounds of sugar. Bring to a rapid boil and cook rapidly until the mixture flakes from a spoon or responds to the jelly test. Cool in the kettle. Pour into jelly glasses and seal.

For a fancy marmalade cut the peel into slivers to resemble tiny fish, flowers, stars, crescents, and so on. They look most attractive suspended in the clear amber syrup. If the marmalade is allowed to cool before it is poured into glasses, the peel will not float to the top.

Orange-Lemon-Grapefruit Marmalade

This is a grand basic marmalade recipe, often known as "amber marmalade." The grapefruit may be omitted, but an equivalent bulk of orange and lemon should then be substituted.

> 1 orange
> 1 lemon
> 1 grapefruit
> Sugar

Shave the fruit very thin with a potato slicer, rejecting nothing except seeds and white fiber. Measure the fruit and add three times the quantity of water. Let stand overnight in a pottery or glass mixing bowl. Next morning boil in the same juice for 10 minutes. Let stand another night. On the second morning add sugar, using pint for pint of sugar and fruit mixture. Bring to a boil and cook until the syrup jells. Stir as little as possible while cooking. Makes about 10 jelly glasses of marmalade.

From Mrs. Lee Hersberg, in Bon Appétit, *compiled by the Junior Service League, Baton Rouge, La.*

Peach Marmalade

> 1 quart ripe peaches, peeled and cut into pieces
> 3 cups sugar
> ¼ cup water

Cook all ingredients together for about 1 hour, stirring constantly. Seal in jelly glasses. Makes 1½ pints.

If peaches are juicy, reserve the juice and combine water to make ¼ cup.

Peach-Orange Marmalade

24 medium-sized ripe peaches
4 oranges
3½ pounds sugar

Peel the peaches and cut into thin strips. Wash and peel the oranges. Cut the skins into thin strips and cut the pulp into small pieces. Combine the fruit and peel, add the sugar, and let stand overnight. In the morning bring the mixture gradually to the boiling point and simmer gently for about 2 hours, or until the mixture is thick and the consistency of marmalade. Pour into hot, clean, sterilized glasses and seal.

From The Episcopal Pantry, *Auxiliary of the Episcopal Church, Danville, Va.*

Baked Pear Marmalade

2 pounds pears
1½ pounds sugar
1 tablespoon candied ginger, finely cut

Peel and cut the pears and remove the cores. Cut the pears into fine pieces. Mix all the ingredients and pack in an earthenware casserole or shallow baking dish. Put in the oven at 200° F. and cook until sugar has dissolved. Increase the temperature to about 325° F., and continue cooking until the fruit is transparent. Pack into small sterilized jars and seal. Makes about 2 pints.

VARIATION

Peaches, damsons, and other meaty fruit may be prepared by the same method. Increase the sugar for very tart fruit.

Quince Marmalade

3 pounds quinces, washed, quartered, and cored
1 whole orange
4 pounds sugar
½ cup orange juice
½ cup lemon or lime juice
2 cups water

Grind together the prepared quinces and the orange. Add the other ingredients. Cook slowly until the syrup jells. Seal in sterilized jelly glasses.

Red-Tomato Marmalade

This marmalade is unusual and very tart; it is especially good with ham.

1 quart ripe red tomatoes
½ cup cider vinegar
1 cup sugar
1 teaspoon salt
1 teaspoon mixed pickling spices

Put tomatoes in boiling water for 2 minutes. Skin, cut into quarters, and put in a saucepan. Add the other ingredients and bring to a slow boil. Cook slowly until thick, stirring frequently. Pour into sterilized jars or bottles and seal. Makes 1 pint.

Sunshine Marmalade

This marmalade has an extra lemon flavor

6 oranges
3 lemons
 Sugar
1 cup lemon juice

Slice the fruits thin. Cover with water and let stand for 12 hours. Next morning boil the fruit and water together for 45 minutes.

Again let stand for 12 hours. Measure the mixture and bring to a boil. Add 1½ times as much sugar as fruit mixture. Bring to a quick boil and cook for 45 minutes. Just before removing from the heat, add the lemon juice. While hot, seal in jelly glasses.

Sunflower Marmalade

This different marmalade is made of watermelon rind and other fruits.

> ½ medium-sized watermelon
> 4 oranges
> 2 lemons
> 5 pounds sugar

Use only the peeled rind of the watermelon, preparing it as for watermelon rind pickle. (See Watermelon Rind Pickle, page 63.) Grind the rind in a food chopper and let it stand overnight in just enough water to cover. Drain, add enough water to cover, and bring to a boil. Do this twice. Squeeze and save the juice from the oranges and lemons. Bring the orange and lemon peel to a boil twice, using enough water to cover. Grind the peel in a food chopper. Combine all the ingredients and cook for 2 hours.
From Mrs. M. E. Hogan, in Chapel Hill Cook Book, *Woman's Auxiliary, Presbyterian Church, Chapel Hill, N.C.*

Tamarind Marmalade

The tamarind nut is a succulent addition to any chutney, relish, or other dish. Growing abundantly in the tropics, it is considered a delicacy when prepared either as a marmalade or as a preserve.

> 1 quart shelled tamarind nuts
> Water
> Sugar

Cover tamarinds well with water and boil until the nuts are soft. Put through a sieve to remove seeds and fibers. Measure equal parts of sugar and pulp and simmer slowly, stirring constantly, until the mixture thickens enough to coat a silver spoon. Pour into sterilized jelly glasses and seal with paraffin or wax. Makes 2 jelly glasses of marmalade.

From The Key West Cook Book, *Key West Woman's Club, Key West, Fla.*

Tutti-Frutti Marmalade

   3 oranges
   1 lemon
   1 No. 2 can crushed pineapple
   1½ cups maraschino cherries with juice
   3 pounds sugar

Wash and thinly slice the oranges and lemon. Discard white fiber and seeds. Mix with other ingredients and cook together for 30 minutes. Seal in hot sterilized jars.

From Mrs. A. K. Thomas, Harrisburg, Pa., in What's Dat Cookin'? *St. Monica's Guild, Christ Episcopal Church, Point Pleasant, W. Va.*

12. Crystallized and Glacéed Fruits; Preserved Flowers

VERY FINE INDEED ARE CRYSTALLIZED AND GLACÉED, OR CANDIED, fruits, which may be prepared from either raw or preserved fruits. The term "crystallized" is usually applied to raw fruits cooked in syrup, and the term "candied" or "glacéed" is used for raw or preserved fruits that are dipped and frosted in cooked grained syrup made of white or brown sugar. It is advisable to use a candy thermometer for cooking the syrup, but the amateur will soon learn to judge by simple tests when the syrup reaches the proper stage.

White Grain Sugar Coating

Before preserved fruits can be coated, they must be washed with hot water to remove all syrup and allowed to dry on a rack. Make a syrup, using ½ pint of water to each pound of sugar, and cook to the "small-thread" stage. To test for proper "thread," take out a drop or two on a spoon. Dip the index finger into the syrup and pull the syrup between thumb and finger. If a fine thread extends between the fingers, the syrup is done. Or cook the syrup until it reaches 215° F., or 10° C. When the syrup spins a thread, take a little in a wooden spoon and rub it around the side of the cooking vessel until it whitens or "grains." Mix the grain down into the syrup. This will cause the mass to begin to granulate. Stick fruit on the tines of a fork and dip them into the syrup until they are thoroughly coated. Spread on racks to dry.

Caramel Coating

Use ½ pint of water to 1 pound of sugar and ¼ teaspoon of lemon juice or vinegar. Cook until the "hard crack" stage—345–350° F.— or until the syrup will crack when dropped on a cool hard surface. Dip the fruit in as for white sugar coating and drain.

Candied Apricots

1 pound dried apricots
1 small bottle maraschino cherries
   Juice of 1 orange
3 cups sugar
1 cup water
   Extra sugar—granulated or powdered

Grind the apricots and cherries twice. Add orange juice, sugar, and water to the fruit and cook for 25 minutes, stirring constantly. When the mixture forms a soft ball in cold water, pour it out on a marble slab. Cover with sugar. When it is cold, cut it into pieces and roll in sugar.

From Laura Hay Braddock (Mrs. James G.), Mount Pleasant, Pa., in The DAR Cook Book, compiled by the Valley Forge Committee, Copyright, 1949, by Aileen Lewers Langston.

Crystallized Cranberries

Serve with turkey or chicken.

    4 cups sugar
    4 cups raw cranberries
    2 cups water

Wash the berries and spread them in a large flat cooking pan. Add water, place over medium heat, and cook 10 minutes. Shake the pan to stir. Do *not* stir with a spoon. Then add 1 cup of the sugar, sprinkling it over the berries in the pan. If the juice boils too fast, turn the heat low. Cook for 15 minutes. Sprinkle over another cup of the sugar. Repeat until 4 cups of sugar have been added to the berries. Cool and pack in sterilized jars.

    This recipe came from my mother, Rebecca McCurdy Robertson, who lived in Alabama.

From Mrs. Walter Merry, in Recipes from Southern Kitchens, *Junior League of Augusta, Georgia, Inc., Augusta, Ga.*

Variation

Use red, sour stoned cherries as a substitute for cranberries.

Stuffed Dates

    Pasteurized dates
    Nuts or fruits or any desired stuffing
    Granulated sugar

Slit dates lengthwise and remove stones. Fill cavities with English walnut, pecan, almond, or any other nut meats. Or stuff with a combination of crystallized ginger, cherries, and nuts or with some other combination of fruit and nuts. Or stuff with marshmallows, fondant, or other candy. Or soak in wine and stuff as for Glacéed Figs (page 209). Shape the dates around the stuffing and roll them in granulated sugar. Let dry and pack in boxes.

From J. Woodall and Son, Midway, Ga.

Crystallized Figs

2 dozen ripe figs
3 cups sugar
1 cup white grape juice (Catawba)
Juice of 2 lemons
¼ teaspon ground allspice

Wash and dry the figs, leaving the stems on. Cover them with the sugar, grape juice, lemon juice, and spice. Bring to a boil and cook very slowly until the syrup begins to thicken. Set aside overnight. Next morning bring the mixture back to a boil and simmer slowly until the syrup is beginning to become a sticky mass. Lift out the figs and lay them on waxed paper to cool. Stuff, if desired, with a mixture of nuts, other crystallized fruits, and so on. Roll in granulated sugar.
Condensed from an early nineteenth-century cook book owned by Mrs. Norman Riddle, Burlington, N.C.

Glacéed Wine Figs

1 pound pasteurized figs
½ pound marshmallows
Wine or brandy
Pecan halves

Pack the figs loosely in a jar and cover with any good wine or brandy. Cut the marshmallows in large pieces and dip them in a little of the wine that the figs were soaked in. Tuck a pecan half in each piece of marshmallow. Put the candy and nuts into the center of the fig, using enough to fill the cavity. Shape the fig around the candy and nuts to give it a natural look. Dip the figs in white or caramel grain sugar syrup and let dry on racks. (See White Grain Sugar Syrup, page 206.)
From Paul Willard, Manager, University-Sequoia and Sunnyside Clubs, Fresno, Calif.

Crystallized Ginger

1 pound young green ginger roots, scraped and washed
1 cup water
1 pound sugar
½ teaspoon cream of tartar

Scrape the ginger before weighing. Let it dry thoroughly. Mix water, sugar, and cream of tartar in a saucepan and bring to a boil. Cook until the syrup begins to thicken. Add ginger and continue cooking until ginger is transparent and syrup has been reduced to a sticky consistency. Lift out the ginger and spread it on waxed paper. Let it cool. Roll in granulated sugar and let stand until the sugar crystallizes. Pack in waxed-paper-lined boxes or other containers. After ginger crystallizes, it may be cut into pieces of any desired size. This is also known as "candied" ginger.

Malaga Grapes Dipped in Chocolate

These are delicious and especially nice for a tea party.

1 pound Malaga grapes
4 ounces bitter chocolate (more if necessary)
Granulated sugar

Wash the grapes and dry thoroughly in absorbent paper or a soft towel. Leave in small clusters of about 3 grapes. Grate the chocolate into the top of small double boiler and set over boiling water. Let the chocolate melt and heat but do not boil. Dip the grape clusters into the chocolate so that each grape will be about three quarters coated with chocolate. Remove and hold the cluster in the air for a moment. Dip in granulated sugar to cover chocolate coating. Spread on waxed paper to dry. Store on waxed paper in covered paper boxes. Do not keep more than a few days, for the fruit may spoil.

VARIATION

Cherries, greengage plums, or any firm small fruit with stems may be dipped in the same manner.

Crystallized Grapefruit Peel

Crystallized grapefruit (or orange or lemon) peel is one of my favorite confections. Each year for Christmas I make many pounds for my own use and for gifts to friends. Some I tint green and red. The peel makes a pretty and refreshing garnish for platters and may also be used as a drink "muddler" and sweetner. A twist of the peel is good in an old-fashioned.

It is easy to save the peel after the fruit has been served. Do not use more than three grapefruit at one time. The thick peel of pink Texas grapefruit makes the best candy.

> Peel from 2 grapefruit
> Sugar
> Water
> Salt
> Vegetable coloring if desired

Pull all pulp from the grapefruit and rinse the peel. Put in a saucepan with water to cover and add 1 teaspoon of salt for each quart of water. Boil the peel for 10 minutes. Drain and save the juice. Cut the peel into strips about ¼ inch wide. Measure the juice in which the peel was boiled and add 2 cups of sugar for each cup of juice. Let the syrup boil for 5 minutes. Add the peel and cook until the peel is transparent and the syrup has been reduced to almost sticky consistency. (If coloring is to be added, add 1 drop for each whole grapefruit peel when the fruit is put in the syrup.) Lift out the peel and spread it on waxed paper. When it begins to harden slightly, roll each strip in sugar. Let the peel get thoroughly dry and candied before storing.

Crystallized Kumquats

Crystallized kumquats are delectable either plain or filled and are prepared in much the same way as kumquat preserves.

> 2 quarts kumquats
> Soda
> Water
> Sugar

Scrub the kumquats well in a mild soda-water solution or in mild soapy water. Rinse and dry. Make a solution of soda water, using 1 tablespoon of soda to 1 quart of water. Bring the soda-water solution to a boil and pour scalding hot over the kumquats. Let stand for about 10 minutes. Drain off the water and discard. Rinse the kumquats in clear cold water three times. Drain and discard the water. Slit each kumquat and remove as many seeds as possible. Put the kumquats in a kettle with enough water to cover. Place a cover on the kettle and boil the fruit for about 10 minutes.

Prepare a syrup by using ½ cup of sugar to 1 cup of water. Put the syrup on in an open saucepan and bring to a rapid boil. Drop the kumquats into the boiling syrup and boil for about 30 minutes, or until the kumquats are transparent. Skim out the fruit and spread on waxed paper to dry. When the kumquats are dry, bring the syrup back to the boiling point. Drop the fruit back into the syrup and cook for 5 minutes. Let the fruit cool in the syrup. Drain the kumquats and place on waxed paper to dry. If they are to be served plain, roll them in granulated sugar and let them dry before packing in cardboard or wooden boxes. If they are to be stuffed, fill the cavities before rolling them in the sugar.

SUGGESTED STUFFING

Ground pecans mixed with chopped dates; whole shelled Brazil nuts; crystallized ginger; crystallized cherries; crystallized pineapple; or any other ground nuts or crystallized fruit.

Rainbow Crystallized Preserves

1 pound crystallized red cherries, halved
½ pound crystallized white cherries, halved
1 pound crystallized pineapple, cut in large pieces
1 tablespoon crystallized orange peel, finely chopped
1 teaspoon crystallized ginger, chopped

Pack an assortment of the fruits in small jars. Cover with enough brandy or whisky to fill each jar. Let stand for at least 1 week before using. These are good for fruit cake topping, on puddings, or on ice cream. They also make pretty party-cooky decorations. Makes 2 pints.

From Mrs. Everette Rogers, The National Hotel, Leesburg, Fla.

Crystallized Pineapple

2 pounds fresh pineapple, peeled and sliced (weigh after slicing)
2 pounds sugar

Peel the fresh pineapple and remove all eyes and dark spots. Cut into slices about ½ inch thick. Cut out the core of each slice. Pour sugar over the pineapple and let it stand overnight. Bring all to a slow boil and then cook rapidly until the syrup thickens and pineapple looks transparent. Do not overcook, for the fruit will darken. Lift out the fruit, spread it on waxed paper, and let it cool. Roll in granulated sugar.

From Mrs. Jack Lindsay, Miami, Fla.

Crystallized Orange Peel

Peel from 3 large thick-skinned oranges
1½ cups sugar, and a little extra sugar
Water

Remove the peel from the oranges in quarter sections. Cover with cold water and boil until the peel begins to soften—about 15 minutes. Drain and remove the inner white portion. Cut the peel into uniform strips. Make a syrup of the sugar and water, using about ⅓ cup of water. When the syrup spins a fine thread, add the orange peel and cook until the peel is transparent and the syrup is very thick. Lift the peel out of the syrup and spread on waxed paper. When the peel begins to cool, roll each strip in granulated sugar. Store in a waxed-paper-lined box.

Glacéed Orange Sections

Peel the oranges and separate into sections, being careful not to break the membrane. Dip into white grain sugar syrup and spread out to dry. (See White Grain Sugar Coating, page 206.)

Glacéed Grapes

Use grapes with stems or those in little clusters. Wash and dry thoroughly. Dip in white grain sugar syrup and spread out to dry. (See White Grain Sugar Coating, page 206.)

Crystallized Papaya

1 green papaya
2 cups sugar
2 cups water

Peel and cut papaya into strips or squares. Bring the sugar and water to a boil and cook until the syrup begins to thicken. Drop in the fruit and cook until fruit is transparent and the syrup is very thick. Remove the papaya and spread out on waxed paper to dry.

Peach or Apple Leather

Once this strange-sounding, but delicious, old form of candy was made professionally by an older generation of "Deep South" ladies, who kept the method a secret. But it has been no exception to the adage that most "secrets will out eventually." This type of leather is cooked in the sun.

Select ripe soft peaches. Peel and mash to a purée. To every cup of purée add ¼ cup of granulated sugar. Mix the sugar with the peaches and simmer over low heat until the mixture comes to a good boil. Boil only 1 or 2 minutes. Remove. Pour into shallow pans or platters in a thin coating (1/16 inch). Cover with mosquito netting and set in the sun for several days (bringing it in each night) until the mixture has cooked down to a tough "leather." Cut into squares and sprinkle with powdered sugar. Roll up into little cylinders and resprinkle with powdered sugar. Store in boxes and serve as a confection or with meats. It will keep for a long time if carefully stored.

From Mrs. William DeR. Scott, Graham, N.C., in The Southern Cook Book.

VARIATION

Apricots may be prepared in the same way.

Candied Strawberries

This is a luscious morsel.

>   Large, firm, ripe strawberries with stems
>   Fondant

Use only large, ripe strawberries that are perfectly formed. Wash carefully or remove grit with a soft damp cloth. Set the berries aside. Make the following fondant:

>   3 cups powdered (confectioners) sugar
>   About 1 tablespoon cold water
>   White of 1 egg
>   Flavoring to taste—about 1 teaspoon
>   (vanilla, lemon, or any other)

Break the egg and pour the white into a regular coffee cup. Add the water. Mix thoroughly with a fork but do not beat. Add enough sugar to make a stiff paste. Add flavoring to taste. Pour the mixture onto a marble slab or flat platter and knead like dough.

Put the fondant in the top of a double boiler or in an earthenware container and set over boiling water. Let the fondant melt, but do not boil. Dip the berries, one at a time, well into the melted fondant. Remove and hold the berry in the hand until the fondant sets. Place on waxed paper to dry.

These are perishable and should be served the same day that they are made. They are pretty if arranged with a few strawberry leaves stuck into the stem end of the berries or on the strawberry.

VARIATION

Figs, dates, prunes, and such fruits may be dipped in the same manner. Pasteurized fruits will keep for several weeks if stored in a dry, cool place.

The Preservation of Flowers in Sugar or Honey

The art of preserving flowers in sugar or honey once flourished on the Continent and in the Americas. It is still popular among the older generations of gourmets. Preserved violets, roses, primroses, orange blossoms, and roselle are among the best known.

The petals of these flowers are not so high in pectin content as the calyx and are used mainly in preserves and wines and for crystallizing. The calyx is best for jelly and syrup. The whole flower gives an even better flavor. The sweeter the flower, the tastier the finished product.

Writers of the thirteenth, fourteenth, and fifteenth centuries spoke freely of sugar and honey flower concoctions: "Vyolette with Almaunde Milk and Sugre"; "Rede Rose with Sugre and Almaunde"; "Primrose"; "Flowrys of Hawthorn putte with sugre or honey, coloure it with the same dat be the flowrys." (*Two Fifteenth-Century Cookery-Books, ed. Thomas Austin, London, 1864, from Harleian Ms, c. 1430, and Ashmole and Douce Mss, c. 1429, published for The Early English Text Society, Oxford University Press, New York.*)

The roselle, which grows abundantly in Florida, is prized for its jelly-making qualities. The sweet pink rose of the United States makes delicate and delicious wine, syrup, jelly, and preserves. The orange blossom is commonly made into syrup for the flavoring of jelly, honey, beverages, and preserves.

A natural orange-flavored honey is often obtained by beekeepers in the Tropics who set the beehives in orange groves. The bees carry the orange-blossom nectar to the honey, thus giving it a pure flavor.

Conserve of Red Roses

"Beat 1 pound of red rose leaves in a mortar. Add this to 2 pounds of refined sugar. Make a conserve. (Put the mixture of rose leaves and sugar in an open kettle, adding a small amount of water to dampen the sugar. Bring to a slow boil and boil rapidly until the syrup reaches the jelly stage. Remove and pour into small jelly glasses. Seal.)

"In the same manner are prepared the conserves of orange peel, rosemary flowers, seawormwood, the leaves of wood sorrel, and so on."

Old Recipe, Wicomico Church, Va., in The Williamsburg Art of Cookery, *by Mrs. Helen Bullock, copyright, 1938, by Colonial Williamsburg, Inc.*

Preserved Violets or Roses (Crystallized Form)

A nostalgic reminder of Old World influence is this recipe, which seems to have had its American inception in New Orleans where so many quaint and charming customs still prevail. The flowers are crystallized and used to decorate cakes and confections or served as any preserve.

Make these and store them in little fancy glasses, giving them for Christmas gifts, just as our contributor does.

    4 cups fresh stemmed violets or whole rose buds
    2 cups granulated sugar
    1 cup hot water

Wash, stem, and drain flowers, being careful not to bruise the petals. In a saucepan dissolve the sugar thoroughly in the hot water. Add the flowers. Put over medium heat and let the syrup simmer until a drop of syrup reaches the soft-ball stage in cold water. Stir the flowers gently with a wooden spoon. Remove from heat and continue to stir gently until the syrup begins to granulate and reaches the consistency of coarse meal. Empty the contents over a wire rack or into a colander and shake off the excess sugar. Cool and pack the flowers in jars. Seal. Use as decoration or serve in little cut-glass compotes.

VARIATION

Orange blossoms or other flowers may be crystallized in the same way.

From Mrs. William Wootton, Baltimore, Md., in The Southern Cook Book.

Honey Rose-Petal Preserves

½ pound sweet pink or red rose petals
½ pound strained honey
   Water
   Juice of 1 lemon

Pick the petals from fresh sweet roses gathered after the dew has dried off. Measure the honey in a cup. For each cup of honey, add 1 cup of water. Mix honey, water, and rose petals and boil until flowers are tender. Strain the syrup into a saucepan. Pour the petals into hot sterilized jelly glasses. Return the syrup to the heat and cook until it begins to jell. Add lemon juice and bring back once to boiling. Remove from heat and pour over the rose petals to fill the glasses. Cool. Seal with paraffin. This is a delicate preserve that has a faint pink tint and light fragrance.

Preserve orange blossoms, violets, or any other fragrant flowers by the above recipe.

Preserved Orange Flowers

Spread the blossoms on a sheet of cloth and pour over them a boiling syrup. Make a syrup by combining 1 cup of water with 1 cup of sugar. Let the syrup boil rapidly for 3 to 5 minutes, or until it is clear. Let stand overnight, and bring to the boiling point on the next day. Spread on platters or trays. Put a sheet of glass over them and let them dry in the sun half a day. Then sprinkle well with powdered sugar. Pack in jars, seal hot in syrup. They are very delicate for flavoring drinks, desserts, and cakes.

From The Puerto Rican Cookbook, *by Eliza B. K. Dooley, San Juan, Puerto Rico, copyright, 1948, by Eliza B. K. Dooley, Dietz Press, Richmond, Va.*

13. Jelly

JELLY IS MADE FROM THE JUICE OF FRUITS AND OTHER FOODS THAT contain pectin. Good jelly is sparkling and clear and is tender yet firm enough to stand after being cut. Fresh fruits are generally used, but good results may be obtained with frozen and dried fruits.

The following suggestions should prove helpful to both the experienced cook and the beginner.

1. Wash, stem, and remove blossom ends of fruit. Unless specifically told to do so in the recipe, do not peel fruit or remove seeds or cores. In these are stored the most abundant supply of pectin—the element that makes the syrup jell. Pectin is extracted from the fruit by heat. Therefore, the fruit must first be cooked; then the juice is strained from the pulp.

2. To extract juice from *soft* fruit, such as berries, use just enough water to prevent the fruit from sticking. Some berries have enough juice of their own and so do not need water. Heat the

219

fruit gradually, stirring constantly. Mash and cook until the fruit has lost its color.

3. To extract the juice from *hard* fruit, such as apples and pears, cut the fruit into pieces, cover with water, and cook slowly until the fruit is tender. Thirty minutes is the average cooking time. Do not crush hard fruit, for it will make the jelly cloudy. Hard fruit, unlike soft pulpy fruit, has minute "grains."

4. Pour cooked fruit into a wet (wrung-out) jelly bag, wet flannel cloth, or other material of sufficient thickness to collect any foreign matter from the juice. Let the juice drip into a large container until the pulp is well drained. The pulp may be cooked a second time in enough water to cover and strained again. *Do not mix the first and second juices,* since they will be of different strength.

5. Too much sugar in proportion to juice will produce a gummy jelly that will not jell. Too little sugar will produce a tough jelly of inferior flavor. Currants, unripe grapes, unripe berries, green gooseberries, and similar fruits require equal quantities of sugar and juice.

6. Work with a small quantity of jelly at one time—not more than two quarts at a time, but four to six cups are even better. Measure the juice; heat rapidly to boiling. Add sugar and stir until dissolved. Boil rapidly until the jelly tests (see page 152). Heated sugar makes the best jelly. Put sugar in a bowl and set it in a slow oven, leaving it there until the sugar looks slightly glacéed and has been thoroughly warmed.

7. If you use one of the commercial pectins, follow the directions provided by the manufacturer. Prepare the fruit just as for pure jelly, extracting juice according to individual recipes, and cook as suggested in the pectin chart. Seal and store in same manner as for other jelly.

8. Before making any jelly, it is a good idea to read the General Instructions pages 5–7, especially those concerned with cooking vessels, containers, and sealing.

Apple Pectin

4 pounds tart apples
2 quarts water
¾ cup lemon juice

Cut apples into pieces, saving peel and cores. Cook fruit in a covered kettle until mushy. Strain twice through a jelly bag or through double thickness of cheesecloth. Do not press on bag, for that will make the juice cloudy. Pour the juice into an open kettle and boil rapidly for 20 minutes. Add lemon juice. Bring back to boiling and remove from heat. Seal in sterilized jars.

Use the apple pectin to make jelly from fruits with low pectin content. Combine equal amounts of pectin and fruit juice. In such combinations of fruit juice and pectin, ¾ cup of sugar is usually correct for each cup of the combined juices. Strawberries, peaches, pineapples, cherries, and other fruits may be made into good jelly by combining them with apple pectin.

Pure Apple Jelly

Apple jelly is a delight in itself, but because of its blandness, it is often used as a basic jelly for other flavors, such as mint, wine, rose petal, rose geranium, lemon verbena, and the like. For the best results in making apple jelly, select tart fruit. Do not peel or remove seeds or cores. Remember that the peel, seed, and core contain a rich pectin supply.

The following is a basic recipe from which other flavors of jelly may be made:

5 pounds tart apples, unpeeled
5 cups cold water
Sugar warmed in oven

Wash apples and cut into quarters, leaving peel, seed, and cores intact. Put into a kettle with a cover. Add the water, place over medium heat, and steam slowly until the apples are tender— about 25 minutes. Pour into a jelly bag and let drip until the pulp is well drained. Do not squeeze the jelly bag—it makes the jelly cloudy. Measure fruit juice and add ¾ cup of sugar for each cup of juice. Heat the juice and add warmed sugar gradually. Bring to a rapid boil and boil until the syrup sheets from a silver spoon or until proved ready by other jelly tests. Skim and pour into sterilized jelly glasses. Seal with paraffin. Do not cook more than 4 cups of juice at a time.

Apple-Mint Jelly

Use very acid apples—the early harvest ones if possible. Proceed as for Pure Apple Jelly (page 221). When ready to pour into glasses, dip a bunch of mint leaves and tender stems down into the hot jelly several times, using 6 to 8 sprays of mint for each pint of jelly. Pour into hot sterilized glasses.

From Mrs. George T. Klipstein, in The Alexandria Woman's Club Cook Book, *Alexandria, Va.*

NOTE: Another way to make mint jelly is to mince 1 cup of mint leaves, cover with boiling water, and steep several hours. Press down the leaves with a spoon to extract all possible juice. Use 2 tablespoons of mint essence to 1 pint of jelly. Add 1 or 2 drops of green food coloring for pretty color.

Rose-Geranium Jelly

Prepare apple jelly, and when the rapid boiling point is reached, dip washed rose-geranium leaves into the hot syrup, dipping up and down until desired taste is reached. When the jelly smells fragrant, it is well flavored. Use from 2 to 3 leaves for each pint. Remove leaves before pouring jelly. Color with red coloring.

Lemon-Verbena Jelly

This is an old-fashioned jelly, and the lemon verbena leaves are just right for flavoring during early apple-harvest season. Dip the leaves as for rose-geranium jelly, using 4 to 5 leaves for each pint. Color with yellow food coloring, if desired.

Crab-Apple Jelly

Crab apples are very fine for jelly, pickle, and preserves. They are not usually edible raw because they are too acid and sour. There are many varieties of crab apples and they are prepared ·for jelly just as any apple. (See Pure Apple Jelly, page 221.)

When the apples have been cooked to a pulp, strain through a jelly bag. Add 1 cup of sugar to each cup of hot juice. Cook rapidly until the syrup coats the spoon. Seal in jelly glasses.

Apple-Peelings Jelly

Apple peelings make a wonderful jelly and should be saved when making pies, sauces, and preserves to be used later in making jelly. Apple peelings are rich in pectin, and the jelly has a fine flavor and color. During apple season, my mother seems to have a little saucepan of peelings perpetually stewing on the stove, thus increasing with no apparent effort, her shelf of jellies. Peach or other fruit peelings may be mixed with the apple.

To make, cover the peelings with water and simmer until tender (add the cores, by all means). Strain through a jelly bag. To each cup of juice add 1 cup of sugar. Cook until the mixture reaches the jelly stage by test. Pour into jelly glasses and seal. The peelings from 6 large apples will make 1 jelly glass of jelly.

Dried-Apple Jelly

Jelly made from dried fruit is easy and economical. Dried apricots, peaches, or combinations of any tart fruit may be used.

        5 cups dried apples
        8 cups water
          Sugar
          Lemon juice

Wash fruit and add water. Put into a covered saucepan. Place over medium heat and boil for 30 minutes, stirring frequently. Drain through a jelly bag. This should make about 3½ cups of juice. Add

1 tablespoon of lemon juice and ½ cup of sugar to each cup of apple juice. Cook until the jelly sheets from the spoon. Seal as any jelly.

From Mrs. M. J. Lea, Jamestown, N.C.

Spiced Apple Jelly

Quick and excellent.

> 8 cups apple juice
> 3 tablespoons whole cloves tied in a bag
> 1 cup vinegar
> 9 cups sugar

Put apple juice and cloves in a wide saucepan and cook over medium heat for 15 minutes. Add vinegar and sugar and boil hard until jelly forms when dropped from a spoon. Remove the spice bag. Seal.

This is my own idea to make jelly this way, and I find it very excellent and a much shorter method.

From Mrs. Edith B. Rawlings, in St. Anne's Parish Recipe Book, *Annapolis, Md.*

Bar-le-Duc Jelly

This famous French currant jelly is said to have derived its name from Bar-le-Duc, the principal city in the Duchy of Barrois (or Bar), on the Meuse River near Lorraine. Sometimes currants are combined with gooseberries or other berries, but true Bar-le-Duc seems to have been made only with currants.

> 1 quart currants
> ⅓ cup water
> 1 pound sugar

Wash and pick over the currants. Drain and put into a saucepan with the water. Cook for several minutes until the fruit is tender. Add the sugar and continue cooking until the syrup jells. Pour into hot glasses and seal.

NOTE: If gooseberries are added, use 1 quart of gooseberries to ½ quart of currants. For each quart of fruit, use 1 pound of sugar.

Pure Blackberry Jelly

7 cups blackberry juice (about 4 quarts berries)
7 cups sugar
Juice of 1 lemon

For best results, have half of the berries ripe and half red. Wash the blackberries and mash thoroughly. Put in a saucepan over medium heat and boil in their own juice for 10 minutes. Strain and add sugar to juice. Cook only 7 cups at a time, adding the juice of 1 lemon. Cook rapidly for 30 minutes, skimming throughout the cooking. Pour hot into jelly glasses. Seal with paraffin. Makes about 6 jelly glasses of jelly.

Calf's-Foot Jelly

No jelly section is complete without this "old faithful." The jelly should be made at least 1 day before using. And it's easy to make.

2 calves' feet
3 quarts water
2 wine glasses sherry
Yellow rind of 1 lemon, grated
Juice of 6 lemons
5 eggs (whites and shells)
1 cup granulated sugar

Put calves' feet and water in a large saucepan over medium heat. Cook for 5 hours, skimming throughout the cooking time. Remove from heat, and strain the liquid through a fine strainer into a saucepan or mixing bowl. Cool to jelly. Remove all oil and fat. Beat together 1 cup of water, sherry, lemon juice and grated rind, egg whites, egg shells, and sugar. Put the jelly into a large enamel saucepan. Add the beaten mixture and place over medium heat, stirring constantly, until the mixture comes to a boil. Remove from heat and put twice through a jelly bag. Pour into molds.

Foolproof Cranberry Jelly

1 pound raw cranberries
2 cups water
2 cups sugar

Wash and stem the cranberries. Put the berries and water in a covered saucepan over medium heat. Bring to a boil and cook for about 5 minutes, or until all the berries "pop." Remove and add sugar. Return to heat and bring back to boiling. Cook at a temperature slightly higher than low for 20 minutes. Strain. If it is to be used as a sauce, pour into a square Pyrex dish and chill. It may be poured into sterilized jars and sealed as any jelly. Makes about 1 pint.
From Mrs. Manly Baker, Burlington, N.C.

Hardimont "Cramberry" Jelly

This recipe is from the files of Hardimont, residence of Mr. and Mrs. J. Crawford Biggs. Mrs. Biggs, long famous for her elegant entertaining, sent the recipe from an old family manuscript cook book that was compiled by an old-time Negro cook. It is quoted in its original form.

"2 cup sugar, 4 cup cramberry, 1 cup water. Cook until all has bust open."
From Mrs. J. Crawford Biggs, Hardimont, Raleigh, N.C.

Cranberry-Quince Jelly

1 quart raw cranberries
3 ripe quinces
1½ quarts water
Sugar

Wash and stem the fruit. Chop separately in a coarse-blade food chopper. Combine the fruits in a saucepan. Add water and simmer until the fruit is tender. Strain overnight in a jelly bag. Discard the pulp. Pour the juice into an open saucepan and boil rapidly until reduced to one half the original volume. Measure the juice, and add 1 cup of warmed sugar (warm in oven) for each cup of juice. Boil rapidly until the mixture sheets from the spoon. Seal in jelly glasses.

Delmonico Cherry Jelly with Kirsch

Very *recherché* is this jelly, which I have refined from an old Delmonico Restaurant recipe.

> 6 ounces cherry stones
> 1 pound red or black currants
> 3 pounds red cherries, sour or tart, stoned (save stones)
> 3 pounds sugar
> ¼ cup kirsch (kirschwasser)

Pound the cherry stones with the currants in a mortar. Collect the juice by draining through a fine sieve. Weigh the juice and save 1 pound. Pit the cherries and put on to cook in their own juice. Simmer the cherries slowly until the fruit and juice reduce to one half the original volume. Add the sugar and the currants and stone juice. Cook until a drop falling on a flat surface will not spread. Add the kirsch and pour jelly at once into jelly glasses. Let cool thoroughly. Cut rounds of brown paper to fit each jar. Dip each round in brandy and put one in each jar on top of the jelly. Seal with melted paraffin or airtight lids. The brandy paper gives extra flavor and will protect the jelly from mold.

Dewberry Jelly

> 4 cups juice from around 3 quarts berries, half ripe, half red
> 3 cups sugar
> Water

Cook the berries as for blackberry jelly. Seal. Makes 4 jelly glasses of jelly.

Key West Cherry Jelly

This jelly is a combination of Florida cherries and apples.

      2 apples
      2 quarts cherries, washed and stemmed
      2 scant cups water
      Sugar

Chop apples and mix with cherries and water in a saucepan. Cook over medium heat until the cherries are very soft. Remove from heat and drain twice through cheesecloth. For each cup of juice add 1 level cup of sugar. Return juice and sugar to the heat and cook for about 25 minutes, or until the jelly stands firm.
From The Key West Cook Book, *Key West Woman's Club, Key West, Fla.*

Gooseberry Jelly

      3 pounds underripe gooseberries
      Water
      Sugar

Wash gooseberries and pick off blossom ends and stems. Cover with water and put on to cook in a covered saucepan. Cook slowly until the berries are soft. Drain through a jelly bag. Measure the juice and add 1 cup of sugar for each cup of juice. Boil rapidly until the jelly sheets from a spoon. Pour into sterilized jelly glasses. Seal with paraffin. Makes about 4 jelly glasses of jelly.

White Currant and Raspberry Jelly

      2 pounds white currants
      2 pounds raspberries (red or black)
      1 cup water
      Sugar
      ½ bottle pectin

Wash and crush currants and raspberries. Add water to mixed fruit and simmer in a covered saucepan for 10 minutes. Squeeze through a jelly bag or cheesecloth. To each 5 cups of juice add 7 cups sugar. Bring to a boil in a large open kettle over high heat. Add the pectin, stirring constantly. Bring to a rolling boil for ½ minute. Remove from heat, skim, and pour into hot sterilized glasses. Seal.

From Recipes Tested and Tried, *selected by Anne Young White, and compiled and edited by Nola Nance Oliver, Natchez, Miss.*

Spiced Grape Jelly

    5 pounds tart grapes (Concord)
    1 cup white grape juice (purple if white is not available)
    1 tablespoon whole cloves
    ½ stick cinnamon, broken
    1 cup vinegar
      Sugar

Wash and stem grapes. Put in a large kettle with grape juice, spices tied in a bag, and vinegar. Cook until the grapes are mushy. Remove spice bag and strain the mixture through a jelly bag or cheesecloth. Discard grape pulp. Return the juice to the heat and boil for 20 minutes. Measure the juice into a wide-mouthed kettle and add 1 cup of sugar for each cup of juice. Boil rapidly to the jelly stage. Pour into sterilized jelly glasses. Seal.

From Mrs. M. J. Lea, Jamestown, N.C.

Grape-Elderberry Jelly

    1½ pounds ripe elderberries
    1½ pounds half-ripe grapes (Concord, muscat, James, or the like)
      Sugar

Wash the fruit and stem. Cook the grapes and berries separately in enough water to cover. When tender, strain separately. Combine the juices, using equal amounts of each. Add 1 cup of sugar for each cup of juice. Boil rapidly until the mixture sheets from a spoon. Other tart berries combine well with grapes.

Iowa Blue-Grape Jelly

This is an unusual grape jelly that jells after sealing.

      1 peck ripe grapes
      Sugar

Wash, stem, drain, and mash the grapes. Cook the mashed grapes in their own juice until they are tender. Pour into a jelly bag, cheesecloth, an old dishtowel, or something similar and drain well. Measure 5 cups of juice and boil for 20 minutes. Remove from heat and stir in 5 cups of sugar. Stir constantly until the sugar is dissolved. This will be very thin but *do not cook* after the sugar has been added to the juice. Pour into jelly glasses and seal. The jelly will gradually thicken.

From Mrs. Joe Cochran, Nevada, Iowa.

Guava Jelly, No. 1

The guava, a crab-apple-like fruit of the tropics, was known in the West Indies as early as the middle of the sixteenth century. Its high sugar content (4 to 10 percent) makes it delicious for jellies, jams, pastes, chutney, and other table dishes.

Cut the guavas into quarters and put in a kettle. Add water to the top of the guavas and boil until the fruit is soft and well cooked, crushing with a potato masher once or twice. Strain through a jelly bag. To 2 cups of juice add 2 scant cups of sugar. Boil rapidly for 15 minutes, or until a web is formed between the tines of a fork when it is dipped into the boiling mixture and cooled in the air.

From Mrs. Kenyon Riddle, in Katch's Kitchen, Women's Club Cook Book, West Palm Beach, Fla.

Guava Jelly, No. 2

      Guavas
      Lemon juice
      Sugar

Wash guavas but do not peel. Cut the fruit into small pieces. Place them in a covered saucepan and cover with water. Bring to a quick boil and cook 5 minutes. Strain through a jelly bag and discard the pulp. Measure the juice into a wide-mouthed open saucepan and bring to a rolling boil. Add 2½ cups of sugar to each 3 cups of juice and 2 tablespoons lemon juice. Boil rapidly to the jelly stage. Pour into sterilized jelly glasses.

Horseradish Jelly

Excellent for cold roast beef or seafood.

> 2 cups sugar
> 1 cup white vinegar
> 1 cup freshly grated horseradish, drained
> ½ bottle fruit pectin

Boil sugar and vinegar together for 3 minutes. Add the horse-radish and bring back to boiling. Add pectin and stir constantly until the mixture reaches a rolling boil. Boil for ½ minute. Remove from heat and cool for several minutes. Skim and pack in sterilized jars. For color, a few strips of pimiento may be added just as the jelly is removed from the heat. Makes about three 6-ounce jelly glasses of jelly.

Japanese Quince and Apple Jelly

The fruit of the Japanese flowering quince, the decorative Japonica, makes an excellent jelly, more tart than that from ordinary quinces. An equal amount of apple juice should be used with the quince juice unless a very tart jelly is desired. Cover the fruit with water and cook until tender. Strain, and add to the strained juice two thirds as much sugar as juice by measure. Finish as any jelly.

From Mrs. Paul Green, in The Chapel Hill Cook Book, Woman's *Auxiliary, Presbyterian Church, Chapel Hill, N.C.*

Japonica Jelly

This is a very old recipe, and the jelly is considered a great delicacy.

Collect the fruit from the Japonica bush very late in the season, just before frost. Wash, cut in quarters, and cook with seeds and skin until tender. Use just enough water to cover. Allow to drip through three thicknesses of cheesecloth. Use equal amounts by measure of sugar and juice. Boil rapidly until the syrup jells when a drop is cooled. Pour into small glasses and cover with paraffin. Makes a clear amber jelly.

From Anna Allen, Baltimore, in Maryland Cooking, *compiled by the Maryland Home Economics Association, Baltimore, Md.* (May be obtained from Mrs. Elizabeth Reitze, 106 Forest Drive, Catonsville 28, Md.)

Old-Fashioned Lemon Jelly

4 lemons, juice and grated rind
2 cups sugar

Combine the juice and grated rind of lemons with sugar and mix well. Put mixture in the top of a double boiler and cook over hot water until it thickens, stirring constantly. Seal in sterilized jelly glasses.

From Mrs. Mary S. Nesbit, Tampa, Fla.

Loganberry Jelly

4 cups juice from 2½ quarts berries, half ripe, half red
3 cups sugar
1 cup water

Proceed as for Pure Blackberry Jelly (page 225). Makes 4 jelly glasses of jelly.

May-Haw Jelly

May-haws are the tiny applelike berries that grow in the swamp-lands of southern Georgia and South Carolina. This is a tart jelly for meats.

Pick over the may-haws, using plenty of green ones. Cover with water and cook until tender. Drip the juice through a bag, but do not squeeze the bag if clear jelly is desired. The juice may be put aside and the jelly made up any time. Use the following proportion:

> 1 cup juice
> ¾ cup sugar

Make as any jelly by boiling juice and sugar together until it jells. Do not make more than 4 cups of jelly at a time. Seal in jelly glasses.

From Mrs. John Mobley, Pelham, Ga., in Recipes from Southern Kitchens, *Junior League of Augusta, Georgia, Inc., Augusta, Ga.*

Mint-Honey Jelly

> 3 cups strained honey
> 1 cup water
>   Juice of ½ lemon
> 2 or 3 drops oil of mint (according to taste)
> ½ cup commercial pectin

Mix honey, water, and lemon juice in a saucepan. Heat quickly to the boiling point. Add pectin, stirring constantly. Bring the syrup to a rolling boil and remove at once fom the heat. Add mint. Skim and pour into sterilized jelly glasses. Seal with paraffin. The mint may be replaced by other flavors or omitted. This is a grand dietetic jelly.

Orange-Blossom Honey Jelly

Use the same proportion of honey, lemon juice, water, and pectin as for Mint-Honey Jelly given above and proceed as in that recipe.

Pick 1 cup of orange blossoms. Cover with boiling water and steep until the water is cold. Press out the juice, and cook slowly until reduced to 1 tablespoon of essence. Add the essence just before removing the jelly from the stove.

Orange Jelly

> 6 large whole oranges
> Juice of 5 large lemons
> Water
> Sugar

Wash and slice orange in thin slivers. Squeeze the lemons and measure the juice. To each cup of lemon juice add 3 cups of water. Pour the lemon-water mixture over the sliced oranges. Let stand in an enamel container overnight. Put in a covered saucepan and cook until oranges are tender. Strain through a jelly bag and discard the orange pulp. Measure the juice into a saucepan. To 1 cup of juice add 4/5 cup of sugar. Bring to a rapid boil and boil rapidly until the jelly stage. Pour into sterilized jelly glasses. Seal with paraffin.

Parsley Jelly

Parsley jelly is delicious with meat or served as an aspic with cream cheese.

> Parsley leaves
> Sugar
> Lemon or lime
> Gelatin

Pick the top tender leaves from sprays of fresh parsley and wash well. Press the leaves down tightly in a saucepan and cover with cold water. Bring to a boil and cook slowly until the leaves are tender. Strain through a jelly bag. Discard the leaves. Simmer the juice until reduced about one third. To each cup of parsley extract add ¾ cup of sugar and the juice and rind of ½ lemon or lime. Boil the mixture for 25 minutes. To each cup of hot syrup add 1 tablespoon of granulated gelatin softened in a little cold water. Dissolve the gelatin thoroughly. Remove from heat and pour into jelly glasses. Seal with paraffin.

Fresh rosemary, thyme, and other herbs may be made into jelly by this recipe.

Peach Jelly

Peaches or peach peelings to make 4 cups juice
4 cups apple pectin (see Apple Pectin, page 221)
Juice of 1 large lemon
3 cups sugar

Wash and cut peaches into pieces. Leave peel on if desired and leave stones in peaches for an almond-like flavor. Put the peaches in a covered saucepan and add enough water barely to cover the fruit. Boil until the fruit is tender. Drain through a jelly bag. Discard the pulp. Measure 4 cups of juice into a kettle and add apple pectin and lemon juice. Bring to a rolling boil and add sugar. Cook until the jelly sheets from a spoon. Pour into jelly glasses and seal with paraffin. Makes 4 to 6 jelly glasses of jelly.

Wild Sand Plum Jelly

The wild sand plum is about the size of a large pecan, but it is round. It grows in the sandy areas of Kansas and Oklahoma and is excellent for making jelly. The plums may be obtained in other sections of the United States from large country markets or sometimes from rural growers. "Buy all they have and persuade them to bring more," our contributor advises.

Plums
Water
Sugar (¾ cup to each cup of juice)

Pick over the plums and wash them in cold water. Put plums in an open kettle with just enough water to cover the second layer of fruit. Cook over medium heat until the plums are soft and all skins are split. Pour plums and liquid into a heavy cloth jelly bag or into a substitute made of flour-sack dish towels. Let drip overnight or for about 5 to 6 hours. Do not squeeze the bag, then the juice will be clear enough to make fine, ruby transparent jelly. The bag may be gently squeezed, but if it is, the jelly will be cloudy. For best results, do not cook more than 3 or 4 cups of juice at one time.

Pour the juice into an open saucepan; bring to a rolling boil and skim if necessary. Add sugar to juice and stir until the sugar is dissolved. Continue cooking the juice rapidly but not at a rolling boil. Skim frequently. Cook until a tablespoon of jelly held over the kettle and slowly poured back into it will leave a thin covering on the spoon and a heavy drop will cling to the side of the spoon. Continue cooking until two large drops form separately and cling to the spoon, then drop slowly back into kettle or cling securely to the spoon—"This is the trick part." Pour the hot jelly into sterilized glasses and seal as for any jelly.
From Mabel Stewart, Oklahoma City, Okla.

Pomegranate Jelly

The pomegranate is an ancient fruit of Africa and Asia which by some mysterious mode of travel and at an unknown time reached America. It thrives in the tropics and in Arizona and California and other sections of the country is often seen as a brilliant hedge. Like many fruits, it has been identified as "the forbidden fruit." It is often mentioned in the Bible (King Solomon had a hedge of pomegranate bushes), and it is revered by the Persians. Its usage is controversial. Most people agree that the pulp that surrounds the seeds is valuable for jelly and that the juice is tasty as a meat seasoner. Some dislike the taste of the seeds and warn against contaminating the pulp with the taste of the seeds; others serve the seeds with sugar and cream or in salads. The juice is said to be cooling to fevers, and a syrup from its pulp makes a refreshing drink.

When in Phoenix, Arizona, some years ago, I had my first pomegranate "dish"—a jelly for breakfast. The ranch house in which I was a guest was half surrounded by pomegranate bushes. The hedge was not in bloom, but I was told that it blossomed beautifully with bright red flowers, similar to those of the Japanese quince. From my hostess, I gathered a few notes on how she made jelly.

Cut the ripe pomegranate in half. Remove the seeds with a spoon or sieve the pulp, being careful not to bruise the seeds. Scoop out the pulp and measure. To each cup of pulp add 1 cup of sugar. Let the mixture stand overnight. Bring to a slow boil. Strain. To the juice add 2 tablespoons of lemon juice to each pint of pomegranate juice. Boil rapidly until the syrup jells. Seal.

It has an elusive taste—rather dry, like quince.

Quince Jelly

Cut quinces into small pieces, being sure to remove the cores. Cover the fruit with water and cook until tender. Strain. Mix cup for cup of fruit juice and sugar. Cook rapidly until the syrup coats the spoon. Skim. Seal as any jelly.

Raspberry Jelly

>   4 cups juice from 2½ quarts berries, all ripe
>   3 cups sugar

Mash the berries. Put over medium heat in their own juice and simmer until soft. Proceed as for any berry jelly. Seal. Makes 4 jelly glasses of jelly.

Raspberry-Plum Jelly

>   4 cups red raspberries, fresh or frozen
>   1 cup large red plums (measure after stoning and chopping)
>   Juice of 1 lemon
>   Sugar

Wash and pick over fresh raspberries and save the juice. If frozen berries are used, thaw out and save the juice. Wash, stone, and cut up plums. Put the fruits together in a kettle and mash with a potato masher. Add ½ cup of water, and cook slowly until the fruit is tender. Strain in jelly bag or through cheesecloth. Measure the juice. To each cup of juice add 1 cup of sugar if fresh berries are used or ¾ cup of sugar if frozen berries are used. Bring to a rapid boil and cook until the syrup sheets from a spoon. Pour into jelly glasses. Seal with paraffin. Makes about 4 to 5 jelly glasses of jelly.

Red-Pepper Jelly

Delicious over cream cheese.

        12 red peppers
         1 tablespoon salt
           Water
        ½ pint white wine vinegar
        1½ pints sugar

Remove the seeds from the peppers and put the peppers through a food grinder. Add the salt and let stand for 3 to 4 hours. Put in a strainer and let cold water run through until the salt is removed. Add the vinegar and sugar. Place over medium heat and boil for 30 minutes. Test as for any jelly. Seal in sterilized glasses. *From Mrs. Hallam Claude, in* St. Anne's Parish Recipe Book, *Annapolis, Md.*

Pure Strawberry Jelly

        3 quarts ripe strawberries (4 cups juice)
           Water
        5 cups sugar
           Juice of 1 lemon

Wash, stem, and crush the berries thoroughly. Drain through a jelly bag. Add 1 cup of water to every 4 cups of juice. Bring to a boil and cook for 3 minutes. Add the sugar and lemon juice. Boil rapidly until the syrup jells. Seal as any jelly. Makes 4 jelly glasses of jelly.

Frozen berries may be used instead of fresh. Thaw the berries at room temperature. Simmer the berries in their own juice for 5 minutes. Strain, measure juice, and proceed as above.

Quick Strawberry Jelly

        3 pints ripe strawberries
     3½ cups sugar
     ½ bottle fruit pectin

Wash the berries and remove stems. Crush well; then drain through a jelly bag. There should be about 2 cups of juice. Add

the sugar to the juice and bring to a full boil. Add fruit pectin, stirring constantly, and bring to a quick boil. Boil ½ minute and remove from heat. Skim and seal as any jelly.

Wine Jelly

     2 cups California wine
     3 cups sugar
     ½ bottle fruit pectin

Measure the wine into the top of a double boiler and add sugar. Mix well. Place over rapidly boiling water and heat for 2 minutes, stirring constantly. Remove from the water and at once stir in fruit pectin. Pour quickly into sterilized jelly glasses. Seal with paraffin at once.

This recipe can be made with California sherry, claret, sauterne, port, muscatel, or Tokay.

From Jessica C. McLachlin, Home Advisory Service, Wine Institute, San Francisco, in What's Cooking on Governor's Island? St. Cornelius Altar Guild Cook Book, New York, 1949.

Youngberry Jelly

4 cups juice from 3 quarts berries, all underripe if possible
4 cups sugar

Crush the fruit and simmer in their own juice for 10 minutes. Strain and proceed as for blackberry jelly. Makes 4 jelly glasses of jelly.

14. Fruit Butter

FRUIT BUTTER IS A CONCENTRATED SAUCE SOMEWHAT SIMILAR TO apple sauce, but it is cooked down so that there is no "free" liquid in it. It is made from many fruits and combinations of fruit and is seasoned with spices, flavoring, or both. It may be stored in a crock, but it is safest to pack it in sterilized glass jars with rubber bands and screw tops.

The general procedure is to wash and cut up the fruit, saving the peelings and cores (unless the recipe states differently, as for quince). The fruit is covered with water and cooked down to a pulp, or until tender and thick. Then the pulp should be refined through a fine sieve or a food mill. (The latter makes the operation simpler and easier.) The sieve or food mill will take out the peelings, seeds, and fibers. The pulp is then cooked again in its own juice to reduce it to a smooth and thick consistency. Sugar and flavoring are then added, and the whole mixture is further reduced.

Many exciting flavors may be given to fruit butter: spices, fruit or flower essence, brandy, or wine.

Apple Butter

4 cups cooked apple pulp or sauce (measure after cooking)
3 cups sugar
1 teaspoon ground cinnamon
¼ teaspoon each ground allspice, cloves, and nutmeg

Wash the apples and cut into quarters, leaving in skins and seeds. Cover with water or fresh apple cider and simmer until fruit is reduced to a soft pulp. Press the fruit through a sieve or food mill to get pulp and juice. Discard the skins and seeds. Measure the pulp and add sugar and spices. Cook slowly, stirring constantly, until the mixture is very thick and has a nice deep reddish color. Pour into jars and seal. Makes about 2½ pints.
From Mrs. R. D. Lea, Chesterfield County, Va.

Italian-Plum Butter

2 cups Italian plums, fresh or canned
Water
2 cups sugar

If fresh plums are used, stone the plums but do not peel. Put the plums in an open saucepan and cover with water. Simmer until the fruit is tender. Press through a sieve or food mill. Save the pulp that has been pressed through the sieve, but discard peels and seeds. Add sugar to the sieved pulp. Put in a saucepan on medium heat and bring to a boil. Reduce heat to simmer and continue simmering until the mixture thickens. Seal immediately in sterilized jars. Makes 2½ pints.

If canned plums are used, add enough water to the juice in the can to cover the plums. Cook and pack as for fresh plums.

Mango Butter

1 pint peeled mangoes (not quite ripe)
Water
¼ cup chopped ginger root
2½ cups sugar

Grind the mangoes through a coarse food chopper. Put into a saucepan, cover with water, and add ginger. Place over low heat and simmer until tender. Remove from heat and press through a sieve or food mill, saving the juice. Discard the ginger. Add sugar and return to heat. Cook slowly until reduced to a thick consistency. Seal in sterilized jars.
From Mrs. Mary Nesbit, Tampa, Fla.

Peach Butter

4 cups peeled peaches, quartered (save stones)
Water
4 cups sugar
2 tablespoons peach brandy

Put the peaches and the stones in a saucepan, cover with water, and simmer until tender. Press the peaches through a sieve. Discard the stones and half of the juice. Measure pulp and use 4 cupfuls. Add sugar and brandy to pulp, and cook until it reaches a thick consistency. Seal in sterilized jars. Add spices if desired. Makes about 2 pints.

Pear Sauce (Butter)

A delightful departure from apple sauce.

7 large ripe pears
1 cup sugar
2½ cups water
1 teaspoon mixed powdered spices (cloves, allspice, cinnamon)

Peel the pears and cut into pieces. Mix all ingredients and cook slowly until the fruit is tender and the sauce is as thick as apple sauce. Seal while hot in sterilized jars, or serve at once. Makes about 1½ pints.

Sweet Potato Butter

Sweet potatoes
Sugar
Vinegar
Vanilla

Cook any amount of sweet potatoes. Peel the potatoes and put them through a sieve. Thin the pulp with water until it is the consistency of apple sauce. Combine sugar with potatoes, using 1 pint of potato pulp to 1 pint of sugar. Cook the mixture slowly until the water has almost cooked out. Add 1 cup of vinegar to each 3 gallons of potato butter. Flavor with vanilla to taste a few minutes before sealing in sterilized jars.
From Mrs. H. D. Dalton, Frederick County, in Recipes from Old Virginia, *compiled by The Virginia Federation of Home Demonstration Clubs, copyright, 1946, by The Federation of Home Demonstration Clubs, The Dietz Press, Inc., Richmond, Va.*

Spiced Apple-Tomato Butter

½ gallon tomatoes, seed and skin removed
½ gallon apples, peeled and diced
2½ pounds brown sugar
½ pint vinegar
1 teaspoon each ground cinnamon, allspice, ginger, and cloves

Mix all ingredients. Bring to a good boil; then cook down slowly until the mixture is thick. Pour into sterilized jars and seal.
From Mrs. E. H. Stockton, in Pages from Old Salem Cook Books, *Dorcas Co-workers of the Salem House, Winston-Salem, N.C., 1947.*

15. Meats and Sea Food

Mincemeat; Smoked and Pickled Meats and Sea Food
Special Meats; Cracklings

MINCEMEAT FOR PIES IS A TRADITIONAL ENGLISH SWEET-SOUR
mixture of minced meat, suet, fruits, vegetables, spices, and flavored according to taste with brandy or other highly seasoned liqueurs.

Mincemeat pies came into being, according to old Vatican formulas, about 600, long before the first English cook books were written. Wild boar, venison, game meat, and fowl were often used instead of the customary beef. Over the centuries the basic recipe seems to have undergone little change, except in the refinement of method and ingredients. The pie had many names; "grete pyes," "bakemete," "bakemete in coffyns," "mete crustards," and "grete cates" were but a few.

The massive pies were made especially for Christmas and other festive and state occasions. They were so treasured that often a king's guard was set to watch them. Frequently, during a banquet of many courses, the mincemeat pie would appear under different guises for four or five courses. One such famous pie graced the coronation banquet of King Henry IV "apud Westmonasterium" in 1399.

A condensation of one of the pie recipes here gives an idea of the typical "grete pye":

"Take faire young beef, and suet of a fatte beste, or of Motton, and hak all this on a borde small; and caste thereto pouder of peper and salt; and whan it is small hewen, put hit on to bolle, and meddle him well; than make a faire coffyn, and couche som of this stuffer in. . . . Than tak Mary (rosemary), dates, resions, prunes, whole clowes, whole mace, canell and saffron, and other stuffer as you thinkest goode; then close the coffyn—and putte hit in the oven."

Good mincemeat should be allowed to ripen for at least 3 weeks before using. It may be stored in a crock or in sterilized jars. If stored in a crock, it must be kept in a cool dry place and the crock should be prepared as for Brandied Fruit (see page 139).

Some may object to the brandy or other spirituous liquor in mincemeat. But any mincemeat worth its meat should have brandy.

Meatless mincemeat is a modern innovation. It makes good pie if plenty of butter and brandy are added at the time the pie is made.

Mincemeat pie should be served warm. A little heated brandy poured over the hot pie adds to the flavor.

Brandy-Wine Mincemeat

Brandy, wine, and rosewater give this authentic old Maryland mincemeat a rich flavor.

    1½ pounds lean cooked beef, finely chopped
     2 pounds cooked suet, finely chopped
     2 pounds seeded raisins

2 pounds currants
1 pound citron, finely chopped
2 nutmegs, ground
2 ounces each ground mace and allspice
1 ounce ground cloves
3 pounds sugar

Wash and dry the raisins and currants. Combine all ingredients and blend thoroughly. Add:

1 quart good brandy
1 quart any wine
1 wine glass rosewater

Lastly, add:

4 pounds sour apples, finely chopped

The Forbes Family Recipe, in Saint Anne's Parish Recipe Book, Annapolis, Md.

Pear Mincemeat

This is a meatless mincemeat that is grand for pies and tarts and as a filling for brown-bread sandwiches. It is also good as a cake filling.

7 pounds firm ripe pears, peeled and cored
2 pounds seedless raisins
1 orange, juice and rind
½ cup wine vinegar
¼ cup chopped crystallized ginger
3 pounds sugar
1 teaspoon each ground cloves, allspice, nutmeg, and cinnamon

Grind the fruit through a coarse food chopper. Add the other ingredients and simmer slowly until the fruits are soft and the mixture thick. Seal while hot in sterilized jars. If used for pies, add butter.

Mrs. Fitzhugh Lee's Mincemeat for Pies

From an old cook book, which bears no identification as to author, title, or date, comes this famous recipe.

"The wife of Governor Fitzhugh Lee of Virginia is a famous housekeeper, and this is how she says she makes the mincemeat for her Thanksgiving pies:

        2 pounds beef
        2 pounds currants
        2 pounds seeded raisins
        1 pound citron, shredded
        2 pounds beef suet, finely chopped (cook the suet, cool, then chop)
    1¼ pounds candied lemon peel
        4 pounds apples, peeled, cored, and finely chopped
        2 pounds sultana raisins
        2 pounds sugar
        2 nutmegs, grated
        ¼ ounce ground cloves
        ½ ounce ground cinnamon
        ¼ ounce mace
        1 teaspoon salt
        2 oranges, juice and grated rind
        2 lemons, juice and grated rind

"Simmer the meat gently until tender, and when cold chop it fine. Mix the dry ingredients; then add the juice and rind of oranges and lemons. Pack in a stone jar, cover close, and keep cool. This mincemeat will keep all winter. The rule is an old one and said to have come from the Custis family in the beginning. According to Virginia tradition, the Widow Custis, who became Mrs. George Washington, made famous mince pies."

From a book owned by Mrs. Norman Riddle, Burlington, N.C.; in The Southern Cook Book.

Homemade Mincemeat

From this good basic mincemeat variations may be made. Substitute veal or pork if desired.

5½ pounds cooked lean beef, ground
1 pound cooked suet, ground
2 pounds seedless raisins, chopped
1 pound currants, washed (leave whole)
6 medium-sized apples, peeled and finely chopped
1 pint white grape juice
½ pint good brandy or whisky
1 quart apple butter
1 pound brown sugar
1 pound granulated sugar
½ cup chopped crystallized orange peel
¼ cup chopped crystallized citron
¼ cup chopped crystallized ginger
2 tablespoons salt
1 tablespoon each ground cinnamon, cloves, and allspice

Boil the beef and suet in salted water until tender. Cool and grind. Mix with the remaining ingredients and bring to a slow boil. Reduce the heat and simmer slowly, stirring often, until the fruits are tender and the mixture is thick. Store in a tightly covered crock or seal in sterilized jars. Should stand 1 month before using.

Small-Family Mincemeat

2½ pounds cooked beef, ground
¼ pound cooked suet, ground
1 quart apple sauce or apple butter
1 quart apples, peeled and finely chopped
1 quart canned red cherries with juice
1 10-ounce package frozen huckleberries, thawed and drained

2 pounds seedless raisins, chopped
½ pound white currants, washed and dried
1 pint watermelon-rind sweet pickle, chopped, with
   syrup
2 pounds sugar
1 cup cider vinegar
1 teaspoon each ground cloves, allspice, nutmeg, and
   cinnamon
½ pint brandy (peach brandy if possible)

Mix all ingredients. Simmer until the fruits are tender and the mixture is thick. Seal in sterilized jars.

Venison Mincemeat

Mincemeat made of venison has a rich gamey taste. Elk or moose meat may be substituted for venison—that is, if you can find such meat.

4 pounds venison rump, cooked
1 pound venison or beef suet, cooked
6 pounds firm ripe apples, not peeled, chopped
1 quart apple cider (or apple juice)
5½ pounds sugar
1½ tablespoons salt
2 pounds seedless raisins, washed and chopped
2 pounds currants (white, if possible), washed
½ cup chopped crystallized citron
1 cup chopped crystallized orange peel
½ cup chopped crystallized lemon peel
¼ cup chopped crystallized ginger
1 teaspoon white pepper
1 tablespoon each ground cinnamon, allspice, cloves,
   and mace
1 pint apple brandy
1 pint sherry wine

Boil the meat and suet until tender. Let cool. Grind in a fine-blade food chopper. Mix all the ingredients, except the brandy and wine, and bring to a slow boil. Simmer until the mixture begins to thicken. Add brandy and wine and cook until the fruits are tender and the mixture is thick. Store in a crock or in sterilized jars.

From R. D. Lea, Chesterfield County, Va.

Green-Tomato Mincemeat

1 gallon firm green tomatoes, finely chopped
1 pound good lean sausage, cooked and broken into
    pieces
5 pounds sugar
1 pint cider vinegar
1 gallon apples, peeled and chopped
1 pound cooked beef suet, ground
2 pounds seedless raisins, finely chopped or ground
1 tablespoon each ground cinnamon and ground allspice
1 teaspoon ground cloves
2 tablespoons salt
½ cup stuffed olives, chopped
½ pint white wine

Mix all the ingredients. Bring to a slow boil and simmer until fruits and tomatoes are tender and the mixture is thick. Seal in sterilized jars. Serve as any mincemeat.

From Mrs. Robert C. Moore, Maplewood Farm, Graham, N.C.

Curing Meat by Brine-Smoke Process
For 100 Pounds of Meat

This is especially good for pork hams and shoulders.

Cover each piece of meat thoroughly with a thick coating of salt and pepper mixed together. Rub the seasoning well into the meat. Let stand for 24 hours. Then, for each 100 pounds of meat, prepare the following brine:

10 pounds salt
4 pounds brown sugar
2 ounces saltpeter

Dissolve the above in 4 gallons of boiling water. Let the brine cool.

Place the meat in a large crock or wooden barrel. Pour the brine over the meat. Weight it down with a heavy stone. Let stand for 6 to 8 weeks, according to the size of the pieces of meat. Then hang the meat in a smokehouse and smoke with hickory wood.

Making Corned Beef

Make a brine "strong enough to float an egg" (see Brines, page 20). Boil the brine and skim. After skimming add:

> 20 pounds beef
> 1 pound brown sugar
> 2 tablespoons whole mixed cloves and allspice
> 1 tablespoon saltpeter

Put the meat in the brine and let stand for 2 weeks. Pour off the brine and boil it again. All the blood will come to the top and should be skimmed off. Pour the brine back over the meat. This will keep all summer.

From Mrs. W. H. Turrentine, in Choice Recipes, *Burlington, N.C.*

Spiced Beef

This is an old recipe and a favorite Virginia way to "pickle" beef.

> 25 pounds beef round, with bone removed
> 4 ounces saltpeter
> Salt

Rub the beef thoroughly with the saltpeter and then lightly with salt, being sure to get both worked down into the cavity from which the bone was removed. Put the meat into a wooden tub or keg and pour over the following mixture:

> 1 quart black molasses
> 1 quart salt
> 2 ounces each ground cloves and ground allspice
> 1 ounce ground nutmeg

Let the meat stand in the mixture for 21 days, turning it each day. Remove the meat from the tub and tie it up snugly in a cloth cover. When ready to use, remove the cloth, cover with cold water, and boil for about 3 hours, or until tender. Let it cool in the water it was boiled in.

From Miss Holladay, in The Guild Cook Book, St. John's Church, Portsmouth, Va.

Curing Ham

There is no single recipe for curing ham. Each person has his own individual method and amount of seasoning. Some smoke the meat with hickory or apple-wood smoke; others rely on the curing with salt and other preservatives, such as saltpeter, sugar, pepper, and so on.

The Honorable Harry Flood Byrd, of Virginia, an authority on the subject, says that hogs should always be killed "when the wind is from the northwest." The first salting should be light. To the salt add a strong solution of water, red pepper pods, and saltpeter (2 heaping teaspoons of saltpeter to every gallon of solution). After the first salting, pack the meat for 3 days. Then take it out and rub it with saltpeter, allowing 1 teaspoon of pulverized saltpeter to each side of one ham. Then mix salt with molasses and rub the mixture well into the meat.

Pack for 10 days. Rub the meat again with molasses and salt mixture. Hang the meat within 3 weeks from the time the hogs were killed. Before hanging, wash each ham in warm water and, while wet, roll in hickory-wood ashes. Smoke in a smokehouse with green hickory wood. About February, the hams are tied in strong cotton sacks and hung up with the hock side down. They will be ready to use in 10 months.

A two-year-old ham is considered the best cured ham, although some prefer a three-year-old.

Brown-Sugar-Cured Ham

An old Maryland method.

The meat should be thoroughly cold before processing. Salt it as soon as it is cut up, using as much salt as it will absorb. Let stand for 3 hours. Then rub each ham for 20 minutes with the following mixture:

¾ pound brown sugar
¾ ounce saltpeter
2½ ounces black pepper

Pack the meat in a large wooden barrel for 6 weeks. Remove and smoke with green hickory or apple wood six times. Tie up in strong cotton bags. They will be ready to use in 10 to 12 months.

Salt-and-Pepper Ham

500 pounds meat
1½ pecks salt
2½ pounds pulverized saltpeter
½ cup red pepper

Rub the meat with the mixture as long as the meat will absorb it. Proceed as for Brown-Sugar-Cured Ham.

Molasses-Cured Ham

500 pounds meat
1½ pecks salt
1½ pounds saltpeter
1 quart black molasses
2 cups ground black pepper

Rub the mixture into the meat for 20 minutes. Proceed as for Brown-Sugar-Cured Ham.

McLoud's "Sweet" Ham

Select a nice salt ham that has ripened until danger of spoiling has passed. Wash off all salt. Mix:

1 quart molasses
½ pound black pepper

Rub the mixture thoroughly into the meat; then sprinkle heavily with additional black pepper. Put the ham into a large (100-pound) brown paper bag. *Do not use a cloth bag.* Tie the end of the bag securely and hang the ham in a cool, dry place. Ham cured in this manner will be as red as beef and will have a sweet, tangy taste. *From Mr. J. T. McLoud, Elon College, N.C. in Soup to Nuts, Woman's Auxiliary, Church of the Holy Comforter, Burlington, N.C.*

Meats Stored in Fat

Preserving meat in fat is an art that is not practiced as often now as it was before the advent of freezing units. It is still a tested and tried way to conserve meat. It is impossible to give individual recipes here for the variety of meats that may be preserved by this method. The basic rules will serve as a guide.

Small pieces of meat, such as sausage cakes, meat patties, chops, and cup-up fowl and game may be stored in glass jars. Large pieces of meat should be stored in earthen crocks.

The meat is always cooked and may be seasoned if desired. When it is taken from the container, as much fat as possible should be scraped off and the meat heated thoroughly.

All containers should be sterilized. A good way to sterilize a crock is to wash it and turn upside down in a large pan of water. Have enough water to come half way up the side of the crock. Boil for at least 15 minutes. When ready to pack, turn the crock upright and drain, but do not dry. Sterilize the jars as for any food.

Use clear, fresh, melted fat, preferably pork fat. Pack the meat in and cover thoroughly so that the fat will seep into all crevices between the pieces of meat. Put in a layer of fat first. *Do not let the meat touch the sides of the container.* Store where the temperature is not above 50° F.

Roasts in Fat

Wipe the meat dry and season with salt and pepper. Roast in a moderate oven (350° F.), allowing 45 to 50 minutes per pound for roasts over 6 pounds, 30 to 35 minutes for smaller roasts. Pack as above.

Sausage or Meat Cakes in Fat

Season fresh meat. Make meat cakes or sausage cakes and fry in fat until thoroughly done, but do not cook too hard. Pack in fat as above. Pack in sterilized jars. Do not store in a place where temperature may go below 40 degrees, for the jars may crack.

Tongue in Fat

Cook tongue by any recipe. Pack in fat as above. Store in a crock or large sterilized glass jar.

Fowl or Game in Fat

Cut the bird into pieces as for frying. Boil in seasoned water until the meat is thoroughly done and tender. Pack in fat as above. Pack in sterilized jars.

Plantation Hogshead Cheese

Hogshead cheese is an old way of congealing the head and feet of a hog. Because of the natural glutinous elements in these parts of the meat, no other gelatin is needed. Other parts of the hog may be made into hogshead cheese or souse meat by the aid of gelatin. The meat is highly seasoned and packed into molds. It is sliced for serving. "A fat medium hog" is the best for this.

    1 fat hog's head cut into quarters
    4 pig's feet or more (8 are better)
    1 cup vinegar
      Salt
      Red pepper pods

Have head and feet thoroughly scrubbed of all hair and the ears cut off. Put the meat in a kettle with the vinegar and enough water to cover. Add 2 tablespoons of salt and the red pepper pods. It is best to cook in a fireless cooker all night. If this is not possible, cook all day on medium heat, adding water if necessary. When the meat is ready to fall from the bones, drain, skin, and remove all bones and gristle. Pick the meat into small pieces until it becomes a mushy mass. Season with:

> 1 tablespoon crushed mixed spices
> ¼ teaspoon red pepper
> 2 tablespoons black pepper
> 1 bay leaf, crushed
> Any other desired seasoning

While hot, press the meat into a long mold, such as a loaf pan. Press down, weight, and chill. The cheese will keep for a long time in the refrigerator.

Gänsegrieven (Goose Cracklings)

Gänsegrieven, or "cracklings," as they are called in the South, are crisp pieces of browned goose skin. They are delicious with cocktails. This recipe, from the *Times Magazine,* is by the chef at Luchow's Restaurant in New York.

"Cut the goose skin into squares of an inch and a half to two inches. Simmer in a very little water with half an onion till the water has boiled off. Continue cooking the skin in its own fat until it has turned a golden brown in color. Cool and serve with cocktails."

The skin used for cracklings is taken from the long neck of the bird.

From Jane Nickerson, Food News Editor, The New York Times, New York, N.Y.

Liver Paste (Foie Gras)

Liver paste is a traditional French delicacy made of the livers of fat geese that are penned in small areas and fed to the limit of their capacity to fatten and enlarge the livers. *Foie gras* was prized by epicures in ancient Egypt, Greece, and Rome, but the art of making it was lost during the Middle Ages. It was revived in the eighteenth century after the discovery of a local *pâté de foie gras* by Clausse (Close), a French chef taken to Alsace by a French governor of the province. This now famous *pâté* is a goose-liver paste flavored with wine and spices and mixed with truffles. The making of *foie gras* has become a notable industry of Strasbourg and Toulouse as well as of other sections of France. It is exported in natural form or as the esteemed *pâté*. Packed in jars, it will keep indefinitely.

Mock *foie gras* can be made from hog, calf, chicken, duck, or any other liver. If one is fortunate enough to obtain truffles, they can be added to the paste.

Pig's Liver Paste

    1 clear pink liver from a young pig
    ½ cup salt
    Water

Put the liver in a container and cover with very cold water to which the salt has been added. Let stand several minutes. Drain. Place in a kettle and barely cover with water. Cover the kettle. Place over medium heat and bring to the simmering point. Continue cooking slowly until the liver is tender. Drain and place the liver in a large bowl with:

    1 medium onion
    1 small clove garlic, peeled and minced
    ¼ teaspoon powdered thyme
    Salt and pepper to taste

Chop all very fine and mash to a thick paste. If the paste is to be stored, add the juice of 1 lemon. Smooth to paste and pack in jars, as for Bibba May's Calf's-Liver Paste. If the paste is to be served within a short time after being made, thin it with a small amount of thin cream or a good wine.

Bibba May's Calf's-Liver Paste

Foie gras made of calf's liver is served often by Mr. and Mrs. W. H. May, Jr., at stately Willeli. This recipe is made especially as an hors d'oeuvre, but it is sometimes served in small molds as a salad. Truffles may be added and any extra seasoning.

2 pounds calf's liver, whole or sliced
Lemon Juice
2 medium onions, ground
3 stalks celery, ground
Salt
Pepper

Boil the liver in water until tender. Remove skin and fibres and put through a food chopper with the onion and celery. Blend to a smooth paste with lemon juice and season to taste with salt and pepper. To store, pack in small jars, cover with melted butter, and seal. Store in a cool place. Small earthenware jars with close-fitting tops make attractive containers—like little German mustard crocks.

From Mrs. W. H. May, Burlington, N.C., in The Southern Cook Book.

Chicken-Liver or Duck-Liver Paste

1 pound cooked chicken or duck livers
4 tablespoons bacon or salt pork fat
1½ teaspoons salt
⅛ teaspoon each ground thyme and ground marjoram
¼ teaspoon ground peppercorns
3 tablespoons sherry wine

Parboil the livers in slightly salted water until tender—about 10 minutes. Do not overcook. Drain. Sauté the livers, spices, and seasoning in the fat. Cook for 4 minutes, stirring constantly. Add the wine and cook for 2 minutes, stirring often. Pour all into a mortar (or onto a wooden board) and pound with a pestle until a smooth paste is formed. If possible, add a few chopped truffles. Pack in small sterilized jars and cover with melted fat. It may be served at once or stored in a cold place. If it is to be kept indefinitely, seal with paraffin and cover.

From Mrs. E. K. Jaquith, Arlington, Va.

Liver Mush

    1 pig's liver
      Fresh pork
      Corn meal
      Salt
      Pepper

Place the liver and a medium-sized piece of fresh pork (about 2 pounds or more if desired) together in a kettle. Cover with water and boil until the liver and meat are tender. Remove the liver and meat and save the liquid. Mash the liver and meat fine with a potato masher and return to the liquid it was cooked in. Bring the mixture to a boil. Add enough corn meal to make a thick mush. Add salt and pepper to taste. Allow the mixture to cook until the corn meal is done, stirring frequently to prevent burning. When done, pour into a shallow dish, and place in the refrigerator. To serve, cut into thick slices and roll in flour. Fry in a greased skillet to a golden brown. The mush will keep for many days if kept in a cold place.

From Old Time Recipes from the Nu-Wray Inn, *Burnsville, N.C., compiled by Esther Wray, third edition revised by Rush T. Wray.*

Pickled Herring

Any salt fish may be pickled by this recipe.

      3 medium-sized salt herring, mackerel, or other salt fish

2½ cups white vinegar
¼ cup sugar
½ cup crab boil (page 11) or mixed pickling spices
(page 12)
1 lemon, thinly sliced
2 medium-sized onions, thinly sliced
Sprig fresh or dried dill
½ teaspoon horseradish
Small whole onions, peeled

Scrub the fish free of salt and rinse well in cold water. Let stand in cold water for at least 12 hours. Drain. Remove the skin and cut the fish into fillets, cutting crosswise into the desired pieces. Put vinegar into a saucepan and bring to a boil. Add sugar and spices. Remove and let cool. Pack the fish pieces in a large wide-mouthed jar, alternating the lemon and onion slices, bits of dill, and a few grains of horseradish. Pour over the vinegar mixture. Put a whole small onion on top of the fish to press down the pickle. Seal and refrigerate several days before using. It will keep for weeks after it is opened if it is refrigerated.

Pickled Oysters

One of the first pickles appearing in American cook books is the pickled oyster. Each recipe differs in the amount of spices, but basically all are alike.

1 quart oysters
½ cup vinegar
1 teaspoon salt
7 whole cloves
7 whole peppercorns
2 blades mace
Red hot pepper pods to taste

Heat the oysters in their own liquor until the edges curl. Lift out the oysters and add vinegar and spices to the hot oyster liquor.

Simmer the liquor for 5 minutes. Pack oysters in hot sterilized jars and pour the hot vinegar mixture over them. Seal at once. Store in a cool, dark place. They will be ready to use in 24 hours.

Pickled Pig's Feet

6 pigs' feet
Salt
Water
1 tablespoon mixed spices tied in cloth bag
1 cup vinegar
1 teaspoon sugar
1 red hot pepper pod, minced

Wash and scrub pig's feet clean with a brush. Rinse and put into a pressure cooker with salt to taste. Cook until the meat falls from the bone. Or cook in a heavy covered kettle with enough water to cover and salt to taste. Boil the spice bag in the vinegar for 5 minutes. Remove the spice bag and set the vinegar aside. Remove all bones from the meat. Stir in the warm vinegar, sugar, and red hot pepper pod. While the meat is still warm, press it into a wide-mouthed jar. Chill so that meat will come out in a nice mold. Slice and serve cold. If the meat is to be stored indefinitely, pack it in sterilized jars and seal. Store in a cool place.

Pickled Pig's Feet

1 set of pig's feet (4)
Water
1 tablespoon salt
Vinegar to cover
½ cup pickling spices (see page 12)
1 tablespoon brown sugar
1 clove garlic
2 red pepper pods

Scrub the pig's feet with a brush and wash thoroughly. Cover with cold water and the salt and cook until easily pierced to the bone with a long-tined fork. Drain and pack in a wide-mouthed jar. Boil the other ingredients together for 2 minutes. Pour over the pig's feet while hot. Seal. The Creoles serve these cold as an hors d'oeuvre. They may also be covered with batter and fried like chicken.

Souse Meat

The Nu-Wray Inn has long been famous for its home-cooked food. This is one of their favorite ways to use the head and feet of hog.

      1 head of hog, well scrubbed
      4 hog's feet, well scrubbed
        Salt
        Pepper
        Vinegar

Boil the hog's head and feet together until the meat is thoroughly done (when the meat falls from the bones). Remove the bones and mash the meat well. Season to taste with salt, pepper, and vinegar. Pour into a shallow dish, such as a square baking dish, and chill in the refrigerator until thoroughly congealed. Slice and serve in vinegar.

From Old Time Recipes from the Nu-Wray Inn, *Burnsville, N.C., compiled by Esther Wray, third edition revised by Rush T. Wray.*

Old-Fashioned Pudding Meat

      1 hog's head with most of the fat trimmed off, boiled
      1 haslet, boiled until it falls to pieces

When the meat is tender enough to fall from the bones and the haslet is tender, remove both from the stock. Take out all skin and bone. Chop the meat fine and season to taste with salt, red pepper, sage, and chopped onion. Press down in jars or shallow pans. Store in a cold place.

From Choice Recipes, *Burlington, N.C.*

Scrapple

Home-made scrapple is often made of any part of the hog. Real scrapple is generally the hog's-head meat combined with meal and seasonings. The pig's feet give a gelatin element.

Boil a hog's head with a set of pig's feet until the meat falls from the bones. Pick out all bones, skin, and gristle. Chop the meat fine. Boil the stock that the meat was cooked in until it is reduced to 2 quarts. To the boiling stock, add 2 cups of corn meal. Stir constantly until a thick mush is formed. Add the meat. Season with:

> 3 tablespoons salt
> 3 tablespoons black pepper
> ½ teaspoon rubbed sage
> ¼ teaspoon cayenne pepper

Mix all the ingredients thoroughly. Taste and correct the seasoning if necessary. Press into pans and set aside for 12 hours before using. Store in a cool place. Or it can be packed in sterilized jars. It is served sliced and browned in hot fat with tart jelly or molasses.

Virginia Sausage

This is an excellent recipe for seasoning sausage.

For each pound of ground pork use the following proportion:

> 1½ teaspoons salt (more if desired; taste for correction)
> ¼ teaspon dry mustard
> ½ teaspoon black pepper
> ¼ teaspoon ground cloves
> ½ pod ground red pepper
> 2 teaspoons ground sage

If more than 10 pounds of meat is used, add 1 extra teaspoon of salt. A pinch of thyme may be added and the sage reduced slightly. *From R. D. Lea, Chesterfield County, Virginia.*

Country Sausage

Tennessee is especially famous for its country sausage. This is a good example.

4 pounds pork meat, ground
5 tablespoons salt
4 teaspoons ground sage
4 teaspoons home-made ground red pepper
1 teaspoon ground allspice
2 teaspoons black pepper
1 teaspoon sugar
1 teaspoon cayenne pepper
½ teaspoon powdered cloves
⅛ teaspoon thyme

Mix the seasonings and then work thoroughly into the meat. Pack into casings or sausage sacks and string them up to smoke with hams. This mixture will cure well and may be eaten all winter and on into the spring—as long as it will last.

From Mrs. B. Frank Womack, former Foods Editor, The Nashville Tennessean Magazine, *Nashville, Tenn.*

Old-Fashioned Sausage

This is a grand savory sausage.

50 pounds meat processed for sausage
50 teaspoons salt
10 teaspoons cayenne pepper
20 teaspoons black pepper
40 teaspoons ground sage

Mix the seasonings well together and rub the meat thoroughly with the mixture. Grind the meat in a food or sausage grinder. Pack in cases (links or otherwise), or store in an earthenware crock and pour melted lard over top. Store in a cold place.

From Mrs. Wallace Broadbelt, in Saint Anne's Parish Recipe Book, *Annapolis, Md.*

Barbecued Shrimp

This is a pickled type of shrimp that will keep for 1 week if refrigerated. It may also be quick-frozen and kept as any frozen food.

    5 pounds fresh shrimp in shells
    Vinegar to cover shrimp
    1 tablespoon each red pepper, celery salt, and dry mustard
    2 tablespoons black pepper
    3 tablespoons salt

Wash the shrimp and drain. Boil the rest of the ingredients. Drop in the shrimp and cook for 25 minutes. Cool in the sauce. Serve in the shells, letting each person shell his own shrimp. If they are to be stored, remove the shrimp from the sauce at once, drain, pack in sterilized jars, and seal. Refrigerate or freeze in regular frozen-food cartons.
From Miss Emily Young, Burlington, N.C.

Easy Brine Shrimp

This brine shrimp may be used later for pickled shrimp or in any way that raw shrimp are used.

    2 pounds raw, fresh medium-sized shrimp
    ½ pound salt
    2 quarts water
    Extra salt and water

Combine salt and water in open kettle and bring to a rolling boil. Drop in the shrimp and cook for about 8 minutes. If "baby" shrimp are used, cut the cooking time to about 6 minutes. Cook for 10 minutes for "jumbo" shrimp, and peel. Remove the black vein down the back. Pack immediately in sterilized Mason jars.

Bring to a boil a weak salt brine made by dissolving 1 teaspoon of salt in 1 quart of boiling water. Pour scalding-hot brine over the shrimp and seal immediately. Process in a hot-water bath according to the time table issued by the manufacturer of the jar. If desired, a sprig of dill may be packed in each jar. Makes about 2 pints.

Pickled Shrimp Quickie

2 cups white vinegar
2 tablespoons crab boil (page 11)
1 pound cooked, peeled shrimp
1 large onion, sliced

Boil vinegar and crab boil together for 1 minute. Pack shrimp and onion in alternate layers in a sterilized jar. Pour over the hot vinegar mixture to fill the jar. Seal, cool, and refrigerate. Set aside for 12 hours before serving. Serve as hors d'oeuvre.

VARIATION

Make a syrup of 2 cups of beer or ale as a substitute for the vinegar. Serve within 24 hours.

Pickled Shrimp

This is grand for hors d'oeuvre or salad

2 pounds raw uniformly sized shrimp
2 tablespoons crab boil (page 11) or pickling spices
    (page 12) tied in cloth bag
Water to cover shrimp
2-quart stone crock or large Mason jar
3 large onions, thinly sliced
3 bay leaves
2 cups vinegar
2 cups salad oil (or olive oil)
2 tablespoons Worcestershire sauce
1 teaspoon paprika
2 cloves garlic, peeled and diced
2 tablespoons salt
1 tablespoon whole black peppercorns
2 small red hot pepper pods

Rinse the shrimp in cold water. Drain and discard the water. In a saucepan combine salt, spices, and water. Put on high heat and bring to a rolling boil. Drop in the shrimp and boil until the shells turn deep pink—about 15 to 20 minutes according to the size of the shrimp. Let stand in water until cool. Drain off liquid and discard it. Peel the shrimp and remove the black vein down the back. Rinse shrimp, drain, and refrigerate immediately.

Meanwhile, prepare a stone crock or large Mason jar by cleansing, scalding, and draining. In the crock put alternate layers of shrimp and onion slices. Put the bay leaves and vinegar in an open pan and bring to a rapid boil. Remove the bay leaves and let the vinegar cool. Combine the remaining ingredients in a mixing bowl and beat with electric or rotary beater until thoroughly blended. Add the cooled vinegar to the salad-oil mixture and blend by beating. Pour the dressing over the shrimp and onion mixture. Cover the crock or jar and refrigerate. They should be ready to serve in 24 hours. If they are to be stored longer, pack into a Mason jar and seal immediately. This shrimp will keep indefinitely if sealed properly and kept in the refrigerator. Once the jar is opened, the contents must be used.

From Katie Lea Stewart, New York City.

Shrimp Paste

2 pounds cooked, shelled shrimp
2 sweet bell peppers
1 medium onion
1 tablespoon Worcestershire sauce
½ teaspoon Creole or German prepared mustard (hot mustard)
1 tablespoon white wine vinegar
$\frac{1}{16}$ Cayenne pepper
3 tablespoons butter
½ cup plain flour
½ teaspoon salt
½ cup thin sweet cream or top milk

Grind shrimp, peppers, and onion together. Add Worcestershire sauce, mustard, vinegar, and cayenne pepper and blend well. Make a thick sauce of the remaining ingredients. Melt **butter** in a saucepan and stir in flour and salt. Mix to a smooth paste. Add the cream. Cook slowly, stirring constantly, to a thick consistency. Stir the shrimp mixture into the sauce. Remove from heat and cool. Pack into molds or sterilized jars and seal with melted fat (butter), then with paraffin. Refrigerate and chill before serving. This will keep indefinitely if refrigerated and not opened.

Pork Pickling Brine

Pork may be pickled in brine, then smoked. Here is a basic brine:

    100 pounds pork
        Black pepper
      8 pounds coarse salt
      4 pounds brown sugar
      2 ounces saltpeter
    ½ pound soda
      4 gallons water

Rub the meat with as much black pepper as it will absorb. Mix other ingredients. Let the meat stand in the brine for 5 to 6 weeks. Hang until dry; then smoke with green hickory wood.

Spiced Salt

If you have an herb garden, this old recipe will be helpful in storing the herbs. It makes an excellent seasoning for soups, vegetables, salads, meats, sauces, catchup, chili, and so on.

    ¼ ounce each dried thyme, bay leaf, and black pepper
    ⅛ ounce each dried marjoram and cayenne pepper
    ½ ounce each ground cloves and grated nutmeg

Dry the fresh herbs and beat to a powder (I use a wooden mortar and pestle). Sift and mix with the powdered spices. To every 4 ounces of this mixture, add 1 ounce of salt. Store in air-tight cans or jars.

Pickled Tongue

Pickled tongue is a delicacy that may be served in many ways after processing. It must be cooked after being pickled.

    2½ quarts cold water
    ¼ teaspoon saltpeter
    1 cup salt
    2 cloves garlic, chopped
    ½ teaspoon red pepper
    1 tablespoon pickling spices (page 12)
    1 fresh beef tongue

Dissolve saltpeter in ¾ cup of cold water and add to the remaining water and ingredients. Put the tongue in a crock and cover well with the liquid. Weight down with a plate and place a heavy weight on it. Let stand for 3 weeks, turning the meat at least three times each week.

Pickled Eggs

My eldest son brought this recipe from St. Louis, Mo.

    Hard-cooked eggs to fill quart jar
    1 pint vinegar
    2 red pepper pods
    1 tablespoon whole mixed spices
    1 tablespoon salt
    1 clove garlic

Put the eggs on to cook in cold water. (This prevents the shells from cracking.) Bring to a boil and simmer for 20 to 30 minutes, according to the size of the eggs. Drain off the hot water and plunge the eggs into cold water. Cool in water 30 minutes. Pack carefully in a quart jar. Mix vinegar with remaining ingredients and pour over eggs. Be sure that the jar is filled with vinegar to cover the eggs completely. Let stand for at least 2 weeks. Keep in a cool place. These eggs are often dyed like Easter eggs before putting in vinegar mixture; they look very pretty in the jars.
From W. W. Brown, II, Burlington, N. C.

Horseradish Mustard

Very hot!

>   4 tablespoons dry mustard
>   4 tablespoons cider vinegar
>   2 tablespoons sugar
>   ½ teaspoon salt
>   2 tablespoons olive oil
>   2 tablespoons fresh horseradish or 1 tablespoon de-
>   hydrated horseradish

Make a paste by blending together the vinegar and mustard. Blend together sugar, salt, and olive oil. Beat the mixtures together until they form a thick paste. Add the fresh horseradish. If dehydrated horseradish is used, mix it with 1 tablespoon of cold water before adding it to the mustard mixture.

An old German recipe.

Storing Venison

This is an old method.

Mix equal parts of sweet milk and water. Wash the meat in the solution and dry it until all moisture has been absorbed. Dust all parts of the meat thoroughly with powdered ginger. Meat treated this way may be hung for 2 weeks. Just before cooking, wash the meat in lukewarm water and dry it off well.

Weights and Measures	Approximate Equivalents
Dash *or* pinch	Less than ⅛ tsp.
60 drops	1 tsp.
2 tsp.	1 dessert sp.
3 tsp.	1 tbsp.
2 tbsp.	1 liq. oz.
4 tbsp.	¼ cup
4 tbsp.	1 wineglass
2 wineglasses	1 gill
1 gill	¼ pt.
16 tbsp.	1 cup
2 cups	1 pt.
2 pt.	1 qt.
4 qt.	1 gal.
8 qt.	1 peck
4 pecks	1 bu.
16 oz.	1 lb.

SUGARS AND SYRUPS

1 lb. fruit sugar	2¼ cups
1 lb. granulated sugar	2 cups
1 lb. brown sugar	2 cups, packed
1 lb. confectioners' sugar	2½ to 3 cups
1 lb. cane syrup	1½ cups
1 lb. strained honey	1½ cups
1 lb. molasses	1½ cups

NUT MEATS

2½ lb. pecans	3 cups
5½ lb. black walnuts	3 cups
2½ lb. English walnuts	4 cups
3½ lb. almonds	4½ cups
2¼ lb. filberts	3½ cups

Fresh Fruits

Bulk

1 bu. plums	50 lb.
1 bu. pears	48 lb.
1 bu. peaches	48 lb.
1 bu. apples	48 lb.

Small Quantity, Approximate

1 lb. apples	2 to 6 apples
1 lb. apricots	8 to 14 apricots
1 lb. cherries	2 cups
1 lb. cranberries	4 cups
1 lb. grapes	1 bunch, 2 cups halved
1 lb. peaches	4 to 6 peaches
1 lb. pears	4 to 5 pears
1 lb. plums	12 to 20 prune plums
1 lb. rhubarb	4 to 8 stalks
1 pt. berries	2 cups
1 pineapple	2½ cups cubed
1 medium grapefruit	1⅓ cup pulp
1 doz. lemons	2½ cups juice
1 doz. oranges	3 to 5 cups juice
1 doz. limes	1½ to 2 cups juice
1 lb. mangoes	2 to 4 mangoes
1 lb. currants	2 to 2½ cups
1 lb. figs	12 to 18

Fresh Vegetables

1 bunch broccoli	1½ to 2½ pounds
1 lb. Brussels sprouts	3½ cups
1 lb. cabbage	3½ cups, shredded
1 lb. carrots	2½ cups, diced
1¼ lb. bunch celery	3 cups, diced
1 lb. Lima beans	⅔ cup, shelled

1 lb. dried onions ....3 large onions
1 lb. tomatoes ....4 small to medium
1 lb. turnips ....3 or 4 medium
1 lb. cucumbers ....3 to 4 small to medium

Sizes of Cans

No. 1 Can ....1½ cups
No. 2 Can ....2½ cups
No. 3 Can ....4 cups
No. 10 Can ....13 cups

Spices, Herbs, Seeds, Etc.

Spices, herbs, seeds, and dehydrated herbs for seasoning are packaged and sold by the trade and are most frequently available in from ½- to 2-ounce containers. They will vary from 1 to 2 tablespoons per ounce. This is an approximate chart for the most common seasonings used in pickles and preserves. However, when procured from a pharmacy, they will probably be sold by apothecaries' weight, 12 ounces to a pound, if not prepackaged.

1 oz. ground allspice, cloves, ginger, mustard ....2½ tbsp.
1 oz. powdered cinnamon, mace, turmeric, mustard ....3 to 3½ tbsp.
1 oz. rubbed sage ....4 tbsp.
1 oz. celery, mustard seed ......3 to 3½ tbsp.
1 oz. whole mixed pickling spices.2½ to 3 tbsp.
1 oz. dehydrated parsley, onion flakes etc. ....4 tbsp.

Density of Sugar Syrup

A sugar hydrometer is very useful in all canning, preserving, and pickling. Either the Brix or Balling scale may be used. Both read directly in percentages of sugar in a pure sugar solution, as shown in the table.

Density	Quantity of sugar for each gallon of water *	
Degrees Brix or Balling	Pounds	Ounces
5		7
10		14.8
15	1	7.5
20	1	14.75
25	2	12.5
30	3	9
35	4	7.75
40	5	8.75
45	6	13
50	8	5.25
55	10	4
60	12	8

* When vinegar is used, the equivalent sugar hydrometer reading would be about 2 degrees higher than that indicated in the table.

Yield of Fresh and Dried Fruits by Measure

Fruit	Unit of Purchase or Size	Yield
apples	1 lb.	3 cups diced or sliced
apricots	1 lb. (3 c.)	1 qt. soaked, cooked, drained
bananas	1 lb.	2–2½ cups diced or sliced 1¼ cups mashed
cranberries	1 lb.	1–1¼ qts. 2–2½ cups ground
dates, pitted	1 lb. (50–60)	2½ cups cut fine
figs	1 lb.	2½–3 cups cut fine
grapefruit	1 large	1¾ cups broken pieces 10–12 sections ¾–1 cup juice
grapes	1 lb.	2¾ cups cut and seeded
lemons	1 large	¼ cup juice 1 tsp. grated rind
oranges	1 large	½ cup diced ½ cup juice 9–12 sections
peaches	1 lb. (3–5)	2 cups peeled and sliced
pineapple	1 med.	3–3½ cups peeled and diced
prunes	1 lb. (30–40)	1 qt. sauce 2⅛ cups cooked and chopped
raisins	1 lb. seedless (3 c.) seeded (2⅓ c.)	2½ cups chopped 2 cups chopped
strawberries	1 qt.	3 cups hulled 1 pt. crushed

INDEX

apple, butter, spiced (tomato), 244
catchup (grape), 118
cider, conserving, 137
chutney (tomato), 106
jelly, 221
  (mint), 222
  dried, 223
  from peelings, 223
  (lemon verbena), 222
  (Japanese quince), 231
  (rose geranium), 222
  spiced, 224
marmalade (pineapple), 195
pectin, 221
preserved, Miss Nellie's, 152
preserve (ginger), 152
quarters, pickled, 54
relish, 90
sauce, brandied, 140
See crab apple.
apricot, in brandy, 131
candied, 207
conserve, 175
jam (dried), 183
marmalade (date), 195
  (raspberry), 194
nectar, 131
preserve (pineapple), 139
artichoke, pickle, 73
  Margaret Pruden's, 71
pickled, French, 70
relish, 89
Bar-le-Duc jelly, 224
beef, corned, 252
spiced, 252
beet, conserve, 176
pickled, party sweet, 73
  whole, 72
relish, 92
blackberry, cordial, 133
jam, Purefoy, 184
jelly, 225
preserve, old-fashioned, 154
syrup, 133
blueberry, pickled, 54
bottled foods, fresh fruits, 130
See catchup, chili sauce, nectar,
  sauce.
brandied fruits, 139–146

brine, fermentation, long, 23
grape-leaf, 16–17
short process, 16
solution, 20
test for acidity of, 20
butters, fruit, 241–243
cabbage, pickle, Miss Chloe's, 91
pickled, 75
sauerkraut, 86, 87
calf's foot jelly, 225
cantaloupe, pickled, 56
pickled stuffed, 55
preserve, 164
  (peach), 164
carissa jam, 185
carrot, jam, 185
pickled cocktail, 76
preserve, 154
relish, raw, 93
catchup, cranberry, Iowa, 116
cucumber, Bandon Plantation, 117
  black pepper, 119
grape, 119
  (apple), 118
home-made, 120
horseradish chili, 129
mushroom, 123
tomato, 127
  red wine, 124
  uncooked, 129
celery relish, 94
"cheese," Damson-Fox grape, 191
cherry, in bourbon, 57
brandied, 140, 141
  Luta's, 56
conserve (raspberry), 180
  (1947), 154
crystallized, 208
jam (raspberry), 189
  red-cherry, 185
jelly (currant), 228
  Delmonico, 227
  Key West, 228
in kümmel, 57
in syrup, 141–142
chestnuts, French, preserved, 155
chili sauce, canned tomato, 115
New York, 116
Thorley's, 115

chilis, Mexican green, 72
chow-chow, Carolina, 112
  Emma Pollard's, 113
  Georgia, 111
  lazy day, 110
chutney, apple-tomato, 106
  mango, 107
  mint, English, 109
  peach, Old English, 108
  pear, Lib Mor's, 109
  rhubarb, 110
citron, preserved, 156
citrus fruit peel, marmalade,
     Normandy Farm, caramelized,
     198
cocktail, mélange, 60
  olives, mock, 80
  onions, 81
  sauce, Ivy House, 117
  tomato juice, 123
cold pack, 7
corn, pickled baby ears, 76
  salad, 94
  relish, 65
corn syrup as sugar substitute, 151
crab apple, jelly, 223
  marmalade, 196
  pickled, 54
  preserve, whole, 153
calamondin marmalade, 196
conserve. See individual fruits.
cracklings, goose, 257
cranberry, crystallized, 208
  jam, 185
  jelly, 226
    (quince), 226
    Hardimont, 226
  relish, Lillian's, raw, 95
    spiced, 96
crystallized fruit, 206–211
  coating, caramel for, 206
    white sugar for, 206
  preserve, Rainbow, 212
cucumber, brined, cooking, 21
  large quantity, 19
  small quantity, 18
  chowder, 98
  curry, 34
  dill, Kosher, 25

pickled, sweet stuffed, 30
pickle. See pickle.
relish, 96
See also pickles, mustard pickles.
currant, jam, black, 186
  jelly, Bar-le-Duc, 224
    (cherry), 228
  shrub, 122
date, marmalade (apricot), 195
  stuffed, 208
dewberry, jelly, 227
  preserve, 154
eggplant, pickled, 78
eggs, pickled, 270
elderberry-grape jelly, 229
fats, meats stored in, 255–256
fermentation, long, 16–18
fig, crystallized, 209
  glacéed in wine, 209
  jam (ginger), 186
  marmalade, 197
  preserve, black, 156
    brandied, 142
    Thousand Pines Inn, 157
  in wine, 149
flowers, preserved, 215–218
frozen foods, 67–69
  rules for using, 65–66
fruit honey, mango, 190
  peach, 191
  pear, Purefoy, 191
  preserve, rose-petal, 218
fruit juices, canned, uses for, 132
gänsegrieven, 257
garlic crisp pickle, 30
gherkins, dill, 26
  sour and sweet, 43
ham, brown sugar cured, 254
  curing, 253
  McLoud's "sweet" cured, 255
  molasses cured, 259
  salt-and-pepper, 254
headcheese, 256
ginger root, crystallized, 210
  preserve, 158
gooseberry, jam, 186
  jelly, 228
  relish, 98
  spiced, 58

grape, brandied, 142
  catchup, 119
    (apple), 118
  conserve, 197
  glacéed, 214
  jelly (elderberry), 229
    from frozen juice, 69
    Iowa blue, 230
    spiced, 229
  Malaga, chocolate-dipped, 210
  preserve, green, 157
  syrup, Muscadine, 134
grapefruit, marmalade (lemon, orange), 201
  peel, crystallized, 211
    in marmalade, 198
Greengage. See plum.
guava, jelly, 237
  paste, 192
herring, pickled, 260
honey as sugar substitute, 151, 216
  See also fruit honey.
horseradish, chili, 129
  jelly, 231
  mustard, 271
  sauce, fresh, 120
hot pack, 7
jalapenas, pickled, 78
jams. See individual fruits.
japonica, jelly, 231
  (apple), 231
jelly, from frozen berries, 69
  from fruit peelings, 223
  rules for making, 219–221
  tests for, 151–152
  See individual fruits.
kumquat, conserve, 187
  crystallized, 211
  jam, 157
  leather, 214
  marmalade, 198
  preserved, whole, 159
lemon, jelly, 232
  peel, crystallized, 211
  pickle, 58
  syrup, 134
lemon-verbena jelly, 222
lime, marmalade, 178

"Old Sour," 121
  preserve, Ogeechee, 160
  relish, 99
liver, pâté, 258
  mush, 260
  paste, Bibba May's calf's, 259
    chicken, 259
    duck, 259
    goose, 258
    pig, 258
loganberry jelly, 232
loquat relish, 99
mango, 160
  bell pepper, 83
  butter, 243
  chips, 161
  chutney, 107
  conserve (pineapple), 178
  jam, 188
  peach, 50
  preserve, 161
  relish, 100
marmalades. See individual fruits.
marrons glacés, 155
may-haw jelly, 233
meats, brine-smoke process for curing, 251
  fat, stored in, 255–256
  venison, storing, 270
  See beef, ham, liver, mincemeat, sausage, tongue.
mélange, brandied fruit, 143
  cocktail, 60
  conserve, 177
  tutti frutti marmalade, 205
mint, chutney, English, 109
  jelly (apple), 222
    (honey), 233
  sauce, 136
mincemeat, 245
  brandied, 246
  green tomato, 251
  home-made, 249
  pear, 247
  pies, Mrs. Fitzhugh Lee's, for, 248
  small-family, 249
  venison, 250
  wine, 246

mushroom, catchup, 123
  pickled, 79
  relish, 100
muskmelon preserve, 164
  See also cantaloupe.
mustard pickle, Barrows House, 26
  Dutch salad, 29
  mixed, Jane Comer's 28
  North Carolina Governor's, 27
  onion, 82
  Toss-in-the-Crock, 31
mustard vinegar for pickle, 22
nasturtium, pickled buds of, 80
Natal plum jam, 183
nectar, fruit and berry, 131–132
olives, mock cocktail, 80
onion, cocktail, 81
  mustard pickle, 82
  relish, 102
orange, baked, Whitlock, 82
  brandy, 145
  crystallized peel, 211, 213
  glacéed sections, 214
  jelly, 234
  marmalade, Scotch, 200
    Sunshine, 203
    Sunflower (watermelon), 204
  My Own Preserved Stuffed, 161
orange blossoms, jelly (honey), 233
  preserved, 217–218
oysters, pickled, 261
papaya, crystallized, 214
  marmalade (pineapple), 199
  preserve, 162
parsley jelly, 234
pâté de fois gras, 258
peach, brandied, 146
    Creole, 144
    white, 144
    old-fashioned buried, 145
  butter, 243
  chips, 163
  chutney, Old English, 108
  conserve (raisin), 179
  jam, 183
  jelly, 235
  leather, 214
  mangoes, 58

marmalade, 201
  (orange), 202
nectar, 131
pickle, Georgia, 61
  Jessamine Gant's sweet, 59
  stone crock, 61
pickles, sweet, 60
preserve (cantaloupe), 164
  plain, 163
pear, butter, 243
  chips, 166
  chutney, 109
  conserve, 178
  marmalade, baked, 202
    (pineapple), 199
  mincemeat, 247
  "Peris in Syrippe (and Wyne),"
    147
  pickle, sweet Seckel, 59
  preserve, easy, 165
    (lemon-ginger), 166
    Martha Washington's, 165
    (peach), 166
  relish, 101
  spiced, 63
  wine, Lucy Street's, in red, 148
pectin, apple, 221
  commercial, 220
piccalilli, 104
pickle, Airlie sweet, 11
  artichoke, 73
  brine for, 18–20
  bread-and-butter, Arkansas, 51
  cabbage, Miss Chloe's, 91
  cucumber, crystallized, Mrs.
      Durant's, 39
    hot, 40
    icicle, 38
    Mil McKay's sweet, 43
    nine-day sweet, 37
    onion, 33
    rings, Mary Rutledge's, 35
    rings, ripe, 45
    twenty-day, 42
  dill, 23
    Kentucky, 25
    Kosher, 25
  English chop, 93
  French, 33

frozen foods, from, 67–68
gherkin, dill, 26
  sweet and sour, 43
  green-tomato, Airlie Plantation, 50
    Champ Clark, whole, 46
    crystal (raisin), 47
    Irene's, 48
    Mary Hopkins's layer, 49
    old-fashioned, 48
    Shamrock Inn whole, 46
    Valeria's, 50
    Holly Hill, 41
    last-of-the-garden, 77
    lemon, 58
    Lord Higden's, 35
    mixed, Elsa Thorley's, 44
    mustard, 26–29, 31
    oil, Barrows House, 36
    peach, 59, 61
    pear, 59
    pumpkin, 184
    salad, "Career Girl's," 67
    sour, 52
    string bean, 73, 74
    watermelon, 62, 63
    See chow-chow, mustard pickle.
pepper, hash, 102
  jelly, red pepper, 238
  mangoes, stuffed, 83
  pickled, red sweet, 86
  relish, 100, 102
  Lily's, 103
pie plant preserve, 180
pineapple, crystallized, 213
  marmalade (apricot), 195
    (papaya), 199
    (pear), 199
  preserve, 167
  relish, 105
  syrup, 135
plum, brandied, 146
  butter, 242
  "cheese," Damson-Fox grape, 191
  conserve, 179
  marmalade, 197
  mock cocktail olives, 80
  preserve, baked Damson, 156
    brown sugar, 167
    Greengage, 158

spiced, 61
  wild sand plum jelly, 235
pomegranate, jelly, 236
pork, syrup, 135
  hogshead cheese, Plantation, 256
  pickling brine for, 269
  pig's feet, pickled, 262
  pudding meat, 263
  scrapple, 264
  souse, 263
  See ham, liver, sausage.
prunes, brandied, 146
pumpkin, chips, 168
  jam, 188
  pickle, 84
preserves. See individual fruits.
quince, jelly, 237
  (cranberry), 226
  marmalade, 203
  paste, 194
  preserve, 169
raisin, cluster, pickled, 85
  pickle (cucumber), 39
raspberry, conserve (cherry), 180
  jam, 188
    (cherry), 189
    Mrs. Green's uncooked, 190
  jelly, 237
    (currant), 228
  jam, frozen berries, 69
    (plum), 37
  marmalade (apricot), 194
  preserve, 168
  shrub, 121
relish, artichoke, 89
  Anne Arundel, 90
  apple, 90
  beet, 92
  cabbage, 91
  celery, 94
  gooseberry, 98
  grape, 119
  India, 97
  lime, 99
  loquat, 99
  mango, 110
  tomato, uncooked catchup, 129
    raw, ripe, 106
  vegetable, fresh, 129

rhubarb, chutney, 110
  conserve, 180
roselle, syrup, 136
roses, conserve of red, 217
  crystallized, 217
  preserve of, 218
rose-geranium jelly, 222
rules for pickling, 5–9
scale, spiced vinegar, 21
salsify, pickled, 84
salt, dairy, 20
  spiced, 269
sand, fruit preserved in, 172
sand plum jelly, 235
sauce, barbecue, Hoskins, 122
  apple, brandied, 140
  green-tomato, 128
  horseradish, fresh, 120
  mint, 136
  pepper, 124
  plum, 119
  soy, tomato, 128
  for spaghetti, 125
  Tartar, Ive House, 126
sauerkraut, 86, 87
sausage, country, 265
  old-fashioned, 265
  stored in fat, 256
  Virginia, 264
Scotch preserve, 170
sealing procedure, 7–8
shrimp, barbecued, 266
  brined, easy, 266
  paste, 268
  pickled, 267
shrub, 121, 122
souse meat, 263
soy, tomato, 128
spaghetti sauce, 125
squash preserves, 171
strawberry, candied, 215
    eight-minute, 109
  jam, from frozen berries, 68
    uncooked, Mrs. Green's, 190

jelly, 238, 239
preserve, Kay Houston's, 169
  Mrs. Holt's, 170
  sun-cooked, 171
  wild, 171
string bean, dill pickle, 74
  pickle, 73
sweet potato butter, 244
syrups, fruit, 133–136
tamarind, marmalade, 204
  preserve, ripe, 174
tomato, butter, spiced (apple), 24
  conserve, Mrs. Gant's, 181
  dill, Kosher, 25
  jam, 190
  marmalade, red tomato, 203
  mincemeat, green tomato, 251
  pickle. See under pickle.
  preserve, Kay Houston's yellow
    pear, 175
    red tomato, 172
  relish, raw ripe, 106
  sauce, green, 126
tongue, pickled, 270
  stored in fat, 256
turnips, pickled, 86
tutti frutti marmalade, 205
venison, storing, 271
vinegar, celery, 22
  mustard, 21
  spiced, 21
  See shrub.
violets, crystallized, 217
walnuts, catchup, 130
  pickled English, 130
watermelon, marmalade, Sunflower
    204
  ginger tea, 62
  Nina Mae's, 63
  preserve, "Sweetmeat," 173
wine jelly, 239
  figs in, 149
  pears in, 147–148
youngberry jelly, 240